Nahum—Malachi

INTERPRETATION
A Bible Commentary for Teaching and Preaching

INTERPRETATION
A BIBLE COMMENTARY FOR TEACHING AND PREACHING

James Luther Mays, *Editor*
Patrick D. Miller, Jr., *Old Testament Editor*
Paul J. Achtemeier, *New Testament Editor*

ELIZABETH ACHTEMEIER

Nahum—Malachi

INTERPRETATION

A Bible Commentary for Teaching and Preaching

John Knox Press
ATLANTA

Library of Congress Cataloging in Publication Data

Achtemeier, Elizabeth Rice, 1926–
  Nahum—Malachi.

  (Interpretation, a Bible commentary for teaching and preaching)
  Bibliography: p.
  1. Bible. O.T. Minor Prophets—Commentaries.
2. Bible. O.T. Minor Prophets—Homiletical use.
I. Title. II. Series.
BS1560.A59 1986   224'.907   85–45458
ISBN 0–8042–3129–X

© copyright John Knox Press 1986
10 9 8 7 6 5 4 3 2 1
Printed in the United States of America
John Knox Press
Atlanta, Georgia 30365

SERIES PREFACE

This series of commentaries offers an interpretation of the books of the Bible. It is designed to meet the need of students, teachers, ministers, and priests for a contemporary expository commentary. These volumes will not replace the historical critical commentary or homiletical aids to preaching. The purpose of this series is rather to provide a third kind of resource, a commentary which presents the integrated result of historical and theological work with the biblical text.

An interpretation in the full sense of the term involves a text, an interpreter, and someone for whom the interpretation is made. Here, the text is what stands written in the Bible in its full identity as literature from the time of "the prophets and apostles," the literature which is read to inform, inspire, and guide the life of faith. The interpreters are scholars who seek to create an interpretation which is both faithful to the text and useful to the church. The series is written for those who teach, preach, and study the Bible in the community of faith.

The comment generally takes the form of expository essays. It is planned and written in the light of the needs and questions which arise in the use of the Bible as Holy Scripture. The insights and results of contemporary scholarly research are used for the sake of the exposition. The commentators write as exegetes and theologians. The task which they undertake is both to deal with what the texts say and to discern their meaning for faith and life. The exposition is the unified work of one interpreter.

The text on which the comment is based is the Revised Standard Version of the Bible. The general availability of this translation makes the printing of a translation unnecessary and saves the space for comment. The text is divided into sections appropriate to the particular book; comment deals with passages as a whole, rather than proceeding word by word, or verse by verse.

Writers have planned their volumes in light of the requirements set by the exposition of the book assigned to them. Biblical books differ in character, content, and arrangement. They also differ in the way they have been and are used in the liturgy, thought, and devotion of the church. The distinctiveness and use of particular books have been taken into account in decisions about the approach, emphasis, and use of space in the commentaries. The goal has been to allow writers to develop the format which provides for the best presentation of their interpretation.

The result, writers and editors hope, is a commentary which both explains and applies, an interpretation which deals with both the meaning and the significance of biblical texts. Each commentary reflects, of course, the writer's own approach and perception of the church and world. It could and should not be otherwise. Every interpretation of any kind is individual in that sense; it is one reading of the text. But all who work at the interpretation of Scripture in the church need the help and stimulation of a colleague's reading and understanding of the text. If these volumes serve and encourage interpretation in that way, their preparation and publication will realize their purpose.

The Editors

PREFACE

The books of the Minor Prophets are often neglected in the Christian church. When we do deal with them, we usually confine our attention to Amos and Hosea and to those few passages from the other books of the Twelve that have been interpreted christologically.

But there are multitudinous riches to be found in the books of Nahum through Malachi, and this commentary is an attempt to mine some of that wealth for the preachers and teachers of the church. Having studied these books closely for several years now, I have become convinced that they should be called the Not-So-Minor Prophets. Through these small canonical gems the word of God speaks to his people, and there are messages to be found here to which the church in our day and every day surely needs to listen.

This is not a historical–critical commentary. That is, its primary purpose is not to illumine critical and historical problems and details of the biblical text. That work has been pursued in most of the books listed in the Bibliography. Yet, at every point, I have utilized the biblical sciences in interpreting the prophetic words, and I am indebted to the vast amount of scholarly research that has gone before me.

There are times, however, when I have had to part company with accepted scholarly views in order to get at what I consider to be the meaning of the biblical text. But because of the homiletical and didactic nature of this commentary, many of my historical-critical positions have not been spelled out beyond the details necessary to make them clear. Nevertheless, I believe they can be defended, and I hope that the reader will find them supported by what actually stands in the biblical texts. My purpose has been to use the biblical sciences to illumine for the church the word of God that confronts us in these prophetic books.

At some points in this commentary, the reader will find brief quotations from sermons on these prophets. Biblical historical critics have never made much use of the vast amount of homiletical interpretation of the Bible that we possess in the church—and scholarship has been the poorer for it. Every time a preacher delivers a sermon, he or she interprets the biblical text in some fashion. Indeed, sometimes giants in the pulpit have illumined the messages of these prophets in a way so searching and profound that their words have driven straight to the heart of what the prophet is saying. Sadly, this is truer of some of the great preachers of the past—J. H. Jowett, Wm. Malcolm Macgregor, Clovis Chappell, G. Campbell Morgan, Charles Haddon Spurgeon—than it is of contemporary homileticians. Especially Spurgeon was a master, not only of the Minor Prophets, but also of the English language. Such preachers have spoken from a depth of faith and theological insight rarely matched in the church today. I have therefore used some of their words in this commentary in order that we modern Christians may profit from this interpretive treasure that has been bequeathed to us by the cloud of witnesses that have gone before us.

This volume is lovingly dedicated with a prayer at the beginning for new attorney Marie, new minister Mark, new mother Katherine, and brand new person Rachel Chamblee Achtemeier.

Elizabeth Achtemeier
Union Theological Seminary in Virginia

CONTENTS

PART ONE

The Word of the Lord During Judah's Last Years:

Nahum

Habakkuk

Zephaniah

These three prophets, along with Jeremiah and Ezekiel, share the distinction of proclaiming the word of the Lord during the last half century of Judah's existence. It was the most turbulent of times. The Assyrian Empire had dominated the ancient Near East for one hundred years, and when that empire fell, an era came to an end. Under King Josiah, Judah enjoyed a brief period of independence and renewal and growth. But Assyria's rod was quickly replaced, first with that of Egypt and then with that of great Babylonia, and Judah's life fell victim to the juggernaut of Babylonian conquest.

According to the prophets, all of these events were intimately connected, however, with the will and working of Israel's God. And it was given to Zephaniah, Nahum, and Habakkuk, in that chronological order, to make clear those connections.

The details of the history of the period can be found in John Bright's book, *A History of Israel,* but the following outline is furnished to the reader for quick and easy reference, since none of the prophetic books can be understood fully apart from such historical background.

1

OUTLINE OF THE HISTORICAL BACKGROUND OF NAHUM, HABAKKUK, AND ZEPHANIAH

Dates B.C.	Events	Prophets/Scripture
745–627	Assyrian Domination of the Ancient Near East	
	Assyrian rulers:	
745–727	Tiglath-pileser III	*740–701 The preaching of Isaiah*
726–722	Shalmaneser V	
721–705	Sargon II	
722/1	Fall of the northern kingdom of Israel; deportation of populace; replaced with aliens.	
704–681	Sennacherib	*The preaching of Micah in Judah*
701	Judah, under Hezekiah (715–687/6), crushed; paid heavy tribute.	
680–669	Esarhaddon	
	Manasseh of Judah (687/6–642), a faithful vassal of Assyria. Widespread syncretism, idolatry, child sacrifice, injustice, persecution of prophets.	
668–627	Ashurbanipal	
	Invasion of Egypt	
663	Sack of Thebes	*Nahum 3:8*
	Power threatened by rise of twenty-sixth dynasty in Egypt under Psammetichus I (664–610), by pressure from Indo-Aryans (Medes, Cimmerians, Scythians), and by revolt in Babylonia. Ammon of Judah (642–640), vassal to Assyria, assassinated.	
640–609	Rule of Josiah in Judah	*Zephaniah chapters 1 and 2*

Dates B.C.	Events	Prophets/Scripture
627	Josiah comes of age; begins independence movement and expansionist policies; abolishes foreign influences.	
626–605	Rise of Neo-Babylonian empire under Nabopolassar.	626–584 *The preaching of Jeremiah*
625–585	Rise of Medes under Cyaxerxes	
622/1	Deuteronomy found during temple repairs; widespread religious reform; abolition of alien cults and priests; centralization of worship at Jerusalem; covenant renewal.	
		II Kings 22—23; II Chronicles 34—35
614	Medes take Asshur	*The preaching of Nahum*
612	Fall of Nineveh to Medes and Babylonians	612–609 *Zephaniah chapter 3*
610	Fall of Haran to Babylonians	
609	Assyrians, aided by Egypt, fail to retake Haran. Assyrian Empire finished. Josiah killed trying to halt Egyptian Pharaoh, Necho II, at Megiddo.	
609–605 Egyptian Domination of Judah		
	Josiah's son Jehoahaz (Shallum) placed on Judean throne; deported to Egypt after three months.	
	Jehoiakim (609–598) put on Judean throne: Egyptian vassal and tyrant, forced labor, syncretism, idolatry, persecution of prophets.	*The preaching of Habakkuk*
605	Egypt defeated by Nebuchadnezzar of Babylonia (605/4–562)	
605–550 Babylonian Domination of the Ancient Near East		
604	Philistia (Ashdod) subdued	
603/2	Jehoiakim transfers allegiance to Babylonia	
601	Babylonian battle with Egypt: Nebuchadnezzar withdraws to recoup; Jehoiakim rebels.	
600/599	Nebuchadnezzar busy elsewhere; guerrilla raids against Judah.	
598	Death (assassination?) of Jehoiakim; Jehoiachin placed on Judean throne; tribute withheld, owing to Egyptian intrigue.	
597	First deportation to Babylonia Zedekiah (597–587) placed on Judean throne	
587	The fall of Jerusalem	

THE BOOK OF

Nahum

Introduction

"All scripture is inspired by God and profitable for teaching, for reproof, for correction, and for training in righteousness, that the man of God may be complete, equipped for every
good work" (II Tim. 3:16–17). We give lip service to such an
acknowledgment of the authority of Scripture, but in actual
fact, we exempt the Book of Nahum from it. Indeed, we often
wish Nahum were not in the canon, and the book has been
almost totally ignored in the modern church. No lectionary
reading is taken from it and no hymn suggests its words, other
than the one line from William Cowper's poem set to music in
"God Moves in a Mysterious Way." ("He plants his footsteps in
the sea, and rides upon the storm," cf. Nahum 1:3c.)

Nahum is, in its historical setting, a prediction and celebration of the fall of Nineveh, the capital of the Assyrian Empire,
in 612 B.C. Some interpreters have therefore scorned the Book
of Nahum, because it seems to be a vengeful, nationalistic expression of Israel's triumph over an enemy. It is the work of a
false prophet, says one. Ethically and theologically it is deficient, writes another.

To be sure, many critics must acknowledge the literary
value of the book. "Nahum's language is strong and brilliant; his
rhythm rumbles and rolls, leaps and flashes, like the horse and
chariots he describes" (G.A. Smith, p. 90). Nevertheless, few
critics approve the message of the book, and many value it
simply as a literary masterpiece.

Nahum is not primarily a book about human beings, however—not about human vengeance and hatred and military
conquest—but a book about God. And it has been our failure to

5

let Nahum be a book about God that has distorted the value of this prophecy in our eyes. We human beings sometimes want to remain the judges of human history, the sole arbiters of right and wrong, and the last warders of proper conduct. In our role, then, as magistrates over human life, we decide what God himself can and cannot do. We decide that God cannot destroy the wicked—that it is God's role only to forgive and that, indeed, there are no wicked and righteous on the earth, but that all are equally guilty. Ancient Assyria was no more evil than Judah, is our decree with respect to Nahum; therefore Nahum is deficient in understanding its people's sin and is an expression only of nationalistic vengeance. A loving God, as pictured in Jonah and in the New Testament, would forgive the sins of Assyria, just as—and this is the final pride—he will always forgive our sins. We dismiss Nahum as inferior to our sense of what is proper.

It is interesting, furthermore, that we have unwittingly used the very tools of scholarship to further our prideful rejection of this prophetic book. The key to the message of Nahum lies in its opening hymn, 1:2–11. This hymn was apparently borrowed by the prophet from an earlier source and adapted by him for his theological purposes. Underlying it are traces of an earlier acrostic hymn, extending at least through verse 8. That is, each line of the hymn begins with a letter of the Hebrew alphabet and runs from a ('aleph) through i (yodh). But the prophet upset the acrostic progression and inserted his own material, notably in verses 2b and 3a. He also extended the hymn in verses 9–11. It is precisely this hymn, however, or portions of it, that is sometimes removed from Nahum or rearranged. By such alteration, the book is deprived of its theological key.

The entire book now lies before us in order, with remarkable symmetry. The opening hymn, 1:2–11, ends in verse 11 with the address to the enemy: "From your midst came forth one who devised/ against Yahweh evil (ra'ah)." The final judgment oracle on Nineveh, 3:14–19, also ends with an address to the enemy in the form of a dirge; and the last line reads in the Hebrew, "For upon whom has not come your continual evil (ra'ah)?" Thus, evil introduced and evil done away form the inclusio of the thought of the book.

Between these two sections, then, stand four judgment oracles against Nineveh: 1:12–15; 2:1–13; 3:1–7, 8–13. Each of

6

these sections ends with a word of the Lord, introduced by "Behold!" (1:15; 2:13; 3:5, 13), and each of these pronouncements of the Lord means salvation for Judah at the same time that it brings judgment on Assyria. Whether this ordered arrangement of the book is the product of Nahum himself or of a redactor is moreover irrelevant, because it is the book as it now lies before us that communicates the message of the one called "Nahum" *(comforting, comforter).* To try to go behind that to some historical figure bearing the name simply vitiates the message of the book.

Internal evidence in the book places its date sometime between 663 B.C., when Thebes was destroyed (Nah. 3:8), and 612 B.C., when Nineveh finally fell to the Babylonians. Some scholars believe that 1:15 refers to the death in 627 of the great Assyrian ruler Ashurbanipal, which marked the beginning of the weakening that led to Assyria's fall. Others have speculated about the relation of the book to the Deuteronomic reform under Josiah, which began in 621 B.C., and have maintained that Nahum says nothing about the sins of Judah because Judah's life has temporarily been renewed by the reform. But most scholars place the book shortly before 612 B.C. and view it as an actual prediction of Nineveh's fall. Certainly the book has that concrete historical setting, but its meaning transcends its historical context and bears a relevance still today.

The book is the only prophetic corpus to have two titles: (1) "A burden *(threatening word)* concerning Nineveh" (cf. Isa. 13:1; 15:1; 17:1); (2) "The book of the vision of Nahum of Elkosh." This is also the only prophetic corpus labeled a "book," but that does not imply that it was originally written and not spoken. "Vision" means simply "prophecy" or "revelation" (cf. Isa. 1:1; Obad. 1). We know nothing else about the prophet. The location of Elkosh is unknown, although the most acceptable traditions place it in Judah and connect Nahum with the tribe of Simeon. Nahum as a person has importance, however, only because of these words of his on behalf of the Lord that have been handed down faithfully to us by Israel and the church.

Nahum 1:2–11

The interpretive riches of this opening hymn are almost beyond enumerating, for we have here only a little less than a complete presentation of the biblical witness to God's person: the testimony to his covenant love and to his patient mercy; his intimate knowledge of his own and his protection of them; his just lordship over his world and his might in maintaining his rule; his specific but also eschatological defeat of all who would challenge his sovereignty. The God portrayed here is really God, different from all lesser imitations, and different too from those impotent idols that we often project upon our universe.

The force of the hymn can be felt more clearly if the Hebrew word order is reproduced:

> A jealous God and an avenger is the Lord,
> An avenger is the Lord and owner of wrath,
> An avenger is the Lord against his enemies,
> and a keeper of anger is he against his foes (v. 2).

The threefold repetition of "avenger" builds to the final "keeper." But there follows the recognition of the Lord's long patience with sin, in verse 3a, and the same two thoughts of his mercy and judgment are once again presented side by side in verses 7 and 8.

The God of the Bible is throughout its pages a jealous God, because he has made for himself a people to serve his purpose; and he wills that that people neither stray from his purpose and devotion to him nor be deterred by any enemy from their covenant calling. The imagery of God's "jealousy" is of his zealous will driving forward toward his goal of salvation for his earth. When any human foes would thwart that drive, God becomes their enemy—an avenger who is master or "owner" of wrath against all challenges to his lordship. That is a threatening picture only to those who want to be their own gods and rule the earth in their own ways, but to those who trust God it is a comfort and an affirmation that he is truly sovereign.

This hymn emphasizes the grace that is to be had from

God. "Good is the Lord," reads verse 7*a* in the Hebrew order, with the emphasis on "good." "There is indeed nothing more peculiar to God than goodness" (Calvin, III, 430). Our very term "God" is a shortened form of "good" and is an acknowledgment that all good flows from him. Human beings cannot have goodness in the world apart from God, and God is dependent on no other source for his goodness. His goodness does not depend on what happens to some person or on what our fortunes are. Thus, our Lord, on his way to the cross, could affirm, "No one is good but God alone" (Luke 18:19), because it is the essence of faith that it confesses in any circumstance, "The Lord is good to all, / and his compassion is over all that he has made" (Ps. 145:9). On a bed of pain, faith says, "Truly God is good." In trouble and affliction and persecution, faith knows God is good—that all his history with his people has been the working out of his good for them and that all the future ahead will be guided by his goodness. So too here, Nahum, at the turbulent end of an age, with kingdoms tottering and armies clashing, affirms, "Good is the Lord."

Nahum gives two illustrations of the goodness of God. He is "a stronghold in the day of trouble" (v. 7*b*), a mighty fortress inside whose protecting arms we need not fear though the earth should change and the mountains shake in the heart of the seas (Ps. 46). He gives enduring protection—for strongholds are no temporary camps—from assaulting foes and safety from destruction. He provides the place of peace and quiet conscience midst the raging warfare of hell's armies. He is the one to whom our Lord on the cross, with the forces of sin and death arrayed against him, could say in confidence as he breathed his last, "Into thy hands I commit my spirit" (Luke 23:46//Ps. 31:5).

God is also good because "he knows those who take refuge in him" (v. 7*c*), that is, he knows those who rely on him for their life and sustenance and guidance. And God's knowledge is far more than simply nodding acquaintance, far more than recognition of a name at a distance. God's knowledge implies intimate care, tender concern, loving communion, like the knowledge of a loving husband for his wife or of a concerned father for his son (cf. Hosea). Indeed, God's knowledge of those who rely on him goes even beyond that, for he numbers the hairs of his beloved ones' heads; he knows their needs, their wants, their sufferings. He besets them behind and before and is acquainted with all their ways. There is not a word they speak

9

that God does not know beforehand. There is not a path they have trod with which God is unacquainted or a road they travel of whose end God is not aware. He knows when they lie down and when they rise and is ever present with them. Such is the goodness of God to which Nahum here gives testimony.

But . . . but . . . twice Nahum uses that word (Hebrew *waw*): "but the Lord will by no means clear the guilty" (v. 3*b*); "but with an overflowing flood/he will make a full end of his adversaries (Hebrew: her place) and will pursue his enemies into darkness" (v. 8). God is enemy of those who defy his lordship; and that too is part of his goodness, for God will not allow evil to triumph in the world. Instead, he will drive it into darkness, pursue it until it disappears into the lifeless realm of chaos and void and nothingness, in short, until it is totally at an end and God's goodness alone remains on earth.

It is almost incomprehensible that our age has so softened these thoughts of God's destruction of evil to which Nahum here gives expression. For if God does not destroy the evil human beings have brought into God's good creation, the world can never return to the wholeness he intended for it in the beginning. To divest God of his function as destroyer of wrong is to acquiesce to the present corrupt state of the world—to accept the sinful status quo and simply to put up with whatever is done by selfish and prideful and corrupted men and women. But surely part of the message of the cross is that evil must be done away by God, if his Kingdom is ever to come on earth as he has promised it will.

Notably, however, Nahum emphasizes that God will be the destroyer of wrong and corruption. Over against all thoughts of human vengeance, of human pursuit of evildoers, Nahum emphasizes that emphatic triad, "an avenger is the Lord . . . an avenger is the Lord . . . an avenger is the Lord" (v. 2). "Vengeance is mine; I will repay," quotes Paul of the Lord (Rom. 12:19; Heb. 10:30; cf. I Thess. 4:6; Matt. 5:39), and Nahum differs in no respect from such New Testament teaching. He expects God to do away with Assyria, and his whole book rejoices over the righteous action of his righteous God. "Our hearts must learn to give way to the wrath of God," wrote Paul Kleinert (p. 21), that is, to step aside for God's requital and destruction of evil, and not take them into our own hands. We must learn what it means to pray, "Deliver us from evil," and what it means to love the enemies of God's goodness. Certainly it

10

does not mean approbation or total passivity toward sin and wrong, any more than it means that we should try to replace God as redeemer of the world. But in dealing with evil, in our world and in our enemies and in ourselves, we are to rely on God's work and not on our own, as he works through both his covenant people and the affairs of nations. "Not my will, but thine be done" is here too the rule of faith.

God's goodness is further emphasized by Nahum in this hymn in his use of the familiar Old Testament phrase, "The Lord is slow to anger . . . " (v. 3a). Surely that must have seemed the case in Judah's experience of the Assyrian Empire. For over one hundred years, ever since the accession of Tiglath-pileser III (745–727 B.C.) to the Assyrian throne, Judah had suffered under the barbarities of the cruelest conqueror of the ancient Near East. She had watched her ten kindred tribes to the north in Israel deported in 722/1, to be lost forever from history. She had become the vassal to Assyrian might under Ahaz in 734 B.C. When she revolted in the reign of Hezekiah, she had watched forty-six of her cities destroyed before the armies of the Assyrian Sennacherib, and she had stayed alive only by stripping herself of treasure to pay heavy tribute. Finally, under Manasseh (687/6–642 B.C.), she had watched Assyrian gods and goddesses set up in her temple, seen her prophets persecuted and killed, and witnessed her court officials parading Assyrian customs and dress (cf. Zeph. 1:2–9).

If one reads Assyrian documents recounting the acts of that empire (see Pritchard), one finds them full of accounts of cruelty, pridefully recounted by the Assyrian rulers. In the face of that, Judah must have thought God was surely slow to anger!

Yet it is a mark of God's goodness that he is forbearing and patient and long-suffering with human sin. "It is a weakness of ours that we want the Lord to take vengeance right now," wrote Luther. "When his vengeance is not immediate, we think it's all over with us" (XVIII, 286). But God is exceedingly slow to anger, because he is exceedingly great: It is the little cur that yaps at every threatening noise—the lion waits and seems to doze. God is forbearing toward his creatures, because he is great in power: The weak cannot bear an insult and they immediately answer back; the lordly smile and shrug off foes and need not deign to harm them, for they know the foe has no real power and cannot prosper long. God always gives his creatures much time to turn to him. He never smites without threatening

11

—by sickness, by providence, by consequence, by his word. Indeed, he is even slow to threaten:

> He doth not even threaten the sinner by his conscience, until the sinner hath oft-times sinned. He will often tell the sinner of his sins, often urge him to repent; but he will not make hell stare him hard in the face, with all its dreadful terror, until much sin has stirred up the lion from his lair, and made God hot in wrath against the iniquities of man. He is slow even to threaten (Spurgeon, "Mercy, Omnipotence and Justice," p. 689).

And then, having threatened, how slow he is to sentence the criminal! In Eden, God had promised that in the day in which the man and woman ate of the forbidden fruit, they would surely die, but God takes a walk in the cool of the day before he levels that sentence (Gen. 3).

Then, having sentenced, how slow he is to carry it out! Surely the cities of earth have lived under the sentencing wrath of God, but how long it has taken for them to fall! Nineveh, Babylon, Jerusalem, Rome have each basked in glory for hundreds of years before the God whose wrath is hard to kindle has said to them, "Be gone!"

However, lest the reader of Nahum's words think God's hesitancy is due to lack of power, the prophet, in the manner of Numbers 14:17 and Romans 9:22, emphasizes also God's might. The Lord is of great might (v. 3a), and Judah is not to think that he has ignored the excesses of Assyria out of weakness, in comparison either with Assyria's armies or with her gods. It is the creator God whom Nahum pictures in verses 3c–5, the God who rebuked the waters of chaos at the original creation (v. 4; cf. Isa. 51:10) and who heaped up the waters of the Reed Sea and of the Jordan to let his people cross over on dry land (cf. Ps. 77:16–20; 106:9; Isa. 50:2). We therefore may have the remnant of a New Year's liturgy here, recited to celebrate God's founding of the earth. But this God can also wither the watered pastures of Bashan and Carmel and wilt the towering cedars of Lebanon (cf. Isa. 33:9); and Assyria, with her irrigation economy and her gods of the waters, is no match for this Lord who controls all water. Indeed, the Lord will use the floods to bring her chaos to an end (Nah. 2:6,8).

12

"The world cannot for a moment stand, except as it is sustained by the favour and goodness of God" (Calvin, III, 427), for its existence depends on the faithfulness of its Lord in preserving it. He has unmatchable power. The whirlwind is but the disturbance of air caused by his striding along. The clouds stretching across the sky are only the dust kicked up by his feet (v. 3*cd*). Mountains—the very pillars of the earth—quake before him (cf. Exod. 19:18; Ps. 114:6–7) and the hills melt (cf. Micah 1:4). The earth heaves up (cf. Amos 8:8) and sinks (RSV: is laid waste) with all its inhabitants.

When God's anger is aroused, therefore, when his patience and pleading have led to nought, when repentance and obedience are not forthcoming and his lordship is scorned or ignored, or when his covenant people have been endangered or themselves have thrown off his yoke, the Lord becomes a "keeper" of wrath (v. 2) who will no longer overlook such sin. He becomes the "Owner" of anger who "will by no means clear the guilty" (v. 3*b*).

The Apostle Paul echoes these thoughts of Nahum's in his letter to the Roman church (Rom. 2:4–10), and Nahum's message is quite consonant with that of the New Testament. Therefore, an age that believes God only forgives is deceiving itself. God can be aroused to wrath.

Then, asks Nahum, Who can stand before his wrath (RSV: indignation; v. 6)? Once again it is God's incomparable power, in his anger, which the prophet has in view. But this time the figure is of fire—some have suggested molten lava—whose heat causes the moisture in the very rocks to expand and burst them asunder. Calvin emphasizes the suddenness of the destruction here, and he may be right. The fire-storm breaks out—whipped to fury, engulfing all before it—the fire-storm of the heat of God's anger against sin.

Obviously, Nahum has in mind God's zealous, jealous destruction of Assyria; and the words, "her place," in verse 8 (RSV margin) probably should not be emended. They are the first hint in the book, other than the superscription, that its words are to be applied to the fall of Nineveh. Then, in verse 9, the enemy is personally addressed and told that no plans they make, no defenses they devise, no counsel they take will be sufficient to turn aside the utter destruction *(full end)* that is coming upon them. God will not have to return a second time. In his first onslaught against her, Nineveh will be totally destroyed. Though she seem dangerous—like tangled thorns that prick those who touch them (cf. II Sam. 23:6–7) or like a drunk man swaggering and boisterous—Assyria will nevertheless be

13

burned up by the fire of God's hot anger, like dry stubble consumed by a racing flame (v. 10).

Nahum saves till last, moreover, the reason for God's wrath against Assyria (v. 11):

> From your midst came forth one who devised
>> against the Lord evil *(ra'ah)*,
> who counseled worthlessness *(belial;* author's trans.; cf. II Cor. 6:15).

The reference is probably not to one Assyrian conqueror but to all of them, and Nineveh's sin, manifested in her cruelty toward subjugated nations, is finally sin against God. Because God is Lord of history, all national and international relations of earth's societies are measured against his justice (cf. Amos 1:3—2:3). The Nuremburg trials following World War II brought Nazi leaders to judgment for their crimes against humanity; but crimes against humanity are, in the last instance, crimes against God and will be dealt with by him—a fact to which Pope Pius XII once gave vivid expression when he addressed a gathering of international leaders in the Sistine Chapel before Michelangelo's painting of the Last Judgment.

Assyria had once been used by God as an instrument of his anger against his own people, according to Isaiah (10:5–6), but power corrupted Assyria, as it corrupts all nations who come to believe that they are in charge of their own destinies and self-sufficient in their own strength. Assyria had boasted:

> "By the strength of my hand I have done it,
>> and by my wisdom, for I have understanding" (Isa. 10:13).

Assyria's sin was that she forgot she was but an instrument in the hand of God:

> Shall the axe vaunt itself over him who hews with it,
>> or the saw magnify itself against him who wields it? (Isa. 10:15).

Indeed, Assyria had even become defiant of the power of God —a defiance evidenced in the boast of the Assyrian commander, Rabshakeh, in the time of Hezekiah:

> "Beware lest Hezekiah mislead you by saying, 'The Lord will deliver us.' Has any of the gods of the nations delivered his land out of the hand of the king of Assyria? Where are the gods of Hamath and Arpad? Where are the gods of Sepharvaim? Have they delivered Samaria out of my hand? Who among all the

gods of these countries have delivered their countries out of my hand, that the Lord should deliver Jerusalem out of my hand?" (Isa. 36:18–20).

The final sin of nations and individuals is the sin of pride— of believing that they can live their lives and conduct their affairs apart from any reference to the King of kings and Lord of lords. But God says to all human pride, as he said to his people in the time of Ezekiel, ". . . surely with a mighty hand and an outstretched arm, and with wrath poured out, I will be king over you" (Ezek. 20:33). God will be king over us, and it is for us to decide whether he will exercise his kingship in love toward us or in wrath.

Nahum incorporated this hymn into his prophecy with specific reference to Assyria and the impending fall of her capital, Nineveh, but this hymnic preface is also valid in every age. It is a testimony to God's goodness, to his patient, forbearing, long-suffering slowness to anger, and his incomparable might; but it is also a testimony to the fact that the Lord will never pass over human wrong.

The church has therefore sometimes used Nahum eschatologically to refer to the final judgment. For example, after commenting on the first five verses of Nahum, John Calvin prayed:

> Grant, Almighty God, that as thou settest before us here as in a mirror how dreadful thy wrath is, we may be humbled before thee, and of our own-selves cast ourselves down, . . . and be cleansed from our vices, until we shall at length appear in confidence before thee, and be gathered among thy children, that we may enjoy the eternal inheritance of thy heavenly kingdom, which has been obtained for us by the blood of thy Son. Amen (III, 427–28).

But Nahum can also be used to remind individuals and church that God levels his judgments against sin throughout the course of history: Evil Nineveh was destroyed.

Indeed, that is the function of Nahum for us today: It is an urgent call to repentance—a call to condemn ourselves for our pride and crimes against God, to cast ourselves on his patient mercy, and to take refuge in his goodness, finally made flesh for us in Jesus Christ. We stand under sentence, and God will by no means clear the guilty. But God is slow—slow to carry out the sentence—and does not wish that we should perish.

15

Nahum 1:12–15

After the key hymn of 1:2–11 that sets the theological context for his prophecy, Nahum now moves from his general testimony to the nature of God to spell out the consequences of that testimony for his own time. Because God will by no means clear the guilty, Assyria will be destroyed.

This oracle is linked to 1:2–11 by its use of *belial* (v. 15; RSV: The wicked; v. 11: villainy), and its principal image is that of cutting off. The Lord will "cut off" Assyria. He will cut off her armies (v. 12), though they be at full strength and fully trained and prepared; military might counts as nothing before the power of God. He will cut off Assyria's gods (v. 14), for they are gods who have no power and who therefore are worthless idols, helpless to protect their people. Finally, he will cut off Belial, which is the image Nahum uses here for Assyria (v. 15).

Belial is a title compounded from two Hebrew words and means "nothingness," "worthlessness." It has almost the force of a proper name in verse 15 (cf. II Sam. 23:6, RSV margin; Job 34:18). Some have thought that it is a Hebrew adaptation of *Belili*, a Babylonian goddess of the underworld and of vegetation, or that it signifies the underworld itself, as in II Samuel 22:5. Others have thought it was originally the name of an evil spirit. In the pseudepigraphal books of the *Testament of the Twelve Patriarchs*, the *Ascension of Isaiah*, and *Jubilees*, it becomes a proper name for Satan, and the Apostle Paul follows such usage in II Corinthians 6:15. In the *Sybilline Oracles*, it is a title given to Nero. Its origin can really no longer be traced, but it certainly is the title which Nahum gives to evil incarnate in the form of Assyria. *Belial*—wickedness, worthlessness, the powers of death in the world—will be cut off by the living God of Israel.

God has given a decree concerning Assyria (v. 14)—and God's word not only created the world but also rules it. "For he spoke, and it came to be; he commanded, and it stood forth" (Ps. 33:9). The decree is that Assyria's name will no longer be "sown" (RSV: perpetuated); that is, she will have no more offspring. She is "vile," literally, she makes a stench; therefore she must be buried (cf. Ezek. 32:22–23).

Assyria's death, however, means good news for Judah, who has suffered under the conqueror's rod for over a hundred years (v. 13). The picture is not of a yoke (as the RSV has it) but of a slavemaster, standing over his captive with an upraised staff. Now that punishing staff will be broken and Judah set free (Isa. 9:4; cf. 10:27). This oracle which pronounces judgment on Assyria means salvation for Judah. Never again will she be afflicted by Assyria's cruelty (v. 12). God did use that empire once to work his wrath against his people, but now Assyria has overstepped her bounds (cf. Isa. 10:5–19) and God will not so use her again.

In verse 15, therefore, Nahum borrows the familiar figure of the herald who ran over the mountains to bring good news (cf. Isa. 52:7) to embody his gospel to Judah. The herald comes announcing *"shalom"*—peace, wholeness, abundant life (cf. Acts 10:36; Rom. 10:15)—and he tells Judah to resume her accustomed life. The last five lines of verse 15 make up the herald's message. Judah can now resume all those festal occasions which she had no heart to celebrate under the tyrant's heel. She can fulfill the vows she made to God. That is, she vowed to offer a sacrifice or to make some return if he would deliver her. It has been done; the vows can be paid. *Belial* will never again overcome God's people. *Belial* is cut off.

That is all a future promise for Judah in the time of Nahum, and if the prophet did deliver his message shortly before 612 B.C., Judah's spirits must have soared as Nineveh went up in flames and the word of the Lord came to pass. But Judah's rejoicing was short-lived. Her wise king, Josiah, the reformer, died in battle against Egypt in 609 B.C. and Assyria's rod was quickly replaced, first by that of Egypt and then that of Babylonia. Indeed, biblical Judah never again knew freedom from the foreigner's yoke until a brief period in the second century B.C., in the time of the Maccabees. What, then, of the word of God that Belial has been fully cut off?

As with one of the interpretations of 1:2–11, given previously, this oracle can be interpreted eschatologically by those faithful to God, who are the true heirs of the promises to Judah. *Belial*—wickedness incarnate, the powers of evil—have been defeated (cf. Rev. 2:27; 12:5; 19:15). The church saw that happen in the cross and resurrection of Jesus Christ, where sin and

17

death met their end and were buried in the grave of our Lord, while he was raised triumphant over them in the fullness of eternal life. The faithful now live by the foretaste of that victory, and they look forward to the full inheritance of it when Christ returns to set up the Kingdom of God on earth.

The City of Nineveh

In the poems that follow in Nahum's book, he gives us a series of pictures of the siege and fall of the Assyrian capital of Nineveh. The pictures are not meant to follow one another in order, as if they described the progress of the battle leading to the city's capture. Rather, the pictures flash before our eyes, illumining first one and then another of the conflict's scenes. So realistic are they that some have thought the prophet must have been an eyewitness to them, but Nineveh's glory was known throughout the ancient world and her armies and their accoutrements familiar to every resident of the Fertile Crescent. Nahum did not need to go to Nineveh to picture that city's fall. As inspired poet, he could see it in his mind's eye. The result was some of the most vivid war poetry ever written.

Surely in Nahum's time Nineveh was a "great city" (Gen. 10:12; Jonah 1:2; 3:2) located on the eastern bank of the Tigris River, some miles north of the Tigris' confluence with the Upper Zab and opposite modern Mosul. It had a history reaching back for centuries, but it attained its greatest glory during the last century of the Assyrian Empire and principally in the reign of Sennacherib (704–681 B.C.). It had a wall almost eight miles in circumference that enclosed the largest fortified space in eastern Asia, and it could accommodate a population of three hundred thousand.

Nineveh was an almost impregnable fortress. On the low hills surrounding three sides of the city forts guarded the approaches to the metropolis, while the Tigris flowed by on the west. Beyond its massive walls the city was guarded by a system of moats and canals, and beyond the latter, outworks added further defenses.

A never-failing water supply was furnished Nineveh by the Khusar, a perennial mountain stream that ran through the city from northeast to southwest and by a canal that had been constructed to leave the Khusar higher up and to flow through the city to the Tigris. Both of these waterways, however, had to pass through the north wall of the city, and thus the city was most vulnerable at that point.

Outside of the wall of the city were suburbs, one added by Sennacherib's successor, Esarhaddon (680–669 B.C.), and others sprouting up as the population grew. Within the city were found Sennacherib's "Palace with No Rival" and Ashurbanipal's huge library of twenty-two thousand clay tablets that now serves as the chief archaeological source for our knowledge of the life and thought of ancient Mesopotamia.

According to the Babylonian chronicle, Nineveh was first besieged by the Medes, under Cyaxerxes, in 614 B.C., without success. However, at the beginning of June (month of Sivan), 612 B.C., the Medes joined forces with the Scythian tribes from the Caucausus and, above all, with Nabopolasar of Babylonia, and laid Nineveh under siege until sometime in August (month of Ab), that is, for about two and one-half months, when the wall was breached and the city taken (Gadd, p. 25).

The Sicilian historian Diodorus (after 21 B.C.) characterizes Sin-shar-ishkun, the Assyrian ruler in power at the time of the city's fall, as "contemptible," concerned only with "luxury" and "effeminate extravagance" (Gadd, p. 27). He also records that Sin-shar-ishkun sent his three sons and two daughters out of the city for safety, despite the fact that he was assured by the words of an ancient prophecy that "none should capture Nineveh by force of arms unless the river first became an enemy to the city" (Gadd, p. 29). It was this prophecy, records Diodorus (XXVII.1) that came to pass:

> . . . in the third year, a succession of heavy downpours swelled the Euphrates (sic), flooded part of the city, and cast down the wall to a length of 20 stades. 2. Thereupon the king realised that the oracle had been fulfilled, and that the river had manifestly declared war upon the city. Despairing of his fate, but resolved not to fall into the hands of his enemies, he prepared a gigantic pyre in the royal precincts, heaped up all his gold and silver and his kingly raiment as well upon it, shut up his concubines and eunuchs in the chamber he had made in the midst of the pyre, and burnt himself and the palace together with all of them (Gadd, p. 30).

Certainly the excavated ruins of Nineveh show marks of fire, although whether Sin-shar-ishkun in fact immolated himself is unknown (cf. Isa. 30:33). We do know that some Assyrians escaped under the leadership of Ashur-uballit to Haran, where the latter was made king, until the empire totally collapsed in 609 B.C.

As for the legend of the river destroying the wall of the city,

19

it cannot be proved or disproved. Nahum 1:8 speaks of an "overflowing flood," and it is possible that the Khusar, which was normally at its highest stage in April and May, was swollen by an extraordinary rainfall and undermined the north wall of the city. Nahum 2:6 also speaks of the opening of the "river gates," and 2:8 describes the conquered city as a "pool." It may be that the besiegers redirected the system of dams and sluices to allow the waters of the moats to flood the city. The traditions are rather consistent in associating the capture of the city with water, but just what supernatural, natural, or man-made events were involved can no longer be ascertained.

Nahum 2:1–13

The text of this judgment oracle, which takes the form of a prophetic vision, is difficult at several points, especially in verses 3, 7, 8, with minor emendations made also in verses 1, 11, and 13 (see RSV marginal readings); but we can reconstruct Nahum's portrayal with some certainty.

A Shatterer (Hebr.: scatterer) "rises up before the face" (Hebr.) of Assyria, who is addressed in verse 1. Like some shadowy spectre rising from the earth, or like some menacing storm appearing on the horizon, Assyria's punisher suddenly looms up before her eyes. The shatterer comes in the form of the scarlet-clad troops of the Babylonian coalition (vv. 3–4; cf. Ezek. 23:14), to confront the Assyrian blue (cf. Ezek. 23:6 [RSV:purple]; 27:23–24); but as in all of Nahum's oracles, he is speaking of more than historical events. This shatterer is God, working his will through the conflicts of nations, restoring in his jealousy (cf. 1:2) his covenant people whom Assyria has plundered (v. 2).

Verses 3 and 4, then, describe the onslaught of the Babylonians against the suburbs of Nineveh, with the polished metal plates of the Babylonian war chariots flashing like lightning in the sunlight and their cavalry whirling on charging steeds.

In verse 5, the outlying districts have been taken and Nineveh's wall is attacked, whereupon the Assyrians rush their commanders and troops to the wall, stumbling in their haste to defend it and setting up a mantelet or "covering" (of whose meaning we can not be sure) to protect themselves from the hail of enemy arrows, spears, and catapulted missiles.

But the "river gates" are opened (cf. 3:13 and see the preceding discussion of the city of Nineveh), the wall is breached, and the attackers pour into the city, which is personified in verse 7 as a woman (cf. 3:5–7) led away into exile, with all her maid servants bemoaning her fate. The first word of verse 7 (which the RSV reads as "its mistress") is literally, in the Hebrew, "it is determined," and it refers once again to the commandment the Lord has set over Assyria (1:14).

When the defenders of Nineveh try to rally their troops and populace, none stay to carry on the fray (v. 8). Many flee in panic, like a pool whose waters are released, and those who are left are terrified and grow pale and weak (v. 10). The attacking troops are therefore free to plunder Nineveh's treasures (v. 9), and the city is left bereft of its riches and power (v. 10).

The prophet therefore utters the taunt of verses 11–12. Great Assyria, so often symbolized in her sculptures and friezes as a proud lion, is lion no more, but has herself become a prey (v. 13).

This oracle is joined to 1:12–15 by the repetition of the word "cut off" in verse 13—that word which furnished the key to 1:12–15—and this connecting word stands at the end of the oracle, just as *belial,* which connected 1:12–15 with 1:2–11, stands at the end of both of those passages. There is an ordered structure here in the Book of Nahum.

Moreover, this oracle is a study in contrasts. In verse 1 Nahum addresses the Assyrians with biting irony, urging them to strengthen their outer fortifications, to guard their roads, and to collect all their strength; but in verse 10 they have become utterly weak. Nineveh has been guarded by her moats and rivers, and in verse 8 her populace is compared to a pool; but in verse 6 her very means of protection have become the instruments of her destruction. In verse 2 Judah has been plundered; but in verse 9 Nineveh suffers that fate. In verse 2 the "majesty" of Judah has been lost; but in verse 9 Nineveh's "glory" (Hebrew: her treasure from booty and tribute) is stripped away. In verse 9 there is no end of Nineveh's treasures; but in verse 10 she is "emptiness," "desolated and wasted" (Hebr.). In verse 12 the lion has filled his cave with prey; but in verse 13 the prey is cut off. And finally, the end of the oracle contrasts with the

21

end of the preceding one. In verse 13 Assyria's "messengers," that is, her emissaries sent forth from Nineveh to exact tribute and compel submission and carry out her royal mandates, will no longer be seen or heard on the earth, while in 1:15 the voice of the one who proclaims *shalom* to Judah will be heard loud and clear. God will bring about a complete reversal of the fortunes of Nineveh, for God is Lord over her and shatterer of her pride and life.

"Behold, I am against you"; that is the determinative word (v. 13; cf. 1:14; 2:7 Hebr.; 3:5), for how we as nations and individuals stand in the eyes of God finally determines our death or life. Israel, because of the unearned grace of God, had been told all her life by him, "I am with you" (Exod. 3:12; 3:14 Hebr.; 33:14; Josh. 1:5; Jer. 1:8, 19; 15:20; Isa. 7:14; cf. 43:5). The disciples of Jesus heard the same merciful assurance when our Lord departed from them (Matt. 28:20; cf. Acts 18:10), and the church has been assured of that divine favor ever since in the presence of God's Holy Spirit with it (Rom. 8:11, 15–17; II Cor. 1:22 and often). Therefore, Paul could write, "If God is for us, who is against us" (Rom. 8:31)? That is ultimate assurance for the faithful. But faith, like unfaith, needs always to ask if it deserves these words that God addressed to Assyria, "Behold, I am against you." Then it needs to contemplate the fate of Nineveh and repent (cf. Matt. 12:41).

Nahum 3:1–7

The fact that this is a "woe" oracle is indispensable to its interpretation. Prophetic woes were pronounced over those who were doomed by God (cf. Amos 5:18–20; 6:1–7; Isa. 5:8–24; 10:1–3; Micah 2:1–4), and it was a familiar form for pronouncement of judgment upon foreign nations (cf. Hab. 2:6–19; Isa. 33:1) as well as upon Israel herself (Ezek. 24:6, 9). Moreover, the form had two sections: that of the accusation, stating what evil the doomed one had done, and that of the announcement, stating the punishment that would come upon the one judged.

22

It therefore follows that this entire oracle is directed to Nineveh and that verses 2–3 picture not the attack upon Nineveh but an example of Assyria's military conquest of a foreign city. Her bloody deeds are being enumerated, and verses 2–3 portray her military juggernaut. They then connect in an unbroken fashion with verse 4. That is, the dead bodies of verse 3 are the result of Assyria's evil trickery of her foreign neighbors. Verses 1–4 form the accusation in this woe oracle, verses 5–7 the announcement of judgment.

This oracle connects with the preceding one by the use of "prey" (RSV: plunder) in verse 1 (as in 2:12, 13) and by the repetition of "Behold, I am against you, says the Lord of Hosts" (2:13; 3:5). In addition, there is a repetition in the Hebrew of *"kabod,"* in 2:9, where it refers to Nineveh's "heaps" of treasure, and in 3:3, where it depicts the "heaps" of corpses that she has caused; but this macabre artistic touch is obscured in the English translation.

This is one of the finest poetic portrayals of a powerful nation to be found in literature. Here we see political, military, and economic power in all its devious corruption. Nineveh is a bloody city because it is full of "lies" (3:1)—because its government practices duplicity, within and without, for its own selfish interests. Here is the nation that proclaims "we want peace" while it prepares for war; that seals a treaty of friendship with a lesser power while secretly plotting the latter's downfall; that denies all responsibility for an international incident which it has covertly brought about. And yes, here too is the government that protects its image in the eyes of its own citizens; whose officials baldly lie about what they are really doing; whose representatives project an image of caring and concern to hide their own greed and corruption; whose official proclamations conceal the truth and can no longer be believed; whose outward image is one of seemliness in the interests of prosperous enterprise, and behind whose mask of etiquette are duplicity and neglect and scorn for the weak and average.

Nahum's picture of Nineveh also shows an overwhelming glimpse of her military might. In the leanest of poetry, with a staccato beat, the prophet portrays Assyria's conquest of a foreign city (v. 2). In a *Blitzkrieg,* all-powerful Assyria defeats an enemy, until the enemy's streets are so full of the slain that the Assyrian soldiers stumble over the corpses (v. 3).

It is all because of Assyria's "harlotry" and "sorcery" (RSV: charms). Normally, these words refer in the Old Testament to the worship of false gods, but they can also refer to international

23

dealings between nations. Assyria is pictured here as a harlot, outwardly beautiful and alluring, who has enticed nations to their doom by their treaties and dealings with her (cf. King Ahaz in the time of Isaiah). Not only is that a comment on the nature of Assyria, but it is also a comment on human proclivity to be fooled by the attractions of this world. We run to those with power, with wealth, with status. We even run to those whom we think have the solutions to our problems. The rich entice us with their ability to buy whatever is needful and desirable. The powerful lure us to their sides with their promises of security. The important shed on us their glory, and the wise seem to ease our perplexities. And so we take refuge in the petty powers of this world and "do not look to the Holy One of Israel" (Isa. 31:1). We "carry out a plan" which is not God's plan and "make a league" that is not of his spirit (Isa. 30:1). And that lures us to our doom as surely as a harlot lures her customers to theirs.

> Her house is the way to Sheol,
> going down to the chambers of death (Prov. 7:27).

Therefore, as Jeremiah also proclaimed in the time of Nahum:

> Thus says the LORD: "Let not the wise man glory in his wisdom, let not the mighty man glory in his might, let not the rich man glory in his riches; but let him who glories glory in this, that he understands and knows me, that I am the LORD who practice steadfast love, justice, and righteousness in the earth; for in these things I delight, says the LORD" (9:23–24).

Because Assyria has lured nations to their death, God therefore pronounces through Nahum his punishment of a harlot (vv. 5–6). In the strongest possible metaphor, the beauty that was Assyria's is shown to be sordid and ugly. The nakedness of the alluring whore is exposed, perhaps shown to be covered with the harlot's sores. Verse 6 may refer to the merciless treatment to which such women were subjected, and it is to be emphasized that Nahum is carrying through the metaphor of the harlot here. She is made the object of scorn and an example to all who see her.

Indeed, finally the harlot will be done to death, and verse 7b is a dirge: "Destroyed is Nineveh!" (RSV: Wasted.) But there are no mourners who will be at her grave, and there are none to comfort her in the present as she sees her doom rise up to meet her. Those who oppose the Lord of hosts are finally bereft of the grace of all community, even the community of those who mourn or of those who comfort one another (cf. Jer. 16:5).

> Grant, Almighty God, that as we have now heard of punishments so dreadful denounced on all tyrants and plunderers, this warning may keep us within the limits of justice, so that none of us may abuse our power to oppress the innocent, but, on the contrary, strive to benefit one another, and wholly regulate ourselves according to the rule of equity: . . . (John Calvin, III, 480).

Nahum 3:8–13

Nahum is a master of metaphor; that is obvious when we remember the primary ways in which he has characterized Assyria. In 2:1–13 Nineveh was a lion deprived of its prey, in 3:1–7 a harlot shamed and exposed. Now, in this taunt song, Nineveh becomes a drunk, weak and dazed. And that image is presented in a daring comparison that only a prophet who was sure of the power of his God could present. Mighty Nineveh, the capital of Assyria, is compared to magnificent Thebes, the capital of Ethiopia and Egypt.

The city of Thebes was the center of the Egyptian Empire for most of the latter's history, from *circa* 2000 B.C. until its fall in 663 B.C. Only during the reign of the Hyksos in Egypt (ca. 1750–1550 B.C.) and of Akhenaten (ca. 1364–1347) was its supremacy challenged. Located on the upper Nile in south Egypt, its god was Amon-Re (hence its name in Hebrew, No-Amon meaning city of Amon), the supreme sun-god; and it was surrounded "by an unrivaled aggregate of sacred precincts and temples" (IDB, IV, 617). Indeed, it was the first great city of the Orient, and it remained one of the world's leading cities for over fourteen hundred years. Allied with Libya on the west and Put (probably Somaliland) on the east (v. 9), it apparently had, like Nineveh, a system of defenses formed by moats and canals, the waters of which were trapped from the rising of the Nile (cf. v. 8).

Yet when Ashurbanipal of Assyria invaded Egypt in 663 B.C., he captured and sacked Thebes, recording his victory in his annals (see Pritchard, p. 295). Even Thebes—glorious

Thebes—went into captivity, says Nahum (3:10). Her children were slaughtered—a familiar sight in ancient warfare. Her nobles were sold by lot as slaves. Her leading citizens were led away or imprisoned in chains—a custom well-attested on Assyrian inscriptions and reliefs. "Even she," proclaims Nahum (v. 10, Hebr.), "went into exile, into captivity." "And," he asks of Nineveh, "are you better than Thebes" (v. 8)?

On the face of it, that is a ridiculous question, because Assyria could immediately answer, "Yes!" After all, she had conquered Thebes. History seemed to show that she was mightier than that Egyptian power.

It is obvious, therefore, that the point of this taunt song is not to compare the relative strengths of the Assyrian and Egyptian empires, but to announce that human might is as nothing before the wrath of God (cf. 1:6). This is an oracle directed against false security, against those nations and individuals who think they can preserve and save themselves in the onslaughts and sea-changes of human history. Those who would save their lives shall lose them, because they are relying on their own powers and not on the power of God. As Paul Kleinert wrote:

> Men may not learn prudence by experience. Ninety-nine godless persons perish in their security, and the hundredth still thinks that his case is a special one, and relies on the same props, which, under others, have been irremediably broken (p. 37).

Nineveh relies on her moats and rivers for the protection of her walls, but Thebes too was protected by waters round about (v. 8). Nineveh relies on her outlying fortifications, guarding the approaches to the city, but those forts will fall like figs shaken into the mouth of the eater (v. 12). Nineveh relies on her mighty warriors, but they will become like weak women (v. 13). Nineveh's gates will be flung open wide to her foes (cf. 2:6), and fire will eat up her barred entrances (cf. 1:10; 2:13). Over against the reasoning that says, "It can't happen to me," Nahum declares, "Even you . . . even you . . ." (v. 11) shall try to hide from the enemy and shall become like a man sotted and dazed, for there is no hiding place from God and no defense against his anger.

Nahum is using in this oracle the familiar Old Testament figure of God's cup of wrath from which all—Israel and foreign nations alike—are forced to drink when they defy God's lordship.

26

> For in the hand of the LORD there is a cup,
>> with foaming wine, well mixed;
> and he will pour a draught from it,
>> and all the wicked of the earth
>> shall drain it down to the dregs (Ps. 75:8; *et al;* cf. Rev. 14:10;
>> 16:19; 19:15).

The results of that cup are staggering, vomit, stupefaction, and helplessness—not a pretty picture, but surely appropriate to the degradation we create on earth by relying on ourselves.

"There's no hiding place down here"—no avoiding the cup of wrath—unless God himself changes the content of the cup into the new wine of the gospel (cf. John 2:1–11; Mark 2:22 par.). "None is righteous, no not one," for we all try to live without God; and Nahum has proclaimed that the Lord will by no means clear the guilty (1:3). But this God of Nahum's—this Lord slow to anger—gives his cup of wrath to his Son in our place (Mark 10:38 par.; 14:36 par.) and offers to us instead a "cup of blessing" (I Cor. 10:16), which is the cup of the new covenant in Christ's blood (I Cor. 11:25). Surely the message of Nahum helps us see anew the mercy in that cup.

Nahum 3:14–19

This final oracle of Nahum's forms the complementary piece to 1:2–11 and ends, as did that introductory hymn, with the word "evil" (*ra'ah,* 3:19f.; 1:11*b*). The opening hymn announced that no evil could stand before the Lord's avenging wrath. This final oracle pictures evil done away—the message confirmed that "the Lord will by no means clear the guilty" (1:3). The oracle falls into two parts: a taunt song, verses 14–17, and a funeral dirge, verses 18–19.

In ironic imperatives, the prophet urges Nineveh to prepare itself for siege—to store up water in cisterns and jars for its trapped inhabitants; to make bricks to repair the portions of its walls knocked down by battering rams (v. 14). All will be in vain, for there in the midst of the city itself fire will devour and sword slay (v. 15; cf. 2:13; 3:13), like locusts eating up a land (cf. Joel 1:4).

27

Indeed, Nineveh can multiply defenders like the very locust horde, verse 15d—and here Nahum picks up the same word that he used for the "heaps" of treasures in 2:9 and the "heaps" of corpses in 3:3, as much as to say, "Heap up your defenders without number; it will do you no good!" A multitude of riches and armies are not sufficient to save. Nahum loves to dwell on Nineveh's multiplicity of worldly possessions. Thus, she also increased her merchants, until they were as many as the stars of the heavens, bringing into the great city a vast treasure of goods and money and sophistication (v. 16). But the possessions and powers of this world do not avail against the Lord of Hosts. All—possessions, powerful persons, princes, officers (RSV: scribes)—all might as well be fleeting grasshoppers who eat and run and cannot bear the heat of God's new day. No one stands before the coming of God's avenging wrath. Nineveh is doomed; God sweeps through; evil is done away.

A funeral dirge is therefore sung over fallen Nineveh (vv. 18–19). Her military commanders (RSV: shepherds) and her nobles are dead (RSV: asleep, slumber), her people scattered upon the mountains like sheep without a shepherd. There is no healing for her hurt. Her wound is fatal.

The prophet then hears a thunderous sound rising over the earth—the sound of peoples everywhere clapping their hands when they hear the good tidings of Nineveh's fall. Some undoubtedly clap in mockery and a spirit of vengeance; others clap as an expression of their joy. But all clap because they are released from the continual evil which Assyria has visited upon them (cf. 3:4). As in 3:7, none mourns Nineveh's demise. The whole earth breathes a great sigh, "Free at last! Free at last! Thank God Almighty! Free at last!"

I use this latter quotation, which some will recognize from Martin Luther King, Jr.'s Washington speech that cited the old Negro spiritual, because it illustrates that there is a legitimate celebration to be held over the destruction of evil on this earth. Nahum, here in 3:19, as indeed in his whole book, pictures that celebration. It is comparable to the celebration of the Israelites after their deliverance from bondage in Egypt (Exod. 15), or it can be compared to the celebration of the Allies when Nazi Germany fell. Human beings can be justly glad when tyrants meet their due and the earth is once again delivered from the corruptions of human power and rule. Such deliverance is a witness to the righteous lordship of God, who is slow to anger

28

but who finally will "by no means clear the guilty." God is not mocked in his world, and what individuals and nations sow they will also reap (cf. Gal. 6:7–10).

Nahum, however, brings two additional and sobering thoughts to that affirmation of God's rule. First, as we have repeatedly seen in connection with the prophet's work, the faithful have constantly to ask themselves if they have so corrupted their own ways that it is they upon whom God will wreak his avenging wrath. We have constantly to examine our deeds and purposes to see if they have become those of a Pharaoh or of a Nineveh, of oppressors or of destroyers. If they have, the judgments of Nahum will fall on us unless we turn from our evil ways and live in Christ. Nahum is, first of all, a great call to repentance.

Second, we must never forget that the whole Book of Nahum is a celebration of divine, not human, action. Nahum leaves vengeance in the hands of God. The prophet firmly believes that God will punish and eliminate evil, just as the faithful throughout the ages have prayed that God will so punish and eliminate it. The prayer of the prophet Jeremiah is typical:

> But, O LORD of hosts, who judgest righteously,
> who triest the heart and the mind,
> let me see thy vengeance upon them,
> for to thee have I committed my cause (Jer. 11:20).

When the faithful pray such a prayer, they replace their own spirit of hatred with God's good purpose, and that purpose works itself out in surprising ways in our world. It by no means clears the guilty, but sometimes it does them to death by taking upon itself their evil in the form of a cross. We also are admonished by our Lord to bear that cross—not only to resist evil, not only to correct it, but also sometimes simply to suffer it, confident in the assurance that God will finally cleanse his earth of all corruption. We are to pray that God's Kingdom will come and God's enemies will be defeated; and we are to walk and work as those who already live in the power of that coming Kingdom. Then, at the end, we will be able to cry, as we watch the kingdom of evil fall:

29

> "Rejoice over her, O heaven,
> O saints and apostles and prophets,
> for God has given judgment for you against her!" (Rev. 18:20).

INTERPRETATION

But that rejoicing will not be a vengeful cry. It will be the celebration of those who know that the God who is very slow to anger—that the God who is undimmed good—has won the victory over all powers who stand opposed to his love:

> "Hallelujah! For the Lord our God the Almighty reigns.
> Let us rejoice and exult and give him the glory" (Rev. 19:6–7).

THE BOOK OF
Habakkuk

Introduction

The Book of Habakkuk is not primarily about the justice of God,
although it is possible to approach the book from that stand-
point. But its principal question is not, Why does God reward
the wicked and punish the righteous? In that sense, Habakkuk
is not a theodicy, a justification of the ways of God to human
beings. It is taken for granted in the book that God is just (1:13);
and indeed, Israel's Mosaic covenant faith in Yahweh, Lord of
heaven and earth, is presupposed throughout the book.

Habakkuk is also not a book about human doubt. Its author,
the prophet Habakkuk of Judah, is unquestionably a man of
faith who engages in constant prayer (1:2) and intimate communion with God (1:12; 2:1), who possesses prophetic powers
and is granted visions and oracles from the Lord, who speaks as
a recognized prophet to his community and feels a responsibility for that community (2:1), and who can unquestionably be
numbered among Judah's righteous (1:4), that is, among those
who trust God.

To be sure Habakkuk is concerned about human suffering
and helplessness before the powers of evil and it instructs persons in how to live in a world of sin. But that too is not the major
message of the book.

Rather, Habakkuk is above all else a book about the purposes of God and about the realization of his will for his world.
It is a book about a God who has promised to Abraham that he
will make a new community of Abraham's descendants and that
he will bring blessing on all the families of the earth through
that community (Gen. 12:1–3). It is a book about a God whose
will for humankind is that they have life and have it more

31

abundantly. It is a book about God's desire that human beings live together in joy and security and righteousness, in a community ordered by his divine will and faithful to his divine lordship. It asks after the accomplishment of that goal and strains toward its fulfillment. In short, Habakkuk is a book about the providence of God; that is, it is primarily concerned with how God is keeping his promises to his chosen people Israel, and through them, to humankind.

The original core of the work undoubtedly comes out of a concrete historical situation in the life of the southern kingdom, Judah, and most of the evidence in the work seems to point to a date around 609–600 B.C. "The wicked" in 1:4 refers to evil persons within Judah itself. The Babylonian defeat of the Assyrians and the Egyptians in 612–605 B.C. and then the subsequent subjection of Philistia and Judah in 603–597 B.C. and after form the background of 1:5–11, 12–17. The book has its original roots in the Babylonian domination of the Palestinian landbridge.

The message of the book is by no means limited to that one historical situation, however. By the author's adaptation of earlier materials (2:5–20), by a strong autobiographical (1:2–3, 12; 2:1–2; 3:1, 16, 18–19) and biographical emphasis (1:1; 3:1), and by subsequent use of portions of the book within Israel's cult (3:1, 3, 9, 13, 19), both Habakkuk himself and later editors have given the work a universal and timeless validity which has made it a witness to every age.

Moreover, this has been accomplished while preserving the book's internal unity. The oracles in chapter 1 build to their climax in 2:3–4. The woes of 2:6–20 illustrate the message of that climax. The psalm and autobiographical portions of chapter 3 give a vision of the future fulfillment of the promise of 2:3–4 and illumine its consequences.

Habakkuk is a book for all faithful people, of whatever era, who find themselves living "in the meantime"—in the time between the revelation of the promises of God and the fulfillment of those promises—in the time between their redemption, when God made his purpose clear, and the final time when that divine purpose will be realized in all the earth. As such, Habakkuk is a book from faith for faith. It speaks of that faith and to that faith which lives in the world as it is and yet which knows that the world is not all there was or is or is to come.

Habakkuk is a book of faith which has already spoken powerfully to faith in the past. It spoke to the Apostle Paul as he wrote his epistle to the church at Rome (Rom. 1; cf. v. 17), and it spoke to the author of the Epistle to the Hebrews (10:36–39). Through Paul's use of it, it spoke to Martin Luther in his monastery and helped shape the Protestant Reformation. Its final verses inspired the poem, "In Him Confiding," from William Cowper (1731–1800) and that in turn gave birth to the Christian hymn, "Sometimes a Light Surprises."

So too today, if Habakkuk's message is heard by faith, it still speaks and shall ever speak to those of us who live "in the meantime" and who look forward to that day when ". . . the earth will be filled with the knowledge of the glory of the Lord,/as the waters cover the sea" (2:14).

Habakkuk 1:1

We know nothing about the prophet Habakkuk, other than what his book tells us and what we can infer from it. Because 1:2–4 and 1:12–17 are framed in the standard language of the Old Testament lament (cf. Pss. 13:1–2; 74:1, 10–11; 88:1, 13; 89:46–51), and because the musical directions in 3:1, 3, 9, 13, 19 indicate that chapter 3 was used in the worship of Israel, it has often been maintained that the prophet was a cultic official and that his book represents his intercessory prayer for or his prophetic complaint on behalf of the worshiping community. Indeed, some have even suggested that the book is to be understood against the background of an autumn New Year's festival in Israel.

Certainly Israel's prophets exercised an intercessory function (cf. Amos 7:1–6; Jer. 7:16; Isa. 62:1, 6–7; Deut. 9:18–29), and Habakkuk gives some evidence that that is his function too. The prophet does not pray for himself alone; his responsibility for his community rests heavily upon him (2:1).

But prophets prayed for their people quite apart from the cult (cf. Amos, who is certainly not a cultic prophet) and cultic forms used in Habakkuk's book have sprung their usual structures. Usually a priestly oracle of salvation, such as those found in Isaiah 41:8–13, 14–16, or 43:1–4, followed a lament (cf. the change of mood in Ps. 22 between vv. 21 and 22). Habakkuk's

33

opening lament, however, is followed by an announcement of judgment (1:5–11) that prompts him to raise still further complaint in 1:12–17 and that in turn is answered only by a promise and a vision concerning faith and the future, 2:2–4. Similarly, while 3:3–15 has the form of a hymn, often sung in the cult (cf. Ps. 97), it has been set within an autobiographical framework (vv. 2, 16–19) that interprets it as a personal experience of the prophet's. Habakkuk is using cultic forms in a manner independent of cultic strictures, just as his contemporary Jeremiah also used them (cf. the lament of Jer. 15:15–18 and its answer, vv. 19–21). We are not justified, therefore, in designating Habakkuk a "cultic prophet."

His name may be a nickname, drawn from the Akkadian *hambakuku*—the name of a plant. The name reoccurs in verses 33–37 of the legendary story of Bel and the Dragon, found in the Apocrypha, but the activities attributed to the prophet there are quite fanciful. We know only that he was a prophet in Judah at the end of the seventh and the beginning of the sixth centuries B.C. and that, in answer to his laments, he received from the Lord a "burden" (1:1; cf. Isa. 13:1; Nah. 1:1)—the oracles and woes and visions now found in his book.

Habakkuk 1:2–4

The key to this initial complaint of Habakkuk's is the Hebrew word *mishpat,* found twice in verse 4 (which has been translated "justice" in the RSV) and which here signifies that order ordained by God for the society of the covenant people (cf. Isa. 42:1–4 and Jer. 5:1–9 for the same meaning of the term). Habakkuk's complaint is that the people of Judah, in the reign of King Jehoiakim (609–598 B.C.), have abandoned the righteous order intended by God for their society, despite the fact that they renewed their covenant with the Lord and underwent a sweeping religious reform only twelve years earlier in the time of King Josiah. That God-intended order was revealed through the *torah* (v. 4, RSV: law), which here has the meaning of the whole religious tradition of Israel, including her Deuteronomic law, her traditions of what God has done in her past life,

34

and the on-going guidance afforded her day by day through the preaching and teaching of priests and prophets. But the inhabitants of Judah have ignored that tradition. They have forgotten what the Lord has done for them, disobeyed the Deuteronomic law, and paid no attention to priestly and prophetic instruction. Indeed, oracles from Jeremiah at this time tell us that priests themselves ignored the *torah* (cf. Jer. 2:8) and false prophets preached their own opinions or the soothing words that the people wanted to hear (cf. Jer. 23:9–40).

The result of the abandonment of God's *mishpat* in Judean society is chaos. On every side, Habakkuk hears and sees "Violence!" (vv. 2, 3)—the violent breach of God's just order. There are moral evils of all kinds which bring the misery of disrupted human relationships (v. 3). There are the oppression of the weak by the strong, endless litigations (v. 3) and quarrels and deceitful dealings between persons (v. 3). God's intended order for the communities of Judah is totally missing (v. 4, literally: paralyzed). When the righteous—that is, those who cling to God and his will for human life—try to set things right, their intentions and actions are so distorted by the evil surrounding them that the result is only a perverted version of God's order—a distortion of *mishpat* that satisfies the wicked that they are doing God's will but that only further frustrates the righteous.

There are faithful persons in Judean society in Habakkuk's time (contrast Jer. 5:1–9), but they are helpless to reform that society. Habakkuk therefore turns to the only source he knows for setting things right. He turns to God in prayer. It is constant prayer, uttered over a long period of time (v. 2), for the healing of his people. But God does nothing to answer that prayer and so apparently has not heard it. (According to the thought of the O.T., if God hears, he acts; cf. Ps. 22:24.)

Habakkuk here faces the dilemma that has confronted faithful people in every age—the dilemma of seemingly unanswered prayer for the healing of society. The prophet is one with all those persons who fervently pray for peace in our world and who experience only war, who pray for God's good to come on earth and who find only human evil. But he is also one with every soul who has prayed for healing beside a sick bed only to be confronted with death; with every spouse who has prayed for love to come into a home and then found only hatred and anger; with every anxious person who has prayed for serenity but then been further disturbed and agitated.

35

Above all, however, Habakkuk here typifies the faithful person who has to live in the world as it is and who has grown weary with the world's ways of wickedness. When he looks about him, he sees those on every hand who do not care a whit for God's will—those who take the word of God and twist it to their own purposes; those who openly break every code of decency and morality and yet who justify their ways; those who seek their own selfish ends and who stamp their self-seeking on a whole generation; those who violate and cheat and deceive and yet who are honored in society's eyes. Habakkuk's time is out of joint, as is every human era, because the world lives under slavery to sin rather than to the righteousness of God. And the prophet is weary—weary with the world as it is. What is the world coming to? is his question and the question of every faithful soul like him. Where will it all end? When will the wicked be defeated and God's order established over all? Is God doing nothing about setting up his righteous rule on the earth? Has his purpose for humankind finally failed? Living in our age, in a society such as ours, those are our questions too.

They are, moreover, not questions that rise out of doubt but out of lively faith in God, for the person who trusts in God and clings to his will knows what God's order for human society could mean. The faithful person has had a foretaste of that order. In communion with God, in daily reliance on God's direction and power, the faithful man or woman has experienced first hand the joy and security and meaning that come from that walk with God. And in company with other faithful persons, the one dedicated to God's ways has known the unity, the peace, the sense of trust between persons that are lent to any company or congregation who live their life by God's commands. The one who trusts God and who walks in his ways longs for— yearns, pants after—that blessed life in God to come on all the earth. His or her prayer is, "Thy kingdom come on earth . . ."; "Come, Lord Jesus, quickly come!"—because the joyful sense of abundant life in God spills out beyond the individual worshiper and the separate congregation and longs to be shared with every person and every community. Faithful persons know the blessing of God and yearn mightily for that blessing to come on "all the families of the earth." But those who trust God also sometimes wonder, as Habakkuk wonders, how such blessing can be realized on earth in the face of such overwhelming human sin and evil.

36

Habakkuk 1:5–11

The answer that Habakkuk receives to his complaint (vv. 2–4) is here recorded in the form of a speech by God to the prophet. The Old Testament tells us that God does not hear every prayer (cf. Isa. 1:15) but he has heard faithful Habakkuk's persistent prayers (cf. Luke 18:1–8), and the answer God gives to those prayers is both comforting and confounding.

First, the Lord reassures the prophet that he is at work. In an age and a society where sinful human beings seem to rule the day and God seems totally absent from the field, God is nevertheless at work to realize his will for the world. The familiar hymn puts it very well:

> God is working his purpose out
> as year succeeds to year.
> God is working his purpose out,
> and the time is drawing near.
> Nearer and nearer draws the time,
> the time that shall surely be,
> When the earth shall be filled with the glory of God
> as the waters cover the sea (Arthur Campbell Ainger, 1894).

God is at work. God is the eternal worker. In a society where all the signs seem to read "Men Working," Habakkuk sees a vastly more impressive sign: "God Working" (Chappell, p. 77). God is not absent from the prophet's world. He has not written it off as a bad experiment. He is not ignorant of what is happening in Judah or throughout the Middle East. All is under his watchful eye, the subject of his concern, and he is at work in the midst of events to fulfill his good purpose. "My Father is working still, and I am working," Jesus told the Jews (John 5:17). That is the ultimate word of comfort to anyone who despairs of society's evil, because God's working leads finally to good for all creation.

The nature of God's work that is told to Habakkuk seems to fly in the face of that assurance, however; for God tells the prophet that he is rousing the Babylonian Empire and its armies under Nebuchadnezzar (605/4–562 B.C.) to march through the

37

Fertile Crescent, to capture nations (v. 6), to inflict violence on all in their path (v. 9), to overrun every fortified city (v. 10), and to take prisoners of war (v. 9). Their march will be swift (v. 6), dread and terrible (v. 7), sweeping through Palestine like the wind (v. 11), and none will be able to escape such force or to turn it aside. The scythe of Babylonia will cut down all in its path. And swinging the scythe—using it as an instrument of his purpose—will be God, the Lord over all nations and history.

Moreover, God makes it very clear in this answer to Habakkuk's prayer just why he is doing such a deed. Judah has rejected God's *mishpat* or order in its society (v. 4); therefore Babylonia's order (*mishpat,* v. 7, RSV: justice) will be imposed upon it. Judah has opted for violence among its inhabitants (v. 2); therefore Babylonia's violence will be its punishment (v. 9). Judah has rejected the ways of God (vv. 2–4); therefore it will have to serve the god of Babylonian might (v. 11). The punishment fits the sin. Indeed, the sin turns back upon Judah to become her punishment, and as Judah has done within her society, so shall it be done to her. The measure she has given will be the measure she will get (Matt. 7:2).

That is an astounding description of the way a good God works out his purpose in our world. Instead of pressing forward toward the realization of his peaceable Kingdom on the earth, God seems by such a work to be going in exactly the opposite direction. Instead of peace, he ordains war; instead of security, violence. Instead of good, he brings about evil; and in place of life, he ordains death. But it is a witness to the working of God that is by no means isolated in the Bible. The Apostle Paul, too, in a section of the Epistle to the Romans (1:15–32) that was written against the background of Habakkuk, declares that God gives us up to our sins as the punishment for them. "If that is what you want," God says in so many words, "all right, you can have it. I give you over to your evil. You can wallow in it, and the very evil that you do will become my punishment of you."

The implications of such a revelation are staggering for our world, for such a word from God implies that the turmoil and violence and death in our societies may not be evidence of God's absence from our lives but instead the witness to his actual working in judgment as he pursues his purpose. No event in human history, therefore, is to be understood as completely divorced from his lordly action and will. God is always at work, always involved, always pressing forward toward his Kingdom.

But the means by which he chooses to pursue that goal may be as astounding as the destruction of a nation or as incomprehensible as the blood dripping from the figure of a man on a cross.

Habakkuk 1:12–17

Habakkuk, as a man of faith, accepts the words of God that have been given him in 1:5–11—an acceptance shown by his confirmation of that word in 1:12. He acknowledges that Babylonia's coming conquest of Judah is ordained by God as the punishment of Judah's sin. (Here, the word *mishpat* has a different meaning than before, is properly translated "judgment," and is parallel to "chastisement.") Such an understanding of Babylonia's role in the seventh and sixth centuries B.C. was proclaimed not only by Habakkuk but also by Jeremiah, Ezekiel, and Second Isaiah. International relations are understood to be always under the sovereignty of God. World history does not take place by chance, according to the Scriptures, nor are human beings ever the sole effectors of it. Human actions result in particular events, to be sure, but human actions are always also accompanied by God's effective actions as he works out his purpose. Thus, Habakkuk, here in verse 12, acknowledges that purposeful working by the Lord.

Moreover, Habakkuk here makes a personal confession of faith about the nature of God. His God ("my God," v. 12*b*) is deliberately contrasted with the false god of might of the Babylonians (v. 11); and his God, unlike the transitory deity of the Babylonians, is everlasting (cf. Deut. 33:27; Isa. 40:28; Ps. 90:2)—the Alpha and the Omega, the One who was there in the beginning and who will be there after heaven and earth pass away; the One who stands above the flux of human history (such is expressed here by "Holy One") and who therefore is the unchanging, sure rock of the faithful midst all the transitoriness of life in the world.

Because Habakkuk understands that the Babylonian onslaught against Judah will be God's judgment and chastisement of his people, the prophet therefore knows that destruction will not do Judah to death. "We shall not die," he states in faith (v.

39

12). God has not ordained the Babylonians for vengeance or to make a full end of Judah or because he has pleasure in the death of the wicked (cf. Ezek. 18:23, 32). God judges his people for a reason, according to the Old Testament. He wishes to correct them, to refine and purify their lives, so that they walk in his ways and obey his will and serve his purpose. God's judgment, according to the Bible—in Habakkuk's time or ours—is always finally an act along the way toward his salvation of his world.

But that does not solve Habakkuk's principal problem. As we have said, Habakkuk yearns for the fulfillment of God's good purpose for the earth. He longs for God's Kingdom to come among human beings and in Judah's society (see 1:2–4). God is bringing the Babylonian Empire against Judah to wipe out Judah's wicked ways. But that does not hasten the coming of God's order. It simply replaces a chaotic society with one that is totally godless—with the rule of a foreign people that makes its own might its god (1:11) and that worships that might as the source of its life (1:16). Thus, Habakkuk's searching question in 1:13 is not a question about God's justice—not a question about the just deserts of the wicked and righteous. Habakkuk's question rather voices his perplexity about the fulfillment of God's purpose. Habakkuk knows that God is absolutely just, morally pure, the enemy of all evil. He knows that there is a basic contradiction between God and all unholiness. Yet, by introducing the Babylonians on the world scene, God has not gone forward toward the establishment of that holiness in all the earth (cf. Zech. 14:20–21). Rather, he has seemed to move even further distant from the goal of the establishment of his right order in the world, and Habakkuk cannot understand that any more than can we. That a God of righteousness replaces one society with another even more idolatrous and evil, that a God of overflowing life may will first that there be destruction and death before he grants abundant living—those are enigmas in the working of God that defy human understanding. It is as if God has abandoned his righteous rule over the earth—as if human society now proceeds on its evil course with no divine ruler over it (1:14).

But Habakkuk knows that God rules history; he knows that God's order will be its outcome—the prophet never abandons God and faith in his purpose. He therefore asks this further question: How long, my God, are you going to allow this reversal of your purpose? How long are you going to seem to move away from your goal (1:17)? It is not the question that Habakkuk

asked in the beginning (1:2). That was a question of how long
God was going to put up with Judah's wickedness. This is a
question of how long God is actually going to intensify that
wickedness by replacing it with a greater evil. God has apparently zigzagged in his march toward his goal. God has turned
and set off in another direction, and the prophet wants to know
if that divine detour is going to last throughout the foreseeable
future ("for ever" in the RSV of 1:17 has the meaning of "continually" in the Hebrew). Habakkuk longed for the end of
Judah's evil, in 1:2–4. God's answer, in 1:5–11, promised Babylonia's greater evil (cf. Jer. 12:1–6). The prophet's principal questions therefore still are, When is it all going to end? Are you, O
Lord, going to fulfill your purpose on the earth?

Habakkuk 2:1–4

> "For still there is a vision for the appointed time,
>   and it pants toward an end, and it does not lie.
> If it delay, wait for it,
>   for it surely comes; it will not be late.
> Behold the one who is puffed up; his life is not upright in him,
>   but the righteous by his faithfulness shall live" (2:3–4 Hebr.,
>   author's trans.).

As has been his habit (1:2, 12–13), Habakkuk now waits on
God for the answer to his perplexity. There is no wisdom in the
world that can find out the ways of God (cf. I Cor. 1:21; Eccles.
3:11; Job 11:7). If we search only nature's workings or history's
lessons for proof of the divine activity, apart from their interpretation by the word of God, we will end up despairing of
God's interest in us and in his world (cf. Isa. 40:27) or we will
become cynically convinced that God does nothing at all (cf. II
Peter 3:3–4; Jer. 17:15; Zeph. 1:12). Worse yet, we may end up
worshiping the creation rather than the Creator (Rom. 1:18–
23). The true revealer of God is the word of God (cf. John 3:13;
17:25 *et passim*).

> As long . . . as we judge according to our own perceptions, we
> walk on the earth; and while we do so, many clouds arise, and
> Satan scatters ashes in our eyes, and wholly darkens our judg-
> ment, and thus it happens, that we lie down altogether con-
> founded. It is hence wholly necessary . . . that we should tread

our reason under foot, and come nigh to God himself . . . let the
word of God become our ladder . . . (Calvin, IV, 59).

Thus, Habakkuk the prophet—the one who is to be the
bearer of the word of God to his people—himself turns to God
to wait for the interpreting word. Prophets have no independent wisdom of their own—they are dependent on the word of
God (cf. Jer. 42:5–7)—as we too are dependent for a true understanding of what God is doing and must ever search the word
now given us in the Scriptures.

Habakkuk speaks of his waiting for the word in a statement
of the utmost resoluteness (2:1). There is no abandoning his faith
here in the face of perplexity, no despairing cessation of a lifetime habit of prayer (cf. I Thess. 5:17), no shadow of suspicion
that God has proved untrue (contrast Jer. 15:18; 20:7); but there
is only the firm confidence that God has yet more to speak and
do, and the persistent, patient waiting and watching for that
divine speech and action (Pss. 33:20; 106:13; Isa. 40:31; Zeph.
3:8; cf. Luke 11:5–12).

The "watchtower" here is purely symbolic—a figure taken
from the custom of ascending high places to look into the distance. This is not a reference to the office of the prophet as a
watchman for his people (Jer. 6:17; Ezek. 3:17; 33:7–9). That
office has a more military connotation and is connected with
warning the people of God's war against their sin. Here the
meaning is similar to that found in Isaiah 62:6–7, and yet does
not even involve that passage's persistent intercession before
God. Rather here the "watchtower" indicates the concentrated
openness, the unwearied waiting of the prophet for the divine
word.

"Seek, and you will find; knock, and it will be opened to
you" (Luke 11:9). The divine word comes to Habakkuk and
gives him the answer to his questions (v. 3). In reply to his query
of whether or not God is going to fulfill his purpose and bring
his divinely ordered Kingdom on earth, Habakkuk is told that
the divine order "surely comes." God's "vision" for his earth—
God's plan to restore his creation to the goodness he intended
for it in the beginning, God's promise to bring blessing on all
the families of the earth through the descendants of Abraham
—still is in effect. It is not an idle dream of the pious, not a lie
(cf. Num. 23:19; Titus 1:2) on which they have set their hearts,
not a vain hope which will bear no fruit or be destroyed by

42

earth's overwhelming evil. The world is not as God intended it, and God is setting it right. His will be the final order established in human society. The hope of all good persons everywhere who have trusted in the Lord is a sure hope, firmly anchored in the providence—that is, the promises—of God.

God has a definite time when his purpose will be fulfilled —THE appointed time (v. 3)—the time fixed by him and not by human beings (cf. Gal. 4:2). He who is the Alpha and the Omega, who is the beginning and the end, whose lordship encompasses all time (cf. Ps. 90) determines when his promises will be delayed and when they will be fulfilled (cf. Ezek. 12: 27–28). In the fullness of his time (cf. Mark 1:15; Gal. 4:4; Eph. 1:10), when the hour has come (cf. John 7:6, 8; 12:27; 17:1 *et passim*), at the *kairos,* when all is fully ripe (cf. Rev. 14:18), God will fulfill his final purposes for his earth. "But of that day or that hour no one knows, not even the angels in heaven, nor the Son, but only the Father" (Mark 13:32). No one can reckon the time. Habakkuk hears only that already in the plan of God the time has been "appointed." From the beginning of his work, God has seen its goal and completion.

Habakkuk is given the assurance, however, that the time "hastens" (literally: "puffs" or "pants") toward its end—almost as if God's fulfillment were personified as a runner speeding toward the finish line. Therefore, that which may seem delayed or halted by our reckoning has not been impeded at all. God's purpose cannot be thwarted (cf. Isa. 55:10–11); it is speeding toward its completion. Indeed, those actions of God that seem to reverse his march toward his goal—as the Babylonian conquest of Judah seemed to Habakkuk to reverse that march (1:12–17)—may not be reversals at all but integral parts of God's purpose to save his earth. Certainly Luke (21:24), Paul (Rom. 9:22–24), and the author of Second Peter were sure that was true:

> The Lord is not slow about his promise as some count slowness, but is forbearing toward you, not wishing that any should perish, but that all should reach repentance (II Peter 3:9).

God's envisioned Kingdom for his earth surely comes and will not be late. Such is the word Habakkuk faithfully passes on to those who live "in the meantime" and who, wearied and dismayed by evil, cry out, "How long, O Lord?" For his contemporaries, he writes the assurance on a placard large enough to

43

be read by every passer-by. For those who come after him, he preserves the assurance in writing. For us, Habakkuk's words have been handed on by a cloud of faithful witnesses, and they bid us still wait in hope for the fulfillment that will not be tardy (cf. Rom. 13:11).

To wait for the fulfillment of God's purposes for his world is not a passive resignation, however—not a clenched-teeth, stoic acceptance of whatever comes along. The end of human history is already foreseen by God, but the route by which that goal is reached, the decision as to who will inherit its abundant life, and the multitudinous events that will work together to bring in the Kingdom are still undecided in the on-going dialogue between God and his creatures. The God of the Bible takes human activity and human decisions seriously and responds to them, acting through and under and sometimes in spite of them, as he works toward his goal, just as human beings also variously respond to his on-going activity. The history of earth is constructed of a continual dialogue between humankind and its Creator in which every action of even the commonest of persons is of utmost importance for shaping the manner and method by which God realizes his goal. We do not delay the Kingdom's coming; but the New Testament suggests we can hasten it (II Peter 3:12; I Cor. 16:22); and we can decide whether or not we will inherit its life (cf. Rev. 22:12–21; Matt. 25:31–46; Luke 18:8).

We can also decide, along the route to the Kingdom, whether we will live under God's curse or under his blessing. In short, we can decide how we will live "in the meantime," for God reckons with his creatures not only at the end but day-by-day as we accept or reject his lordship. It is this decision—to have blessing or curse—with which the second part of the word given to Habakkuk deals. God's answer to the prophet's perplexity is made up of two parts: (1) the assurance that the vision comes and will not be late (vv. 2–3); (2) God's instructions as how to live "in the meantime"—how to inherit already that life of the Kingdom which comes in its fullness at the end (v. 4). The faithful can have a foretaste, as it were, of the Kingdom's abundant blessings. The "not yet" can already partly become their "now" (cf. Rom. 8:23; II Cor. 6:1–10). The vision of the end makes certain who is in charge of human history now. It therefore mandates how to live in the present (cf. II Peter 3:11).

As a result, Habakkuk 2:4 has become one of the central

affirmations of those of biblical faith because it summarizes the manner of the faithful life. Not only was its teaching of utmost importance for Paul (Rom. 1:17; Gal. 3:11; cf. Heb. 10:37–38), and not only did it form a kind of foundational summary of the faith of the Protestant Reformation but, as it has been mediated through the New Testament, it now also forms a common ground of agreement between Protestant and Roman Catholic (see the 1983 Catholic–Lutheran statement on justification by faith). So too the Talmud agrees that it represents a summary of the law: "In this one sentence, The just shall live by his *'emunah* (faith), the 613 precepts, which God once delivered from Sinai, are collected into a compendium" (quoted in Kleinert, p. 31). How, then, does this summary teaching envision a life pleasing to God?

First, 2:4 tells what the faithful person is not: He or she is not "puffed up" or "lifted up;" that is, there is no reliance on one's own self or personal resources to secure and sustain one's life. Certainly this divine word is contrasting the life of faith with that of the Babylonians, who make their own might their god (1:11) and who rely on their merciless plunder to furnish them with the good life (1:16–17). But the word given the prophet goes far beyond that historical reference. Wherever human beings rely on something of this earth—whether it be intellectual achievement or wealth or military might or aesthetic ability and appreciation or pride of birth and status or even the ability to cope and solve problems and master the complexities of modern life—wherever confidence is placed in human prowess and not in God for the achievement of a satisfying and secure manner of living, there true life cannot be had.

Rather, such false reliance makes one's life crooked or curved or distorted in some way—in short, not "upright" or straight or true to the divine intention for it (2:4a). True life— life as it was intended—can only be had by relying on God daily to give it. He is the Creator and Giver and Sustainer of all life. Our vital principle, which makes us living beings, shrivels and withers, curls and dries up, and then dies apart from him (cf. Ps. 1).

We see such distortions of God's gift of life in a thousand manifestations—in our broken human relationships and the poisons of our festering hatreds; in our crippled efforts to achieve security and the shadows of destruction that haunt us; in our despoiling of the beauty of the earth and of the loveliness of

45

human society; in our proud boasts of self-sufficiency which are always undermined by our anxieties and fears and loneliness; in our futile efforts to escape our guilt and in our pathetic attempts to deny death's reality. On our own, our lives are indeed curved and bent and distorted images of what they were intended to be, because they were meant to have their base and sustenance in an on-going fellowship with God.

Habakkuk's vision then turns to a positive description of the faithful person (v. 4*b*). Those who will have true life, those who will fully live, those who will blossom and flourish and bring forth their fruit in due season are those "righteous" (cf. 1:4) who live in faithfulness to God. Both words—"righteous" and "faithfulness" (RSV: faith) need explanation.

To be righteous means, throughout the Bible, to fulfill the demands of a relationship (see the author's article on "Righteousness in the OT"). Since the relationship here under discussion is the relationship with God, Habakkuk further makes the affirmation that the relationship with God is fulfilled by "faithfulness." That does not mean moral steadfastness, rectitude, and earnestness. It does not signify the proper performance of ethical or cultic duties. Rather, faithfulness here means trust, dependence, clinging to God; it means living and moving and having one's being in him alone; it means relying on him for the breath one draws, for the direction one takes, for the decisions one makes, for the goals one sets, and for the outcome of one's living.

> The faith which saves is not one single act done and ended on a certain day: it is an act continued and persevered in throughout the entire life of man. The just not only commences to live by his faith, but he continues to live by his faith: he does not begin in the spirit and end in the flesh, nor go so far by grace, and the rest of the way by works of the law. . . . Faith is essential all along; every day and all the day, in all things. Our natural life begins by breathing, and it must be continued by breathing; what the breath is to the body, that is faith to the soul (Spurgeon, "A Luther Sermon at the Tabernacle," p. 715).

Faithfulness means placing one's whole life in God's hands and trusting him to fulfill it, despite all outward and inward circumstances; despite all personal sin and guilt; despite all psychological and social and physical distortions. Faithfulness is life by God's power rather than by one's own (cf. I Cor. 1:30–31); and therefore it is truly life, because it draws its vitality from the living God who is the source of life.

It is with this meaning that Paul uses 2:4*b* in Romans 1:17. Verse 17 is an integral part of Romans 1:15–23, and verses 16–23 are the explanation of verse 15 (see *Romans*, by Paul J. Achtemeier). Paul is explaining why he is eager to preach to the gentile Romans, and he says that he preaches to the Gentiles because salvation (life) has been offered by God to all—to both Jews and Gentiles (v. 16 [RSV: Greek]). The Jews have no privilege of birth. Life is not given as the reward of what we are or because of our status or for anything we possess in ourselves. Rather, life is given to faith—to those who rely on God through Christ Jesus to give it. In the same manner, in Galatians 3:11, Paul states that life is not given to those who do the works of the law. As in Habakkuk, nothing we do on our own suffices to give us life. Indeed, reliance on doing the works of the law for our salvation leads us further from reliance on God. Rather, once again, life is given to those of faith, "that in Christ Jesus the blessing of Abraham might come upon the Gentiles" (v. 14). Apart from reliance on God we live under his wrath and curse and God gives us over to the chaos we have created for ourselves (Hab. 1:12–17; Rom. 1:18–23, 24–31; cf. Gal. 3:13). But in sole reliance on his lordship, we inherit his blessing—his abundant vitality—his never-failing life (cf. Jer. 2:13; John 4:13–14).

Obviously, the New Testament's use of 2:4 includes an eschatological interpretation of that verse: The life referred to in these New Testament passages is eternal life—the resurrected life after death, which is equivalent to salvation for Paul (Rom. 8). That eschatological dimension is the sense, too, of Hebrews 10:37–38, where a persecuted church is urged to await "the coming one," namely Christ, who is identified with the coming "vision" or Kingdom of Habakkuk 2:3. If the faithful do not relinquish their trust in God in Christ, they will have eternal life or they will enter the place of "rest" (Heb. 3—4) or they will become inheritors of "the land of promise," with its "city which has foundations, whose builder and maker is God" (Heb. 11). Thus, the New Testament use of 2:4 has extended the latter's meaning beyond that found in Habakkuk's prophecy to encompass the full sense given to the term "life" by God's act in Christ.

But the New Testament also includes Habakkuk's sense of "life" as a gift of God given to the faithful in the immediate present. We shall see the joy and certainty given to the prophet in the midst of his turbulent and evil world when we discuss his closing hymn (chap. 3). But Paul, the justified, was no stranger to those immediate gifts from God. "Rejoice in the Lord al-

47

ways," he could write from his Ephesian prison, "again I will say, Rejoice" (Phil. 4:4)! ". . . I have learned, in whatever state I am, to be content" (Phil. 4:11). "We are afflicted in every way, but not crushed; perplexed, but not driven to despair; persecuted, but not forsaken; struck down, but not destroyed" (II Cor. 4:8–9). "Who shall separate us from the love of Christ? Shall tribulation, or distress, or persecution, or famine, or nakedness, or peril, or sword" (Rom. 8:35)? The life given by God to the faithful righteous was for Paul also an immediate gift —that same foretaste of the future Kingdom's blessings that Habakkuk knew—and that same foretaste that every faithful person has known who has clung to God, come what may.

By such faithfulness, God tells Habakkuk, the prophet can live an abundant life in his time and place. That is the message Habakkuk passes on to his contemporaries, to us, and to all the faithful who find that they must live "in the meantime," between the revealing of God's purposes for his world and the final realization of those purposes. Countless faithful in Israel and in the church for over twenty-five hundred years have found God true to his word.

Habakkuk 2:5–20

Everything that follows in Habakkuk's book is confirmation of the vision given him in 2:3–4. Specifically, the series of woes in 2:6–20 is intended to reinforce the promise given in 2:4 by showing that those who rely on their own powers and not on God cannot sustain their self-contained life or find permanent satisfaction in it.

Verses 5–6a: The fact that the woes are intended to illustrate 2:4 is shown by the transitional verses, 5–6a, that lead from 2:4 to 2:6b following. Verse 5ab is corrupt in the Hebrew and many emendations have been suggested for it, but it probably should be read, "Yea, moreover, for wealth is treacherous; a mighty man is proud, and he does not rest (or abide)." The "mighty man" refers to the might of the Babylonians (1:11), their "wealth" is that of 1:16, and their inability to "rest" or "abide" reiterates the impossibility of finding true life, as in

48

2:4*a*. The remainder of verse 5 then describes the Babylonians' accumulation of such wealth, as in 1:14–17.

The crucial question in connection with the interpretation of these woes, however, is Why? Why cannot the proud and mighty abide or rest? And it should be noted that the prophet leaves behind the specific illustration of the Babylonians to discuss the mighty and wealthy and proud in general. Why is true life impossible to such persons and nations?

Certainly the thought is not that tyranny is automatic suicide, as in some Wisdom theology, because it defies the God-given order of the creation. Such an interpretation is much too divorced from God's active involvement in his world to be true to Habakkuk's understanding. For this prophet—and indeed for all of them—there is no automatic working out of the purposes of God. God acts in Habakkuk's view "doing a work" (1:5), "rousing the Chaldeans" (1:6), ordaining them as a judgment (1:12). God subjects Judah to the Babylonian conqueror ("thou makest," 1:14). And so too in the words of these woes, God—in distinction from the dumb idols of metal (2:18) that cannot "awake" or "arise" or "give revelation" (2:19)—will give the cup of judgment to make the mighty and proud drunk and ashamed (2:16). God is at work in his world fulfilling his purpose, and part of that working is his active judgment, described in these woes, on all who have been proud and mighty—the "puffed up" of 2:4*a*.

There are similar series of woe oracles to be found in Isaiah 5:8–23 and 10:1; 28:1 and 30:1 and 31:1; Amos 5:18 and 6:1. These here probably have their background, not in funeral laments over the dead but in the genre of curse. Those who do not live in God to receive his blessing of life live under his curse and therefore will be done to death. They cannot "rest" in this world (Hab. 2:5). Their lives are crooked and bent (2:4*a*). They shall not abide (2:5). God's judgment will come upon them in this "meantime" in which we live.

What form will God's judging curse upon the righteous take? Once again, as in 1:12–17, the punishment will fit the sin; and that evil which the unrighteous have done will return upon their own heads. (This is explicit in 2:6–8, 15–17, implicit in 2:9–11.) If such wickedness is what you want, God decrees, then you shall have it. Thus, the judgments are spelled out:

49

Verses 6*b*–8: Those tyrants who have oppressed their subjects and their captives with heavy debts and taxation will find their debtors rising up against them to plunder their wealth. The booty taken by violence and war and oppression will become spoils in the revolt of the peoples against their captors. (We might note that the picture is true to the history of most people's revolutions that have taken place in our world.)

Verses 9–11: That family or dynasty or national government *(house)* which has gained power for itself by robbing and deceiving and oppressing its populace, and which has thought itself safe from every challenge to its power and propriety, has not understood the limits set by God on its sovereignty (cf. Ps. 127:1). In a stunning figure, Habakkuk says that the very stones of such a "house" will be the plaintiff against it, and the very beams the witnesses who will judge the "house" guilty and sentence it to death.

Verses 12–14: That government which thinks to glorify itself by its own achievements—by establishing a city or putting up public buildings or instituting new laws or providing services —and which does so by forced and unjust measures is making its subjects labor for that which cannot last, for that which is "nought," and which will be burned up by the fire of God's wrath. "Is it not, behold, from the Lord of Hosts?" reads verse 13*a* in the Hebrew; that is, has the Lord of Hosts not decreed it (contra RSV)? For he is working his purpose out to fill the world with the knowledge of his glory (cf. Exod. 9:16; Num. 14:21; Isa. 11:9). Therefore the attempts of human beings to gain glory for themselves by public works built on injustice are empty and vain endeavors that will fall before God's universal sovereignty.

Verses 15–17: That military power which thinks to gain respect and admiration ("glory," v. 16) for itself by ruthlessly lording it over its neighbors and by subjecting them to humiliation will find the cup of wrath that it has made its neighbors drink (cf. Jer. 51:7) forced back upon itself. But this time the cup will be in the hands of the Lord (cf. Jer. 25:15–16; Lam. 4:21; Isa. 51:17; Ps. 75:8), who will make the mighty conqueror ashamed instead of glorious, staggering instead of powerful (cf. Obad. 16). The violence done to other nations—here symbolized in verse 17 by the use of Lebanon's forests for constructing military machines and buildings—will return upon the head of the violent and overwhelm him; "for the blood of men and violence to the earth, to cities and all who dwell therein"—the refrain is repeated from verse 8 as a summary of the evil nature of the nation cursed.

Verses 18–20: Finally, the subject changes and the woe is pronounced over all those who have worshiped false gods. The subject shifts so radically that many have thought this to be an addition, but this woe is very appropriate as an ending to the series. It is saying that the false gods of the tyrants and oppressors and military powers will be unable to save their people from the curse of the only true God. The Lord is in his heavenly temple (cf. Ps. 11:4)—he is not some false god made of stone or of anything else in all creation. And he stirs himself to bring about the curses pronounced in these woes (cf. Zech. 2:13). Let the earth therefore be still and learn who is truly God (cf. Ps. 46:10) as he works his lordly will upon those who have defied his lordship (cf. Zeph. 1:7).

There is a limit set on human wickedness by the lordship of God. Those who practice violence and oppression and injustice in the earth have fallen victim to the primary sin of pride. They think themselves gods who can legislate over human life and use it as they will for their own selfish purposes of greed and might and glory. They think others' lives belong to them and that they themselves are no longer creatures but lords, who can take to themselves the absolute right over human weal or woe —the absolute right to say who will live and who will die. But no, Habakkuk has been told, No. The earth's way is subject to God's will; and in the affairs of men and nations, God is working out his purpose.

> For the earth will be filled
>   with the knowledge of the glory of the Lord,
>   as the waters cover the sea (v. 14).

It is significant that in this verse Habakkuk has added the phrase, "the glory of" (cf. Isa. 11:9, where the phrase is omitted), for it encompasses the goal of human history of which Habakkuk has been told: the establishment of God's glory—that is, of esteem for him as true God—over all the earth, the establishment of an order in the world over which God alone reigns— in short, the promised coming of the Kingdom of God.

Because that is God's goal for his world, and because he is true Lord, he therefore brings his judgment on those who chal-

51

lenge his lordship "in the meantime." There are judgments that take place now; tyrants are given their due—not because there is a moral order in the world that works automatically, but because the Lord of all so decrees and acts: The proud challengers of God's rule cannot rest or abide or live (2:4a, 5).

On an individual scale that puzzles us, because the wicked in the world who have made themselves or their own might their gods do not always seem to get their due. On the contrary, they often seem to be highly successful (cf. Ps. 73:4–10). It seems much easier to see God's judgments at work in the rise and fall of nations: A Hitler commits suicide in his final bunker and a Mussolini is strung up by his heels. And yet, even wickedness in high places often seems to go unchallenged: Evil King Manasseh of biblical Judah enjoyed forty-five years of unparalleled peace and prosperity, just as some contemporary tyrants have enjoyed untroubled years and then gone peacefully to their graves, old men and full of years. Where, then, are God's judgments to be found "in the meantime"? Sometimes we think we can point to them, but often we cannot. History read from its own evidence is opaque here too, just as it was opaque to Habakkuk in 1:12–17 (see the comment there). The interpreter of Habakkuk 2:6–20 should not try to prove the truth of these woes in Habakkuk from a reading of past history. It is not history which proves the truth of the word of God but the word of God which illumines history, and always that word is to be read with the eyes of faith.

In the rise and fall of rulers and nations, these woes in Habakkuk are telling us, the Lord of all history is actively at work, sustaining the faithful and returning the evil of the wicked on their own heads. And that work is not postponed until some final judgment but also takes place now, in this "meantime" in which we live out our earthly lives.

The answer to our perplexities about the ambiguities of human history is the word of God—his promise that he rules in every age and that evil receives its just due. That is the illumining word to which we are to cling, and it is a promise that can instill in us a quiet heart and confidence, as we struggle with injustice and wickedness. But it is a promissory word that can be comprehended only by faith. In the words of Psalm 73:

52

> . . . when I thought how to understand this,
>   it seemed to me a wearisome task,

until I went into the sanctuary of God;
  then I perceived their [the wicked's] end.
Truly thou dost set them in slippery places;
  thou dost make them fall to ruin.
How they are destroyed in a moment,
  swept away utterly by terrors!
They are like a dream when one awakes,
  on awaking you despise their phantoms (vv. 16–20).

Habakkuk's message here in 2:6–20 calls us to that wide-awake
faith.

Habakkuk 3:1–19

The autobiographical framework of 3:2 and 3:16, which
surrounds the hymn of 3:3–15, connects the hymn directly with
the woes of 2:(5)6–20 and with the promise of 2:4. Habakkuk has
heard that the proud, who do not rely on God, cannot rest or
abide or live (2:4–5) and that the Lord will return their sins on
their own heads to destroy them (2:6–20).

O LORD, I have heard the report of thee,
  and thy work, O LORD, do I fear (3:2).
. . . .
I heard, and my innards were moved,
  at the sound, my lips quivered,
rottenness came into my bones,
  and my legs trembled (Hebr. obscure) (author's trans., v. 16).

Such is the effect on the prophet of God's word concerning his
judgment on the faithless. That is a fearful judgment, before
which the prophet can only tremble in awe and terror and
before whose frightful wrath Habakkuk can only pray for mercy
—not only for himself and the faithful but even for the wicked
(v. 2e). In such a framework, verses 3–15 are then elaborations
of that judgment; and the hymn is characterized as a word
whose "sound" the prophet has heard (v. 16). In the context of
such a revelatory word, he therefore waits in confidence for
God's judgment to overtake those who have invaded Judah (v.
16ef)—a specific reference to the Babylonians of chapter 1.
  The hymn, however, is not merely an auditory revelation.
It is a vision, in which the prophet is given to see not only God's

53

judgment on the Babylonians but also on all the nations of the earth (v. 12). The hymn really concerns God's final reckoning with the wicked and the establishment of his order in all the earth. It therefore is the confirmation not of 2:4 but of 2:3—of the time when God brings his purpose for the earth to completion.

Because this is true, it is possible that 3:16 is displaced and that it belongs immediately after 3:2. Up to this point, the book has had a decided dialogic character, with the prophet crying out (1:2–4), the Lord answering (1:5–11), the prophet questioning further (1:12–17), and the Lord giving further reply (2:3–4, 5–6a; 6b–20). Verse 2 with verse 16 of chapter 3, then, form the prophet's shaken and yet faithful reaction to 2:4, 5–6a, 6b–20.

But that is not the end of the matter. The word of 2:3 has yet to be confirmed—the promise of God to establish his Kingdom upon the earth—and that confirmation is supplied by the vision of 3:3–15, whereby all the prophet's questions are stilled and he ends with the confession of 3:17–19.

The hymn in 3:3–15 has the form of a prophetic description of a theophany or appearance of God and shares many features with the theophanies found in Deuteronomy 33:2; Judges 5:4–5; Psalm 18:7–15//II Samuel 22:8–16; Psalms 68:7–8, 17, 32–34; 77:16–19; 97:1–5. It may, therefore, have been used as an independent piece in the cult, and its later superscription (v. 1) and postscript (v. 19d) attest to such usage. Nevertheless, such theophanies come from prophets; this hymn's placement in Habakkuk has attributed it to him, and there is no reason to deny it to him. Indeed, the structure of the book and its theology demand its present position.

Verses 1–2, 16: This prayer of 3:2 forms Habakkuk's "amen" to God's revelation—his faithful response to the words of the Lord that have been granted him. "Yes, O Lord," he as much as says, "do that work of which you have spoken to me. Here in our 'meantime,' when all seems hopeless—when the righteous are defeated by the wicked and when the proud and mighty make themselves gods and their pride struts through the earth—yes, O Lord, renew that work of which I have heard from of old and of which you now have once again reassured me." It is as if the prophet were praying, "Thy kingdom come, thy will be done . . . Yes, O Lord, do it."

No verse reveals more clearly than this one that Habakkuk's concern is not with his own ineffectiveness as a prophet. Habakkuk does not pray here, "Lord, prosper my work." He prays, "Lord, renew thy work." He wants God's purpose to be fulfilled, God's work on earth to be done, God's actions to be seen clearly by faith in the passages of history. This prophet concentrates on God and not on human beings. And so should the church when it uses this text.

The Kingdom of God—that is the church's proper concern, is it not?

> Let goods and kindred go,
> This mortal life also;
> The body they may kill:
> God's truth abideth still;
> His Kingdom is forever ("A Mighty Fortress Is Our God").

There is our focus—the kingship of God. What does it matter if some cause is defeated, if some nation totters, if some suffering is borne? The question in the midst of it all is, Has the time of the Kingdom drawn nearer? Has God's purpose been advanced? Is his banner still on high? The church's goal is every knee bent and every tongue confessing Christ's lordship. The church's concern is the glory of the Lord known over all the earth. The church's cause is one Lord, one faith, one baptism, one God and Father of us all, in all and through all. And so the church's prayer is and must ever be, "O Lord, in the midst of the years, renew thy work. Bring in thy Kingdom on this earth, even as it is in heaven."

It is quite certain that we ourselves cannot achieve that goal. There is the delusion abroad in our time that the achievement of liberation for the oppressed in society, or the sharing of wealth with the poor, or the achievement of nuclear disarmament will usher in the Kingdom of God. But noble and necessary as they may be, human causes, in whatever age, are always marred by that creaturely pride and selfishness that war against the Creator. And finally God himself will have to establish his reign in the hearts and societies of sinful human beings, transformed to accord with his lordship. In the power of the Spirit, we can work in accord with God's purpose, to be sure. We can choose to promote it, and not oppose it. But we cannot finally achieve that salvation that only God can give.

The coming of the Kingdom will mean salvation (cf. 3:13), that is, God's abundant life. On the way to the achievement of

his goal, God puts down the wicked and rids the earth of the
proud evil that opposes his rule. But when the Kingdom comes,
evil is gone and good alone remains.

> Steadfast love and faithfulness will meet;
>   righteousness and peace will kiss each other.
> Faithfulness will spring up from the ground,
>   and righteousness will look down from the sky.
> Yea, the LORD will give what is good . . . (Ps. 85:10–12a).

Good will be our name and the character of our people. Good
will be our hearts and our relationships with one another. Good
will be the earth again, as God intended it in the beginning. For
God is good, and his goodness will rule his creation. Seeing that
is the goal of God, and the future that he promises, Habakkuk's
prayer is surely the prayer appropriate to God's faithful people:
In the midst of the years, renew thy work, O Lord; in the midst
of our years, make it known.

Verses 3–15: As final answer to the prophet's prayer in 3:2
and as final confirmation of the word of 2:3, Habakkuk is given
to see in a vision that which he has been promised: God's victory
over all the earth and the establishment of his Kingdom. Like
Moses at the top of Mount Pisgah looking over into the promised land (Deut. 34:1–4), like Jeremiah inheriting a piece of
property as a first fruit of the restoration (Jer. 32), like Christians
being offered a foretaste of the new wine of the messianic banquet when they sit at the Lord's table (Mark 14:25 par.), or like
Peter, James, and John being given that vision of the resurrected Lord on the Mount of Transfiguration (Mark 9:2–8),
Habakkuk is granted a foresight of God's purpose accomplished
(3:3–15). The passage forms the most extensive and elaborate
theophany to be found in the Old Testament.

As in the days of old, when God first began his work with
Israel in the Exodus and at Mount Sinai—that time when God
became King in Israel (cf. Deut. 33:2–5) and Israel became his
holy nation, set apart as instrument of his purpose (cf. Exod.
19:4–6)—God in this vision of the prophet's comes once more
from the southern desert of the Sinai peninsula (v. 3). But this
time he comes as King over all the earth: His glorious manifesta-
tion so illumines the heavens that all the earth responds in
praise (cf. Ps. 48:10). Light dominates the sight of him: Rays, like
those of the sun, come forth from his sides (cf. Ps. 18:12), but the
light is only the veiling of his power (v. 4; cf. Job 26:14). He has

such might that his enemies fall before him as if struck by pestilence and plague (v. 5).

He stands—the one calm figure midst all the tumult of the nations—measuring, that is, sizing up the peoples for judgment until they tremble before his gaze (v. 6). Even the eternal mountains are cleft by his look, and the everlasting hills sink low, for this is the God who determined his purpose in the beginning and is now bringing it to completion (v. 6e; RSV: His ways were as of old; Hebr.: everlasting are his ways, cf. 1:12). Cushan, which is synonymous here with Midian, remembering the past judgment which has fallen on it (Num. 31:7–8; cf. Judg. 3:8–10?), trembles in its tents.

Why has the Lord come forth (v. 8)? Is it to turn the rivers to blood once again, as the Nile was turned (Exod. 7:17–24)? Is it to divide the Reed Sea as it was divided when God's people passed through (Exod. 14:16, 22, 29)? Is it to heap up the Jordan, as it was heaped when the Israelites entered into the land (Josh. 3:16)? The questions are rhetorical, because those rivers and that sea have been subdued and the natural world now serves its Creator. Why then has God appeared with his horses and chariots of salvation (cf. Deut. 33:26; Pss. 18:10; 68:17)?

The answer is clear. God has come once again to conquer the chaos, as he did at the creation (Gen. 1; cf. Pss. 74:12–13; 89:9–10; Isa. 51:9); but this time the chaos symbolizes the evil of all nations, and God is portrayed in the figure of the divine Warrior-King. Verses 9–15 therefore picture the final battle.

God removes the covering from his battle bow (v. 9; apparently there is some reference in this verse also to an oath to the tribes of Israel, but the Hebrew is unreadable and the RSV's rendering is conjectural). At the same time, God calls forth the elements to aid him (vv. 9–10), cleaving the earth with rivers, shaking the mountains, summoning forth the great deep to roar against the enemy, commanding the sun and moon to remain in their dwelling so that darkness covers the earth (cf. Josh. 10:12–14). The picture tempts one to see God taking up that battle bow that he laid aside, according to Genesis 9:13, and using the great deep this time to defeat the wicked.

The only lights in the midst of the darkness are the lightnings of God's arrows and the flashing of his spears (v. 11). He tramples his enemies under his feet like a man treading out the grain (cf. Isa. 63:1–6). He sends panic among his enemies, so they turn their arrows against their own leaders (v. 14, RSV

57

margin). And as in the original defeat of chaos (cf. Pss. 74:13–14; 89:9–10), God crushes the head of the wicked, laying him open from neck to thigh (v. 13). Thus does he defeat the chaos of the nations, that is, the wicked who would oppose his rule, symbolized in verse 15 in the figure of the "sea" and the "mighty waters."

Moreover, God's whole battle is fought for one purpose—to bring salvation to those who trust him and who therefore are his people (v. 13)—to give life to his "poor" (v. 14) who depend on him as their sole helper. The vision is of the victory gained, when evil is no more and those faithful, who have relied on God, have inherited his Kingdom.

In short, Habakkuk in this vision granted him foresees something of an equivalent of Armageddon (Rev. 16—19)—evil fallen, God triumphant in his final battle with wrong. Indeed, there is even mention in 3:13 of the salvation gained for God's "anointed," which is a reference to the Davidic king, who is "saved," as in Zechariah 9:9 (Hebr.), along with God's people. It is an isolated reference in Habakkuk; some would doubt its genuineness. Certainly it has nothing to do with King Jehoiakim of the prophet's time. Rather, we can only say that Habakkuk's vision of the Kingdom come includes a Davidic ruler.

Verses 17–19: When the vision fades and its battle sounds die and the prophet returns to his present, no more questions rise to his lips and no further anguish disturbs his peace. His outward circumstances are no different from what they were at the beginning. Destruction and violence still mar his community, strife and contention still arise (1:3). Nations still rage and devour those weaker than they (1:13). The arrogant still rule (2:5), the poor still suffer (2:6–7), the enslaved still labor for emptiness (2:13). And false gods still are worshiped in the earth (1:11; 2:18–19). But Habakkuk knows who is working his purpose out, unseen, behind the turmoil. And Habakkuk now knows what the end of it all will be. He therefore sings the magnificent song of trust that we find in 3:17–19.

Three interpretations of the conditions pictured in verse 17 are possible if the verse is compared with others similar to it in the prophetic writings. (1) It may be that the failure of fig tree and vine, of field and flock are due to the invasion of the Babylonians, as in Jeremiah 5:17, and that Habakkuk is expressing his confidence in God's salvation of him in the face of the enemy. (2) In Amos 4:9; Micah 6:15; and Haggai 2:16–17, such deprivations are the effect of God's covenant curse upon the land. In this case, Habakkuk would be expressing his confidence that God will save him and the faithful while judging the unfaithful. (3) In Joel 1:10–12, such conditions are present at the Day of the Lord, and Habakkuk's song, then, would be an expression, once again, of deliverance at the time of the final judgment.

Probably the first interpretation is to be preferred as the original. Habakkuk is setting forth the faith that knows how to live "in the meantime" (2:4), and the primary threat that faces him and his countrymen in 600 B.C. is that of the Babylonians. And yet, certainly the similar passage in Jeremiah 5:17, in an oracle on the foe from the north, also has about it dimensions of the Day of the Lord and of the final judgment. The foe in Jeremiah is not only Babylonia, but also God, who comes as the Divine Warrior to wreak his final judgment on his people. Habakkuk may therefore be referring not only to the historical threat of Babylonian invasion and destruction of the land, but also to God's final reckoning with evil in his world.

In summary, Habakkuk is saying that come what may— injustice and violence in his own society, desolating foreign invasion, God's destruction of the wicked in his world—nevertheless, he and the faithful like him can rejoice and even exult, because God is their salvation (cf. 1:2; 3:13). The Lord is their strength—the Hebrew word can also mean "army"—who not only sets them in the heights where no harm can reach them but who also sustains their lives. It is Habakkuk's final "Amen" to the promise that the righteous shall live by their faithfulness (2:4)—his final affirmation that nothing can separate him from the love of God, and that therefore nothing can cloy his joy in the God of his salvation.

Can we live with that? Can we affirm Habakkuk's faith and know with certain joy that God is working his purpose out and will bring it to completion? Can we therefore join Habakkuk's song of trust and confess that nothing can wrest us from the protection and sustenance of such a sovereign Lord? Can we, in the midst of our evil world, or on a bed of pain—can we when enemies confront us, or friends and family prove untrue—can we when facing death or the powers of hell unloosed—nevertheless join in Habakkuk's song?

> Though vine nor fig tree neither
> Their wonted fruit shall bear,
> Though all the field should wither,
> Nor flocks nor herds be there;
> Yet God the same abiding,
> His praise shall tune my voice,
> For while in Him confiding
> I cannot but rejoice (Wm. Cowper [1779] hymn, "Sometimes a Light Surprises").

Countless faithful souls have shared Habakkuk's faith and therefore also found his joy. Let me quote only two: Dietrich Bonhoeffer from his Nazi prison cell: "By good powers wonderfully hidden, we await cheerfully, come what may." And Charles Haddon Spurgeon in a sermon on this passage:

> ... We have been assured by people who think they know a great deal about the future that awful times are coming. Be it so; it need not alarm us, for the Lord reigneth. Stay yourself on the Lord ... and you can rejoice in His name. If the worst comes to the worst, our refuge is in God; if the heavens shall fall the God of heaven will stand; when God cannot take care of His people under heaven He will take them above the heavens, and there they shall dwell with Him. Therefore, as far as you are concerned, rest; for you shall stand ... at the end of the days ("The Middle Passage," p. 723).

Yes, truly, the word is sure: The God and Father of our Lord Jesus Christ is at work, fulfilling his purpose. His Kingdom comes. And "in the meantime" and for evermore, the righteous shall live by their faithfulness.

THE BOOK OF
Zephaniah

Introduction

The ministry of the prophet Zephaniah spanned the years of King Josiah's reign in Judah (640–609 B.C.). His was the first prophetic voice to be heard in Judah since the time of Isaiah and Micah, that is, since 701 B.C., and the message he brought from God was radical and universal in its scope:

> I will utterly sweep away everything
> from the face of the earth, says the Lord (1:2).

The great Day of the Lord—of the Mighty Man of War—was about to break over all creation.

Zephaniah announced that message in Jerusalem in the years following the syncretistic reigns of Kings Manasseh (877/6–642 B.C.) and Amon (642–640 B.C.); but the church has understood the prophet's words to be relevant to its life in every age, and they have been handed down to us as a word of God for our time also.

It has often been noted that Zephaniah is the one prophet for whom four generations of ancestors are named, among them one "Hezekiah" (1:1). It is doubtful, however, that the name is a reference to King Hezekiah of Judah (727–698/6 B.C.); and whatever Zephaniah's ancestry, it does not determine the content of his message.

The book has been preserved for us in what appears at first glance to be the familiar editorial tripartite pattern found in much of the prophetic literature. That is, there is judgment on Judah (1:2—2:3) followed by oracles against the foreign nations (2:4—3:8) and then promises (3:9–20). However, there is an organic wholeness about the book that argues against its overall

61

arrangement by an editorial hand. The theme of sinful human pride runs through the whole work, and its separate parts are held together by similar and contrasting images. These latter will be pointed out in the commentary, but for example, there is the "mighty man" in 1:14 and 3:17, or the picture of "exulting" in 2:15 and 3:17. At the same time, Hebrew rhetorical structures prevent the separation of the supposed three parts of the book: 2:3 belongs inseparably with 2:4, and 3:8 joins with 3:9—connections that are obscured in the English translation. J. H. Eaton has written:

> . . . the true significance of the work lies in its wholeness. Broken apart, it loses its essential meaning. Its components must indeed be distinguished, but only that their mutual relations can be appreciated.
> . . . it is the finished work which has the best claim to our attention. And it is, after all, the finished work which the Jewish and Christian Canon commends to us (pp. 123, 124).

With that judgment, I wholeheartedly agree.

It has also often been noted that 3:14–20 contains phrases similar to some found in the Deuteronomic portions of Jeremiah. And it may be that Zephaniah was a member of that levitical-prophetic reform group that was responsible for the collection of Deuteronomy which gave rise to the Deuteronomic reform of 622/1 B. C.—a group that also included among its members the prophet Jeremiah and, later, the authors of Third Isaiah (see the author's *Deuteronomy, Jeremiah,* and *The Community and Message of Isaiah 56—66*). Such reformers not only shared a common cause but also apparently a common rhetoric, and Zephaniah gives evidence that he has sometimes used such manner of speech. I do consider, however, that chapters 1 and 2 of the book date shortly after 640 B. C., before the Deuteronomic reform, while 3:1–17 was delivered sometime in 612–609 B.C., after the fall of the Assyrian capital Nineveh and the failure of the reform in Judah. Verses 18–20, on the other hand, represent later Deuteronomic updatings of the work.

Zephaniah 1:2–6

In 1939, a British preacher named W.E. Bowen published a sermon entitled "Black-Robed Years" on the text of Zephaniah 1:2. In that sermon, he did what so many Christian interpreters are tempted to do with the Book of Zephaniah. He softened the judgment announced by the prophet by pointing to our salvation in Christ. He did this by juxtaposing Zephaniah 1:2 with John 3:16, both read aloud, and he commented this way:

> Can we, "who profess and call ourselves Christians" doubt which of these sayings is from a spiritual standpoint the finer of the two (p. 33)?
> ... there is surely nothing in His (Jesus') teaching to justify the supposition that He would have endorsed such a prophecy of general extermination ... (p. 31).

Zephaniah's radical pronouncements of God's judgment upon the whole earth were thereby rendered irrelevant and unimportant to the Christian reader or hearer of them.

By way of parenthesis, it might be pointed out how ironical was Bowen's interpretation of this text in his particular historical setting of 1939, for there was taking root across the English channel in Nazi Germany a thorough-going perversion of the biblical faith—a fact that Bowen noted in his sermon, but dismissed rather lightly. And that perversion was finally done away only by being swept from the face of the earth.

Perhaps there are some lessons there for us as we begin with the Book of Zephaniah, for the prophet's words have come down to us through the centuries as part of the canon of the church. We are therefore instructed by the historical church not to hurry by Zephaniah's judgments but rather to listen to them as words addressed to us also.

Certainly these words in 1:2–3 present one of the most radical pictures in the Bible—of God's wrath burning up a creation gone wrong. As in Jeremiah's awful vision of God's act of creation reversed (Jer. 4:23–25), everything is to be destroyed

63

—human being and beast and bird and fish: in the familiar biblical phrases, "anything that is in the heaven above or that is in the earth beneath or that is in the waters under the earth" (Exod. 20:4). The picture parallels that of Paul's in Romans 1:18: "For the wrath of God is revealed from heaven against all ungodliness and wickedness of men. . . ." And as is always the case in the Bible, the sinfulness of human beings drags down nature itself to participate in the sin and the subsequent judgment on it (cf. Gen. 3:17; Jer. 12:4; Rom. 8:20–21).

But the Old Testament never deals only in generalities. It moves always from the universal to the particular. So in verse 4 of our passage, the judgment centers down on Judah and Jerusalem. Because they are that portion of the Chosen People who survived the fall of the Northern Kingdom to Assyria in 722 B.C., they are not to believe that they are exempt from God's judgment that will encompass the earth (cf. Amos 3:2).

Their sins against their covenant Lord are carefully specified, and the sins are three: (1) idolatry, (2) syncretism, and (3) indifference toward God (vv. 4–5). These are the fruits of the long reign of Manasseh and of the short reign of Amon in Judah, when both were vassals of the Assyrian Empire. From the pictures that are presented to us in II Kings 21:1–5 and 23:4–14, we know that when Judah served Assyria it served Assyria's gods as well, worshiping those astral bodies which the Assyrians —like modern–day astrologers—believed to control the fate of earth. In addition, the age–old worship of the ba'als, the fertility gods of Canaan, continued, with its abominable practices of sacred prostitution and child sacrifice. And left over from the example of Solomon was allegiance to the Ammonite god Milcom (cf. I Kings 11:5, 33; II Kings 23:13). This idolatry infected the very center of Judah's religious life, the temple, where there were sacred cult objects kept for the worship of the Canaanite goddess Asherah (II Kings 23:4; 21:7) and statues dedicated to the sungod Shamash (II Kings 23:11), as well as altars for sacrifice to the Assyrian astral deities (II Kings 23:12; 21:4). At these idolatrous shrines, Judean priests led in worship.

Furthermore, the Judeans saw no harm in their confusion of gods. They could take an oath by the name of the Lord, binding themselves to his character, and yet equate him with the foreign god Milcom (v. 5) as if there were no difference between gods—much like modern syncretistic attempts to equate Jesus with Buddha or Allah or Sun Myung Moon or some

64

shadowy mystical "presence." The holy God of the covenant, beside whom there was no other, whose name was One and whose character was absolutely unique among gods (cf. Deut. 6:4; Isa. 45:6), had become for the Judeans just another name in an endless pantheon of powers.

But indifference to God, absence from his worship, and neglect of his commands follow hard on the heels of his disappearance into a row of nondescript divinities. Where God's character, revealed through the Bible's sacred story, is blurred from sight and lost, obedience and prayer and praise and commitment to him become matters of indifference. Thus, Judah had become a "backslider" (v. 6), neglecting the only One who gave her life. God's reaction to her sin was to condemn her to that death she had chosen.

We Christians sometimes believe that the cross will always shield us from similar condemnation, but there is no automatic guarantee in the gospel of Christ against such death. Where the worship of his lordship becomes mixed with allegiance to other lords, where there is belief that luck or the stars or the powers of this world ultimately control our destiny, where we therefore neglect the worship of the Lord and conform to the ways of society and water down his commands for convenience or ideological servitude, we too are confronted by a God who can say to us, "I will utterly sweep away everything from the face of the earth." And perhaps in this nuclear age we have had a glimpse of the instruments of that sweeping.

Zephaniah 1:7-13

It may well be that this passage is made up of what were originally very short prophetic oracles, but the whole has been joined together—by the prophet himself or by some other—to form an impressive initial announcement of the coming of the Day of the Lord and the central reason for that coming. Here Zephaniah pronounces God's basic indictment of his covenant people.

The thought of the Day of the Lord is perhaps more explicitly prominent in the Book of Zephaniah than in any other prophetic writing, although it receives sustained treatment also in the Book of Joel, and in order to understand Zephaniah's preaching, we must understand the nature of the Day.

The concept of the Day of the Lord has its roots in the ancient theology of Israel's holy wars, which were conducted in the period of the tribal league (ca. 1220–1020 B.C.) and actually up through the time of Saul (1020–1000 B.C.), according to fixed cultic or sacral rules (hence the name "holy" war). The Lord was the Divine Warrior in such battles, leading the hosts of Israel, and in fact winning the battle for them with cosmic weapons of thunder (I Sam. 7:10), falling stones (Josh. 10:11), darkness (Exod. 14:20; Josh. 24:7), water, and earthquake (Judg. 5:4–5). Most important, the Lord inspired terror and panic among the enemy (Exod. 15:14–16; 23:27; Josh. 2:9, 24; 5:1; 7:5), leading them to bring about their own destruction. This whole complex of ideas was much later used by Deuteronomy to give assurance to embattled Judah in the time of Zephaniah and Jeremiah (cf. Deut. 20).

The prophets of Israel, however, put a new twist on that message. Beginning with Amos, they announced that on the Day of the Lord, God would turn his warfare, not only against Israel's enemies but also against Israel herself, as punishment for her sin. Such an announcement is explicitly made, not only here in Zephaniah 1 but also in Amos 5:18–20; Isaiah 2:6–22; Ezekiel 7:5–27; Joel 1:15; 2:1–11; and Malachi 4:5 (cf. Lam. 2:1, 21–22; Ezek. 34:12). Indeed, that divine warfare against Israel probably forms the background of Amos's entire message and most of Jeremiah's. So too it is the fearful backdrop of the whole of Zephaniah 1:2—3:8.

The title "Day" designates not a definite extent of time but a definite event in time, whose nature is to be determined entirely by the Lord (so Wolff); and thus the phrases, "at that time" or "on that day" indicate not fixed periods but particular events, whose nature is then spelled out. According to the prophets, the nature of the Day is as follows:

1) It is near (Zeph. 1:7, 14; Amos 6:3; Ezek. 7:7; Joel 1:15; 2:1; cf. Isa. 13:6; Ezek. 30:3; Obad. 15; Joel 3:14).

2) It is a day of God's wrath and anger against the wicked (Zeph. 1:15, 18; 2:2, 3; Jer. 4:8; 12:13; Ezek. 7:3, 8, 12f., 14, 19; Lam. 2:1, 21–22; cf. Isa. 13:9, 13).

3) It is a day of darkness and gloom (Zeph. 1:15; Amos 5:18; 8:9; Joel 2:2) or of clouds and thick darkness (Zeph. 1:15; Ezek. 34:12; Joel 2:2; cf. Ezek. 30:3).

4) The heavenly bodies are darkened (Amos 8:9; Joel 2:10; cf. 2:31; 3:15; Isa. 13:10).

5) God is pictured as a warrior (Zeph. 1:14 [see the comment on this verse]; 3:17; Jer. 20:11; Isa. 59:15–18; 63:1–6; 66: 15–16; Zech. 14:3; Joel 2:11).

6) It is a day of battle, of trumpet blast and battle cry (Zeph. 1:16; cf. Ezek. 7:14; Jer. 4:5, 19, 21; 6:1; Isa. 13:2–22; 22:5–8; Ezek. 30:4–5; Obad. 8–9; Zech. 14:2–3). Of sword (Zeph. 2:12; cf. Ezek. 7:15; Jer. 4:10; 12:12; 46:10; Isa. 13:15).

7) The enemies are dismayed and rendered impotent (Ezek. 7:17, 27; cf. Jer. 4:9; 6:24; Isa. 13:7–8; Ezek. 30:9; Zech. 14:13).

8) God searches out his enemies to destroy them (Zeph. 1:12; Amos 9:2–4; cf. Isa. 13:14–15).

9) The wealth of the enemies cannot save them and becomes useless (Zeph. 1:18; Isa. 2:20; Ezek. 7:11, 19; cf. Isa. 13:17).

10) Human pride is destroyed (Zeph. 3:11–12; Isa. 2:11–17; cf. Ezek. 7:10, 24; Isa. 13:11; Obad. 3–4).

11) It may be that some are hidden in the Day or saved as a remnant (Zeph. 2:3, 7, 9; Amos 5:14–15; cf. Joel 2:18–32; Jer. 4:14; Obad. 17).

The prophets therefore pictured the Day of the Lord in the terms of a fixed tradition, and there is actually nothing basic in Zephaniah's portrayal of the Day that is not found already in the prophecies of Amos and of Isaiah and that is not passed on to the prophets coming after. Yet each man of God painted the Day in the peculiar colors of his own situation, some more freely than others, and perhaps the most creative use of the tradition is to be found in the prophecies of Jeremiah.

Zephaniah too contributed his own portrayal, notably that of the Lord's sacrifice in 1:7. "Be silent before the Lord God!" is the priestly cry before the sacrifice, and it has usually been thought that Judah is the offered "animal" in this verse that God is going to share with his guests. That would be true if this were the *ḥerem* sacrifice which, in the holy war tradition, came at the end of the battle (cf. Deut. 20:16–18; 25:17–19; I Sam. 15:3; Jer. 46:10; 50:26–27; Isa. 34:5–7). But the battle has not yet begun here in Zephaniah's portrayal. It is threat, but not yet present, and Zephaniah 1 really serves as the prelude to the call to repentance in 2:1–4. The sacrifice of 1:7, therefore, is that which always preceded the holy war (cf. I Sam. 13:9; II Sam. 15:12), when the soldiers were consecrated for battle (Zeph. 1:7; 67

Isa. 13:3; cf. "prepare war" in Jer. 6:4; 22:7; 51:27). God is preparing his army in this portrayal—an army whose members are as unknown and as mysterious as Jeremiah's foe from the north. God readies himself to destroy all nations, including Judah, and who knows what mysterious agents he uses to bring his judgments upon them? This is not an apocalyptic picture, however, any more than it was in Amos 1—2. It signals not the end of the world but the transformation of it.

Most important for our understanding of Zephaniah as the word of God are the reasons for God's judgment on Judah, and, as in the preceding passage, those reasons are spelled out in sharp specificity.

First of all, as a vassal of Assyria, the leaders of Judah have accommodated their ways to those of a foreign culture, shown by their attire in the latest foreign fashions (1:8). Assyria's ways have become Judah's ways, and Assyria's customs hers. Yet, from the beginning, Israel was supposed to have been a unique nation (cf. Exod. 33:16), "a people dwelling alone" (Num. 23:9), as it were, unlike any other society. They were "not to do" as all those peoples did who dwelt around them (Lev. 18:1–5), but they were to do as God commanded in his covenant law. Like the church, Israel was not to be conformed to this world but solely to the will of her covenant Lord (Rom. 12:2), and now she had exchanged that uniqueness for accommodation to her situation.

As in the preceding passage (vv. 4–5), she therefore had fallen victim to pagan idolatry, once again symbolized by a specific act—that of stepping over thresholds where, pagans believed, evil spirits dwelt (1:9; cf. I Sam. 5:5 and the ancient Roman custom of carrying a bride over the threshold).

Further, in her desertion of her unique God, she had deserted his covenant commands that specified special succor to the poor and helpless (Exod. 22:21–27; 23:6–10). Violence and fraud against the weak had become the way of life in law court, commerce, and social intercourse (1:9). Indeed, the luxury items in the leaders' houses were the proceeds gained from such rapacity.

Judah, like our modern society in this so-called "post-Christian era," believed that a new situation demanded new ways of getting along in the world. She had to be practical. She had to compromise. She had to adjust to reality. After all, Assyria ruled the day; and if one is wise, one will be as pleasant

68

and as accommodating as possible to those who hold the reins of power—to one's boss, to one's social leaders, to one's organization, to one's government officials. Ancient commandments, delivered by an unseen God, hold little force and importance in a world that is clearly run by other, human powers.

This attitude of Judah's is summed up by the prophet in 1:12, which forms the central indictment in his book: The Judeans are men and women who are "thickening upon their lees." The figure is taken from the process of wine making. The lees are the sediment of the grapes, and new wine is allowed to sit undisturbed upon its lees only long enough to fix its color and body. It must then be poured to another vessel or drawn off before it becomes thick and syrupy and too sweet and subject to mold (cf. Jer. 48:11; Isa. 25:6 is therefore a figure for very sweet wine).

The Judeans therefore are those who have become "thickened wine," and the meaning of that is spelled out in the lines that follow. They are "those who say in their hearts, 'The Lord will not do good, nor will he do ill.' " That latter saying has the form of a proverb and thus is common parlance in Zephaniah's Jerusalem; indeed, as the prophet points out, it characterizes the attitude of the hearts of the citizens of Judah. It reveals their inner thoughts and the motivating center of all their actions. And what the proverb means is that the Lord will do nothing at all (cf. Gen. 31:24; and the application of the saying to idols in Isa. 41:23; Jer. 10:5)! The citizens of Zephaniah's Jerusalem believe that God no longer governs the world. Not even good things are attributed to his actions, for he does not act at all, and his influence and the effective working out of his purpose are believed absent from the earth. That reminds me of the man in one of our congregations who once remarked, "Sure I believe in God, but I don't believe he does anything." Surely that is a picture also of modern secular society, which believes that God is absent from the world and that therefore "anything goes"— that there is no one to see what we do (cf. Ezek. 8:12; 9:9) and therefore there are no consequences to be paid. In such societies, human beings have committed the ultimate idolatry—the final sin of trying to make themselves their own gods (cf. Gen. 3:5).

In the face of this supreme idolatry, this total breach of the covenant (cf. Exod. 20:3), Zephaniah announces that the Day of the Lord is near and hastening fast. That Day will reveal who

69

really rules the world and who has power to act (cf. the reference to God as "King" in 3:15, a title for God often connected with the Day of the Lord: Jer. 51:57; Ezek. 20:33; Zech. 14:9, 16).

God's battle day against his rebellious people and against his rebellious earth will begin in the heart of Jerusalem—judgment begins with the household of God (I Peter 4:17). But appropriate to the secular society that Jerusalem has become, God's destruction of his sinful people will start not at the temple but in the commercial quarter—at the Fish Gate in the north wall (cf. Neh. 3:3; 12:39; II Chron. 33:14), where fishermen from Tyre entered with their catch (cf. Neh. 13:16); in the Second quarter (II Kings 22:14//II Chron. 34:22), a suburb added to the city by Manasseh's wall, near the Fish Gate; and in the Mortar (the name means pounding place, cf. Prov. 27:22), a basin in the city between the east and west hills on which Jerusalem was built, where apparently traders and merchants dwelt. There in her commercial center—her ancient Wall Street—Jerusalem will experience God's first attack (vv. 10–11).

Zephaniah's poetry lets us hear the sounds of battle—voices crying out in distress and wailing over ruin; crashing and the noise of destruction echoing off the hills of the city (cf. Jer. 50:22; 51:54).

God will begin his Day in the commercial center. But then like Diogenes with his lamp searching for truth, and like Jeremiah searching Jerusalem for one righteous person (Jer. 5:1; cf. Gen. 18:22–33), God will search out every corner of Jerusalem, illuminating its dark crannies with an oil lamp, until he has found all those who think he is not in charge of his world (cf. the same picture in the holy war passages of Amos 9:2–4 and Isa. 13:14–15; also see Jer. 16:16–18 and Ezek. 9:4–6). He will make a minute and diligent search, and it will be impossible to escape him (cf. Ps. 139:7–12). The well–to–do, comfortable, self-sufficient idolators, who think themselves to be gods, will find their accumulated goods have become only the spoils of God's war (cf. v. 13; Jer. 15:13; 17:3) and themselves helpless before him.

The last four lines of verse 13 are made up of the covenant curses found in Deuteronomy 28:30, 39 (cf. Amos 5:11; Micah 6:15, and the reversal of the curse in Isa. 65:21–22; Ezek. 28:26) —curses which would come upon those who broke covenant with God. And that is finally Judah's sin—she has broken her covenant with God, not in little ways of temporary straying, not

70

in minute infractions of the covenant commands, but basically, from her heart. In the place of God, she has put herself. She has thought God unnecessary. And that total breach of covenant faithfulness will bring her total end. For a secular age like ours, and for a church as conformed to the world as we are, that pronouncement by Zephaniah is a fearful and terrible word from God.

Zephaniah 1:14–18

Few passages from the Old Testament have been more widely represented in the liturgy of the church, in literature, and in both sacred and secular music than has the hymn on the Day of the Lord which forms the first two verses of this passage. The Latin Vulgate reads the beginning of verse 15 as *"Dies irae,"* and in the thirteenth century, a Franciscan monk composed a seventeen-verse poem on that text. (He was probably not, however, the friend of Francis of Assisi, Thomas of Celano, *ca.* 1250, to whom the poem is often attributed [Treach]). The first part of the poem gave a description of the Last Judgment, a summary of Christian eschatology. The second part passionately appealed to Christ's mercy. Like the Scriptures, the poem circulated in several different manuscript versions, and no other hymn has ever had more numerous translations—all of which differ—into vernacular languages (for the beginning of one translation, see Taylor, VI, 1012). In the fourteenth century, the poem began to be included as a sequence in Requiem masses, and it was officially incorporated into the Roman Missal in 1570 (Sadie). From there it passed into numerous literary and musical works, both ancient and contemporary.

Until 1969, the use of the *Dies Irae* in some masses was obligatory for the Roman Catholic Church, but perhaps symptomatic of our times, it has now fallen into disuse. Nevertheless, with such a long history of interpretation behind it, we need to ask, What is happening here in Zephaniah 1:14–15?

In anticipatory prophetic vision, Zephaniah sees the beginning of God's holy war against his people: "The mighty man—there—utters a war cry" (v. 14d Hebrew)! The scene opens with the battle cry of the Lord (cf. 3:17; Isa. 42:13; Jer. 25:28–31;

71

Amos 1:2; Joel 3:16; for the words of a war cry in the Holy War, see Judg. 7:18). Thus, "the sound of the day" in verse 14c should be read "the voice of the day," for the reference there too is to the voice of the Divine Warrior, initiating the fray.

> . . . lo, he sends forth his voice, his mighty voice" (Ps. 68:33).

> The voice of the LORD is powerful,
>> the voice of the LORD is full of majesty (Ps. 29:4).

That voice of God, at whose rebuke the chaotic waters fled at the creation (Ps. 104:7), whose thunders give hailstones and fire (Ps. 18:13; cf. Job 37:5); that voice that was heard at Sinai with ". . . thunders and lightnings and a thick cloud upon the mountain and a very loud trumpet blast, so that all the people who were in the camp trembled" (Exod. 19:16); that voice, "whose words made the hearers entreat that no further messages be spoken to them" (Heb. 12:19)—that is the voice that will be heard at the beginning of God's holy war against his people.

As at Sinai, when the covenant with Israel was established, the voice here is accompanied by "darkness and gloom," by "clouds and thick darkness," and by trumpet blast—all cosmic manifestations of the Lord's overwhelming presence. But the awful message of Zephaniah is that the covenant Lord has broken out on his Day, not in saving love toward his people—not to enter into fellowship with them as at Sinai—but in wrath and fury. And so this Day of the voice of the Lord will be a day of "distress and anguish," of "ruin and devastation," of straits (RSV: distress, v. 17) that may be felt in the very bones of one's being.

No fortifications are adequate to turn back this Warrior (v. 16). No silver or gold will be able to buy deliverance from his attack (v. 18)—a strategy sometimes effective against a human enemy (II Kings 15:19–20; cf. 16:7–9; 18:13–16). Under the stresses and straits of the Lord's attack, the Judeans will grope like blind men, unable to find their way—the fulfillment of God's covenant curse in Deuteronomy 28:29. This beloved people of the Lord, this chosen nation, this peculiar treasure, will be as worthless in God's sight as dust and as unclean dung. Dust they are, and to dust they shall return (cf. Gen. 3:19).

But the sin which the Divine Warrior now attacks in his fury is not Judah's alone. The sin of trying to live life without

72

God—the awful, terrible attempt of trying to run the world without him—is the sin of all the earth (cf. Gen. 3—11). And so God, in the fire of his jealousy—that exclusive claim he makes to the allegiance of all his creatures—will show his lordship over all flesh by consuming them in their rebellion (v. 18). Sin has reached universal proportions. The destruction of it must therefore be also universal.

The end will come suddenly, according to verse 18. "Men, we know, are wont to extend time, that they may cherish their sins" (Calvin, V, 221), but their time of rebellious independence from God will come to an end when they least expect it (cf. Mark 13:32–35).

The contemporary church has made large use of this passage in Zephaniah 1:14–18. In some lectionaries, Zephaniah 1:7, 12–18 are coupled with I Thessalonians 5:1–10 or I Thessalonians 4:13–18, and with Matthew 25:14–15, 19–29 or Matthew 25:1–13, thus equating Zephaniah's Day of the Lord with the *parousia*, the resurrection from the dead, and the last judgment. That is the same interpretation as that given in the *Dies Irae* in the Roman Catholic Church. Thus the Day which, in Zephaniah, was "near and hastening fast" is used by the church to form its eschatology, as is the case with so many of the prophetic pictures of the future judgment and salvation.

The Old Testament picture of the Day of the Lord is also used for realized eschatology in the New Testament, however. The darkness of the Day is pictured as present at the crucifixion of our Lord, from the sixth to the ninth hour (Mark 15:33//Matt. 27:45; omitted by Luke), and that is similar to John's understanding of the cross as God's judgment on this world, with its darkness (John 12:31–32, 35–36).

Either way, the church has always connected the awful judgment pictured in Zephaniah 1:14–18 with the figure of Jesus Christ, who has come and who is coming again. And that judgment is not to be softened or bypassed. According to Jesus, faithless, unwatchful, negligent servants can find the door shut (Matt. 25:10):

> . . . the door for ever locked, the road which
> leads nowhere, the lie, the everlasting dark (Bernanos, p. 23).

In our attempts to rule our own lives, we can find ourselves cast "into the outer darkness" where "men will weep and gnash their teeth" (Matt. 25:30). And the only remedy for that is to

73

surrender our self-rule and to trust in that One who comes on God's Day to deliver us from his wrath, that we may "obtain salvation" (I Thess. 5:9) and be forever "with the Lord" (I Thess. 4:17). The great Day of the Lord is near and hastening fast. But we can have a comfort (I Thess. 4:18) "in life and death," if we will receive him in our hearts (cf. Zeph. 1:12). It is with the same thought that Zephaniah 2:1–4 proceeds.

Zephaniah 2:1–4

Zephaniah 2:3, along with 3:11–13, is a stated Old Testament lesson for Epiphany in many denominations. It is also the central announcement of the Book of Zephaniah, consonant with all that has gone before and all that comes after.

Zephaniah 1 has proclaimed the near and hastening Day of judgment of the Divine Warrior on all humankind for its ultimate sin of pride—of trying to live in a world where there is no God and human beings have become their own gods. And as the New Testament lectionary readings often coupled with 1:14–18 have anticipated (see the previous section), there is only one way of being saved from such universal judgment—by renouncing reliance on one's own powers and by casting oneself on the mercy of God; in short, by renouncing the final sin of pride and humbling oneself before one's Creator. It is exactly that one hope of salvation to which Zephaniah here calls his sinful nation. Midst the gloom and thick darkness of the awful Day, there is one gleam of light—the mercy of God which desires that his people live rather than die (cf. Ezek. 18:30–32; John 3:17).

But Judah's basic problem is that she is a "nation that is not ashamed" (v. 2:1*b* Hebr.). As in the preaching of Jeremiah, shortly after Zephaniah's:

> ". . . no man repents of his wickedness,
>   saying, "What have I done?"
> Every one turns to his own course,
>   like a horse plunging headlong into battle (Jer. 8:6*c–f*).

74

No one judges his actions in the light of God's will. No one repents that her ways are not in accord with God's wishes, set forth in the covenant law.

Zephaniah therefore calls his people to "hold assembly" (2:1)—probably figuratively or literally, an assembly of fasting and repentance and of seeking God for help and guidance (cf. II Chron. 20:3-4; Joel 1:14). Zephaniah's call is urgent, emphasized by the threefold "before" in verse 2. (The text of v. 2*ab* is difficult and probably has the meaning, "before another day passes without such an assembly"; it reads, literally, "before bringing forth a decree [to hold such an assembly], a day passes away like chaff.")

"Seek the Lord" is Zephaniah's call (2:3; cf. Amos 5:6; Isa. 55:6), for in turning to God the people will acknowledge that they themselves are not gods and that they are dependent on the One who is really God and Lord of their lives. That seeking, that turning, that acknowledgment will yield three results:

First, it will instill humility (v. 3*a,c*; cf. 3:12)—that meekness of spirit (cf. Isa. 11:4), the brokenness and contriteness of heart (cf. Pss. 34:18; 51:17; Isa. 57:15; 66:2) that is appropriate before God, because it realizes that it is, in fact, not self-sufficient but dependent on him for the very breath of life—for the light of every morning and the walk of every day. Knowledge that in God alone we live and move and have our being —to that humble but joyous realization Zephaniah beckons (cf. I Peter 5:6).

Second, turning to God leads to obedience, to doing his commands (v. 3*b*; cf. Isa. 58:2; Jer. 5:4-5; 8:7). If we give up running our own lives—if we resign as rulers of our own private universes and turn to God's direction—we find ourselves obeying his will set forth in his teachings and commandments. And it is precisely such obedience to God's covenant commandments in the Decalogue and Covenant Code and prophetic and priestly *torahs* that Zephaniah calls his people.

Such humble dependence, then, and such obedience are, in the third place, "righteousness" before the Lord (v. 3*c*)— which means that they are the fulfillment of the demands of the covenant relationship with God. (See the author's article on "Righteousness in the Old Testament"). We should note, however, that the covenant relationship is not fulfilled simply by obedience to the law. Up until the post-exilic period, the Old Testament never indulges in such legalism. Rather, righteousness in the Old Testament, as in the New, is primarily by faith —by that trusting and loving dependence of the heart (cf. 1:12) on God alone for life and good and guidance (cf. Deut. 6:5),

75

which issues in a daily walk of surrender and fidelity and obedience (cf. Deut. 10:12–16; 11:1, 13, 18–20; 30:16, 20). To this righteousness, gained by seeking God, Zephaniah calls his unrepentant people; for this alone can save them from the imminent Day of the wrath of the Lord.

It is significant, therefore, that in the Epistle (I Cor. 1: 26–31) and Gospel (Matt. 5:1–12) readings that are sometimes coupled with this passage in the lectionaries, the characteristics of faith are dealt with—humility over against the wisdom and independence of the world, obedience over against self-rule, the righteousness of God through Christ over against the proud and sinful claims of human beings. Such lectionary readings afford an opportunity to examine the nature of the life of faith, and that opportunity should not be passed up.

Zephaniah is addressing not only a faithful remnant in Judah, who are already humble and obedient, however. He is imploring his whole nation to turn to God and become faithful. Like Paul addressing "saints" in Corinth (I Cor. 1:2)—that godless lot—and urging them to live up to their sainthood in Christ, Zephaniah here implores the covenant people of God to become in fact faithful to the covenant.

But the invitation is qualified: "Perhaps" they will be hidden when the flood of judgment engulfs the earth (v. 3; cf. Amos 5:14–15; Isa. 26:20–21; Job 14:13; Ps. 57:1). Sin has reached universal proportions; the judgment on it also will be universal. And no human being—not even a prophet—can say who will be spared in that reckoning (cf. Matt. 24:40–42); "perhaps you," perhaps not; it is a call that makes one tremble.

The effects of the promised Day of wrath on the nations of the world are then pictured. And that picture must begin here in verse 4 because it forms the backdrop of the urgent appeal of verses 1–3. "Seek the Lord," is the call. Thereby learn humility and obedience and righteousness; for the Day that comes will sweep away all (1:2), and the first illustration of that engulfing word is that it will sweep away the Philistines (v. 4). Beginning at the south on the coastal plain and moving northward, Zephaniah enumerates the four remaining cities of the old five-tribe Philistine league (cf. Josh. 13:3), which, from 1150 B.C. on, formed a constant threat to Isreal and in the time of Saul almost snuffed out her life.

God's war against his enemies, within and without Israel, is about to begin (cf. 1:14). ". . . the Hebrew crackles with alliteration and ominous puns" (Eaton, p. 137). The word for "Gaza" sounds much like the word for "deserted" in the Hebrew, the word for "Ekron" much like "uprooted." Thus, by the use of such assonance, Zephaniah proclaims that these cities will fulfill the omens of their names. Superb poetry is set at the service of the wrath of the warrior God.

Zephaniah 2:5-15

The call has been issued, "Seek the Lord!" which means, "Cast yourself on his sovereignty and mercy," for the Day comes when the Lord will sweep away all who have tried to live without him (see 2:1-4). This universal judgment is now pictured in detail.

The nations that are mentioned here are intended to symbolize all the known world: Philistia on the west (vv. 5-7); Moab and Ammon on the east (vv. 8-11); Ethiopia, here inclusive of Egypt, to the south (v. 12); as climax, Assyria to the north (vv. 13-14, 15), for the North was the most sinister of regions, according to the prophets (cf. Jer. 1:15; 4:6; 6:1, 22), and Assyria was its embodiment in this time of Zephaniah.

The reasons given for the judgment on the world are noteworthy. Philistia's sin is not specifically mentioned but her proud arrogance and blasphemy against the God of Israel had already given birth to legend in Israel (cf. I Sam. 17). And it is precisely the pride of the nations (cf. Gen. 11:1-9) which primarily characterizes them in these oracles, and which is the object of the divine wrath on his Day (cf. Isa. 2:6-20): pride of wealth, alluded to with the word "Canaan" in verse 5, a synonym for greedy traders, and with the mention of fine "cedar work" in verse 14; pride of power, embodied in the boasts and scoffings of Moab and Ammon (vv. 8, 10; cf. Isa. 16:6; Jer. 48:7, 14, 17; 49:4) and in their grabs for territory (cf. Amos 1:13; Ezek. 25:1-7); pride of independence and security and sovereignty, set forth in the taunt of verse 15 against Assyria (cf. Isa. 47:8, 10). The nations exulted in their pride (v. 15; cf. Isa. 22:2; 23:7; 32:13; Zeph. 3:11), but God's exultation was to be the last word (3:17).

77

The results of the Day of wrath against humankind's proud independence are vividly pictured by the prophet. The busy fortified cities along the coast will become quiet and open resting places for flocks (vv. 6–7). Moab and Ammon will be desolated, indistinguishable from the barren salt pits and nettle-covered territory around the Dead Sea (v. 9) The Ethiopians and Egyptians will fall by God's sword (v. 12). And the fertile, green regions of Assyria, with their rivers and canals, will become blown desert, with vultures and hedgehogs (both unclean, according to Lev. 11:18; Deut. 14:17) lodging in the capitals of Nineveh's fallen pillars, and owls hooting in broken window frames, and ravens cawing from deserted doors (cf. Isa. 34:11–15). Such will be the end of those who have claimed to be great in the earth.

> Pride goes before destruction,
> and a haughty spirit before a fall (Prov. 16:18).

The passage ends with a separate taunt song against Nineveh (v. 15), because her claim, "I am and there is none else," is equivalent to saying, "I am the lord, and there is no other" (Isa. 45:5, 14, 18, 21). No God who is really God can let such a claim go unchallenged. Nineveh's is a boast common to those who wield power in the world: Hitler claimed a thousand year Reich; many were sure there would "always be an England and its colonies beyond the seas;" the petty tyrant Haile Selassie named himself "the King of kings, Elect of God, Lion of Judah, his most Puissant Majesty;" and we in the United States are fond of saying that we are the greatest nation on earth and that we can do anything because after all we put a man on the moon. But verse 8 of our passage reads, "I have heard . . .!" God hears, God knows what we are about in our pride, and as verses 9 and 10 emphasize, he is "the Lord of hosts," that is, the Lord of all power, supremely alive (cf. v. 9, as I live), supreme Sovereign over his world. Therefore,

> . . . the LORD of hosts has a day
> against all that is proud and lofty,
> against all that is lifted up and high; . . .
> And the haughtiness of man shall be humbled,
> and the pride of men shall be brought low;
> and the LORD alone will be exalted in that day (Isa. 2:12, 17).

78

There is a remnant here in Zephaniah's picture of the future—the remnant of the house of Judah, which has in fact been preserved in the universal judgment (vv. 7, 9). The prophet will describe the characteristics of that remnant later (3:9–13). The noteworthy fact, however, is that the remnant will move out into the territory of the foreign nations (vv. 7, 9; cf. also 3:10) where they will dwell in peace and security (v. 7), inheriting the fruits of God's victory over all (v. 9). In short, Zephaniah is proclaiming, as we shall see, that the meek shall inherit the earth (Matt. 5:5).

That is a switch on usual prophetic pictures of the future. The Isaiah tradition always portrayed the nations streaming to Jerusalem to join with Israel (cf. Isa. 2:2–4//Micah 4:1–3; Isa. 45:14, 22–25; 55:1–5; 56:3–8; 60; 61:5–6; 66:18–20), as did perhaps Micah (7:11–13) and later, Haggai (2:6–7) and Zechariah (8:20–23; 14:16–21). Here in Zephaniah, the remnant of Israel moves out to the nations and forms in their lands the new people of God. The "perhaps" of 2:3 has become a promise for the future in 2:5–15, and those who survive for the Kingdom of God will be those who have acknowledged his sovereignty by their humble, obedient, righteous seeking of their true Ruler (2:3).

It is not easy to interpret Zephaniah 2:5–15 in our day in any but eschatological terms, equating its promised universal judgment with the *parousia* in the New Testament. But in one of the great evangelistic sermons on this passage, Charles Haddon Spurgeon took as his text, 2:5c—"The word of the Lord is against you." After setting the text in its historical context, he then enlarged its meaning to refer to the Scriptures ("the word") as a whole.

The word of the Lord is against us—the entire proclamation of the Scriptures—unless we confess in our hearts and lives the sole sovereignty of the God to whom they witness. For the God of the Bible, in Calvin's words, "is no idle spectator, who only observes what takes place in the world" (IV, 248). And human pride will always stumble, in this age as well as the next, and nettles and salt pits and desolation in our hearts will always be the accompaniment of life apart from God, the bitter fruit we eat in the secret gardens of our rebellious self will. The Word —the word here of Zephaniah, and the word in the rest of the Scriptures—the word made flesh in Jesus Christ—stands against us and our sinful pride. It will now and always so stand if we ignore it or reject it or think it a word intended only for someone else. And what a terrible pity that would be! For the word of the Lord throughout the Bible is a word intended to be for us and not against us—a word intended to restore our life and

79

to lead us into quiet pastures and to allow us to lie down at
evening time in peace and security. Therefore, "Seek the Lord
. . . seek righteousness, seek humility."

Zephaniah 3:1–20

After chapters 1 and 2, Zephaniah 3 reads like a new series
of proclamations on Zephaniah's part; and it may well be that
its oracles were delivered later in the prophet's career, possibly
after it became apparent that the Deuteronomic reform would
bear no fruit (cf. v. 2) and after Assyria's final collapse at the
defeat of Nineveh (cf. v. 6). Thus, it would date in the period of
612–609 B.C., and it would seem significant, then, that many of
the phrases are echoed in Jeremiah. Such fact seems to support
the view that there was a rhetoric connected with the Deuteronomic reform that was shared by those prophets such as Jeremiah and Zephaniah who supported it.

Yet it must be said that such an attempt to locate Zephaniah's separate pronouncements in specific historical contexts
is not absolutely necessary for the overall interpretation of the
book. Chapter 3 is consonant with all that is found in chapters
1 and 2 and forms an organic whole with them.

Indeed, structurally, 3:1–5 is intimately related to 2:15, for
it continues Zephaniah's practice of moving from the universal
to the specific (cf. 1:2–3, 4–6), by which the prophet reminds his
people that they are not exempt from the judgment coming on
the earth. And it makes this move by focusing on the figure of
the city, whether that sinful entity be Nineveh (2:15) or Jerusalem (3:1). As in 2:1–4, then, 3:1–8 move once more from concentration on Judah (3:1–7) to the nations (3:8). All the themes of
chapters 1 and 2 are resumed in chapter 3. But it is now apparent, in 3:1–8, that Zephaniah's call to repentance has gone un-
heeded.

Verses 1–8: God has not left himself without witnesses (cf.
Acts 14:17): Such is the testimony of 3:1–7. By four means the
God of Israel has continually tried to correct his faithless people
and restore them to trust in him, and each means has been an
instrument of his love for his chosen folk. First, he has sent his

80

prophets to them, including Zephaniah (the "voice" of v. 2; cf. the frequency of the thought in Jer. 7:23; 11:4, 7, *et al.*). Second, he has given them his covenant law (correction, v. 2—perhaps indicative of the Deuteronomic reform and again a favorite phrase of Jeremiah's: 2:30; 5:3; esp. 7:28; 17:23; 32:33; 35:13). Third, he has manifested his unfailing care for them in the preservation of the round of day and night (v. 5; "justice" here signifies the order in the natural world). Fourth, he has destroyed various nations around them in military battle (v. 6). To this people, who foolishly think that God is absent from the world (see comment on 1:12), Zephaniah points to God's presence in their midst (cf. Jer. 14:9) and to his working on every hand.

It is almost inconceivable that Judah is blind to such a divine companion. "Surely," God is pictured musing, "she will fear me" (v. 7; cf. Isa. 63:8), that is, turn to me in obedience and reverent trust. Verse 7 is extremely difficult in the Hebrew and many emendations (including that of the RSV) have been suggested. The Hebrew can be read:

> I said, Surely she will fear me,
>   she will accept a fetter (i.e., God's yoke of the law, cf. Jer. 2:20);
> and she will not cut off her refuge (i.e., her security in God's presence and commandments)
> all that I have visited upon her (i.e., all that God has given her in word and done for her in deed).

God could equally be pictured in the same thought about his church, which has been given the same sure witness and refuge in word and sacrament, in holy history, and in the unfailing round of nature.

Judah, however, has not been moved even by the fall of other nations. She has never once considered that there is a God and that he may destroy her too if her deeds are corrupt (v. 7) —a state of affairs upon which Calvin has commented: "When the next house was on fire, how was it possible for you to sleep, except ye were extremely stupid" (IV, 277)? But stupid Judah is (cf. Jer. 4:22; 5:20–25, esp. v. 21)! And so she not only continues to ignore her God but she eagerly continues in her corrupt freedom from God's yoke (v. 7; the Hebrew gives the sense: "They rose up early to corrupt all their doings"—a contrast to God's faithfulness every dawn, v. 5. The figure is found elsewhere only in Jer. and in II Chron. 36:15).

Judah rejects each of God's four witnesses to himself (vv.

81

1–2). Specific illustration of this is then given in an indictment of Judah's four leading classes (vv. 3–4). Her princes (cf. 1:8) or government officials who should be shepherding the people instead devour them like hungry lions. Her judges who are supposed to defend the weak accept bribes and seek gain for themselves with wolfish greed. Her prophets who should give guidance from the word of the Lord are instead (literally) "light," frivolous windbags who are full of hot air. Her priests whose office demands that they distinguish between the holy and the profane—between God's things and human things (cf. Lev. 10:10)—have instead secularized their world and ignored the *torah;* that is, they have failed in their duty to teach the people all the sacred story with its commands and the proper response to it.

"Therefore, wait for me" is the command (v. 8)—not just to the faithful but to Judah as a whole. "To wait" for God means to expect him to act, whether in blessing (Isa. 40:31) or, as here, in judgment. God's Day of wrath comes when he rises up as a witness in his courtcase against his earth. God's attempts to guide and correct and warn his people have failed. Judah, like all the earth, is defiant and polluted (*rebellious* and *defiled,* v. 1). God will begin a new people and a new earth by wiping out the old.

Verses 9–13: Verse 9 is connected with verse 8 by its structure in the Hebrew, the last line of verse 8 and the first line of verse 9 both beginning with the Hebrew particle *ki,* translated "for" (the RSV obscures this by translating "yea"). The parallelism is, moreover, theological; and this passage is to be read not as a doctrine but as a witness to holy history. From the thought of the fire of God's jealous wrath (cf. 1:18) that will consume the earth (v. 8), the proclamation moves immediately to God's transforming action that will establish his new people (v. 9). God's word never ends with judgment, for God's goal for his world is finally not death but life. He is the God not of the dead but of the living. He is a God finally not of wrath but of love.

That Zephaniah pictures here what is tantamount to God's new beginning with his creation is shown by the fact, as Eaton has suggested, that verses 9–10 bear echoes of Genesis 11:1–9. In that ancient story, rebellious humankind was punished by the confusion of its language and its scattering abroad over the earth. Here, pure language is restored and the peoples worship

God "with one accord" (literally, "with one back" or "shoulder to shoulder"), in unity.

But who is this new people of God in verse 10? As we have seen in Zephaniah 2:7, 9, it is the remnant of Judah that moves out into foreign lands and inherits the earth. God's humble, dependent, righteous remnant will worship him throughout his creation, even in those regions beyond the limits of the imaginable world ("beyond the rivers of Ethiopia").

When we consider that the one universal fellowship in the world, begun with the Spirit's transformation of its language (Acts 2), is now the church of Jesus Christ, this proclamation by Zephaniah is seen to contain within it wondrous glimpses of God's future.

Zephaniah's vision of the future is not yet fulfilled, however, not even in the Christian church, for though we claim a universal fellowship of those who trust Jesus Christ as Lord, the prophet's vision stretches beyond the worldwide confession of God's sovereignty to the consequences of it. Those consequences are embodied in the figure of Jerusalem, to whom verses 11–13 are addressed.

Jerusalem! There is the center of God's work. There he abided in the midst of his people. There he began his alien work of judgment. There his Son confronted the powers of the world and the principalities of darkness. There the initial victory was won which will finally cleanse the earth of evil. And there that cleansing will be first and fully manifest. Jerusalem will become the city that does no wrong, the symbol of God's Kingdom come on earth—in the words of John of Patmos, "the holy city, new Jerusalem, coming down out of heaven from God, prepared as a bride adorned for her husband" (Rev. 21:2). We all well might follow the ancient psalm's admonition to "pray for the peace of Jerusalem" (Ps. 122:6), for when she is whole, the earth will be whole and God's good purpose finally consummated.

In verses 11–13, Zephaniah portrays the future peace of Jerusalem. Pride—that final, rebellious, defiant human sin with which the whole Book of Zephaniah has dealt—will be gone from the Holy City (v. 11). The shameful (3:1), shamelessly unrepentant (2:1) society will be no more. She who was like Nineveh in her godless, independent, exultant pride (2:15) will no longer be haughty (cf. Isa. 3:16); but her people—the remnant of Judah (v. 12; 2:7, 9)—will in humility (cf. 2:3) and lowliness find their sufficiency in God (cf. II Cor. 3:4–5).

83

The most important words follow, however, in verse 13. Jerusalem's people, relying on God, will take on his character. He does no wrong (3:5) and neither will his new people (v. 13). Their faith in him will issue in the ethical transformation of their lives.

The prophets were always sure that what one worshiped determined one's character (cf. Jer. 2:5). Thus, the pure worship of the God of Israel results in lives conformed to his (cf. II Cor. 3:18; I John 3:1–3)—in Ezekiel's images, hearts and spirits transformed by his Spirit (Ezek. 36:26–27). Ethics, according to the Bible, are the fruit of a living relationship with the Lord and have neither base nor motive power unless that relationship be present (cf. Hos. 5:4). But if the fellowship with God exists, it must issue in transformed deeds (cf. James 2:17; Rom. 12:1; Gal. 3:22–24 *et al.*). No one can meet the Lord and live without being changed into his new creation (cf. II Cor. 5:17).

The nature of the change that Zephaniah describes is significant—the banishment of lying and deceit and fraud from the community (v. 13; cf. Jer. 9:2–8)—in short, the faithful and trustworthy fulfillment of one's covenants with one's fellow human beings, akin to God's fulfillment of his covenant with his creation (cf. 3:5).

> Our society is slowly being undermined these days by those who will not keep their covenants—those government officials who cynically violate the public trust, those businessmen and laborers who do not make reliable goods or give honest return for the consumer's money, those husbands or wives who consider their marriage a bond to be easily broken, those parents who turn over the responsibility for guiding their children to the TV set for hours on end, day after day (*Preaching as Theology and Art,* by the author, p. 112).

In the new Jerusalem that Zephaniah envisions, God's new people will keep their covenants, as God has so faithfully and lovingly always kept his. "They shall do no wrong," for they will be like their Lord. And the fruit of that ethical transformation of Jerusalem will be peace and security for the Good Shepherd's flock: ". . . they shall pasture and lie down, and none shall make them afraid." Well should our discordant world "pray for the peace of Jerusalem!"

Verses 14–20: In this section verses 14–17 are completely consonant with what has gone before. God is once again pictured as the Divine Warrior (v. 17*b*), as he was in 1:14 (see the commentary there); but now the terrible destruction of his Day of wrath is over. He has taken away his judgments, that is, his condemnations or indictments (cf. 3:8) of his people (3:15*a*), because he has destroyed all the faithless proud from her midst (v. 15*b*; cf. Jer. 50:20). His war against his people is no more.

In this connection, verse 17*d*, which the Revised Standard Version emends on the basis of the Septuagint to read, "he will renew you in his love," should be read from the Hebrew, "he will hold his peace in his love"—the war cry of 1:14 is stilled. No more need Judah's hands be paralyzed with fear (v. 16*c*). She need not any more fear evil and the destroying judgment evil brings (v. 15*d*). God's warfare against his covenant people has come to an end (cf. Isa. 40:2; Ezek. 37:26–28).

Since the people are now cleansed of their faithless pride, God dwells in their midst (cf. 3:5) as their King (v. 15*c*). That has been the issue of the book throughout—the question of who rules Judah's life. Can she construct for herself a world without God and get away with it (see on 1:12), or is he truly Lord over her? Actually the answer, throughout the Scriptures, is never in doubt. God, the mighty Man of war, is King over nature and human history.

But the miracle is that this king, this warrior, is, in the words of the Hebrew of verse 17*b*, "a mighty Man to save" (cf. Jer. 14:9). The King of the universe is finally the King of love, and he wills to save his people. And so he works his purging and transforming work of love and creates on Zion a new people who fully trust his rule and who can therefore celebrate his reign with all their hearts (v. 14*c*; cf. "hearts" in 1:12).

The pictures Zephaniah paints for us in 3:14–17 are awesome. There, in the streets of Jerusalem, are the faithful people of God holding carnival—shouting out their joy to one another, exulting with dance and timbrel and laughter over the fact that God rules their lives (v. 14; cf. Zech. 9:9; Isa. 54:1). It is a celebration that we Christians sometimes have known on Easter morn, when God's trumpets have sounded in our sanctuaries and in our hearts his victory over death and evil. Equally, it is a joy we have known in those quiet moments of prayer and meditation when the sure knowledge has flooded over us that God holds our lives secure and precious.

85

But the further picture of Zephaniah's is the one before which the whole universe must catch its breath: There, in the midst of his celebrating people, is God rejoicing and exulting over them (v. 17c,e; cf. Isa. 62:5; 65:19)—a father holding a home-coming party for the son who was lost and is found (cf. Luke 15:11–32); a shepherd exuberantly calling out to friends and neighbors that the sheep lost from the flock has been recovered (Luke 15:3–7). In the heavens the morning stars sing together again to laud this new creation (cf. Job 38:7; Luke 15:7, 10), and a great multitude of heavenly hosts sings "Hallelujah!". (cf. Rev. 19:6–8), while on earth the sea roars out its approval (Isa. 42:10; Pss. 96:11; 98:7), the hills sing together for joy (cf. Ps. 98:8), and the trees of the field clap their hands (cf. Isa. 55:12). Such is the celebration of love, the Bible says, when God saves his people—when he is worshiped as King in their midst and no longer need war against them. The Book of Zephaniah ends in almost unimaginable joy (v. 17).

Obviously, in the text as we have it, verse 17 is not the final verse of the book, however, and in fact, by an emendation based on the Septuagint, the Revised Standard Version has connected the first line of verse 18 with verse 17. Verse 18 is unintelligible in the Hebrew, yielding something like, "Those that are afflicted for the solemn assembly, I will gather from among you. They shall bear the reproach that is upon you." That sounds like a reference to a persecuted group within the community whose suffering is understood as the atonement for the sins of the community. We may therefore have here a later veiled reference to that Deuteronomic reform group within Judah which considered itself to have taken over the role of the Suffering Servant of Second Isaiah (see the author's *The Community and Message of Isaiah 56—66*). At the same time, verses 19 and 20 (though v. 20 *ab* is obscure in the Hebrew) contain promises much like those in Third Isaiah (cf. Isa. 56:6–8; 60:14, 18; 61:7; 62:7; 66:22), and the whole of verses 18–20 may be later Deuteronomic editorial contributions to the work of the prophet, who himself may have been a member of the reform party in the time of Josiah. The Deuteronomists have simply appropriated the work and updated it as a word of God applicable to their later situation after the return from exile—a procedure fully appropriate to the nature of Scripture. As C.H. Spurgeon, who had a way of getting inside the word of God, said in a sermon,

86

> The fulfillment of a divine promise is not the exhaustion of it. When a man gives you a promise, and he keeps it, there is an end of the promise; but it is not so with God. When he keeps His word to the full, He has but begun. He is prepared to keep it, and keep it, and keep it for ever and ever ("A Sermon for the Time Present," p. 733).

Thus, the word comes to us also, ever afresh, and applies to us.

It is appropriate therefore that Zephaniah 3:14–20 is a stated Old Testament reading for Advent (coupled with Phil. 4:4–9, a call to rejoice, and with Luke 3:7–18 the Baptist's preaching of the good news) in some lectionaries, and that Roman Catholics and Episcopalians also use 3:14–18 to celebrate the Feast of the Visitation, or for Unity Sunday.

In an Advent sermon, Lutheran Larry A. Hoffsis saw the promises of Zephaniah 3:14–20 fulfilled in Christ: the King of Israel, present in our midst (v. 17a), as we gather around his table; God's judgments removed (v. 18a) by the peace with God offered in the outstretched and nail-printed hands of our Lord; our enemies cast out (v. 18b) at the empty tomb and the last enemy, death, destroyed; our hands and hearts strengthened (v. 16c) and made courageous down through the centuries by Christ's abiding presence; the church caught up in the song of victory (v. 14) by the "angels, archangels and all the company of heaven." But Hoffsis added that future note always present in these promises of God that he keeps and keeps and keeps until his Kingdom comes:

> The prophet's words are fulfilled in Christ. Even so, there remains for us, too, the element of the future about them. Certainly all is not past in Christ. He points us to his coming again. He is in our midst now, of that we can be assured. But there is a nearer presence still to come, when we shall have our final homecoming with God. That will be a greater celebration . . . a higher festival than when the prodigal returned (pp. 30–31).

The church can run its race, knowing that joy is set before it.

PART TWO

The Word of the Lord in Post-exilic Times:

Haggai

Zechariah

Malachi

These three prophets, along with Third Isaiah, proclaimed the word of the Lord to the struggling community of Jews in the region of Judah after the return from Babylonian exile. Haggai was first on the scene, with Zechariah and Malachi following after. But their setting was far different from that known to their fellow prophets before the fall of Jerusalem and the exile to Babylonia. Judah no longer existed as a national entity. Her territory was now a tiny sub-province of the vast Persian Empire. Her Israelite populace no longer made up a nation but a religious congregation of Jews. And her daily existence was a matter of staying alive in the face of hunger and devastation, of inflation and hostility from neighbors.

As the God of the Bible was present and working in the days of Israel's glory, however, so he was also at hand and active in her darkest days of trial, and it was the task of these post-exilic prophets to proclaim how that was so.

Once again, the reader is furnished with an outline for quick historical reference, in the hope that it will help to anchor the prophetic messages in their specific times and circumstances. But for further details, the reader is referred to John Bright, *A History of Israel*.

OUTLINE OF THE HISTORICAL BACKGROUND OF HAGGAI, ZECHARIAH, AND MALACHI

Dates B.C.	Events	Prophets/Scripture
605–550	**Babylonian Domination of the Ancient Near East**	
597	First deportation to Babylonia.	
	Zedekiah (597–587) placed on Judean throne.	
587	July–The fall of Jerusalem.	
	Second deportation	
582	Third deportation to Babylonia	
597–538	**Jews in Babylonian Exile**	593–571 *The preaching*
	Had their own colonies, religious leaders (Ezekiel), commercial enterprises.	*of Ezekiel*
	Priestly Code assembled by Zadokite priests.	
	Final form of Deuteronomic History compiled.	
	Chapters 40—48 added to prophecies of Ezekiel	
550–330	**Persian Domination of the Ancient Near East**	
	Persian rulers:	
550–538	Cyrus	ca. 538, *Second Isaiah*
539	Defeated Babylonia	*written in Babylonia*
538	Cyrus decreed restoration of Jewish community and cult in Palestine.	
	Temple ordered rebuilt at Persian expense,	Ezra 1:2–4; 6:3–5
	captured temple vessels restored.	
	Allowed Jews to return to Palestine. Project placed in charge of	Ezra 1:7–11
	Sheshbazzar of Judean royal house, who is appointed prince (governor?)	
538/7	Small group of exiles and Zadokite priests returned to Judah	
	with Shesh-bazzar.	
	Restoration of Temple foundations begun.	Ezra 5:16
	Work soon discontinued. Samaritan opposition	Ezra 4:4–5
	Some sort of regular cultus resumed. Levitical priests replaced	
	by Zadokite priests as leaders in sacrifice.	
	A protest against Zadokites, reflecting views of combined	538–515 *Third Isaiah*
	Isaian–Jeremian–Levitical–Deuteronomic reform movement.	
	Some members of this group also the authors of . . .	
	Continuing hardships, droughts, crop failures, inflation, disorder,	II–III *Zechariah* (9—11; 12—14)
	and injustice in Judean community.	

Dates B.C.	Events	Prophets/Scripture
530–522	Cambyses	
522–486	Darius I Hystaspes	
522–520	Series of upheavals and revolts in Persian Empire put down; the zenith of the Empire.	
521	Second, larger group of Babylonian exiles returned to Judah under the leadership of Zerubbabel, grandson of the Davidic Jehoiachin. Accompanied by Zadokite high priest, Joshua ben Jehozadak, and by the author of I Zechariah.	*Ezra 2:2*
520	Urging the rebuilding of temple. September 21—foundation of temple laid.	*520 The preaching of Haggai* *520–518 The preaching of I Zechariah* *(Chapters 1—8)*
515	March 12, Temple rebuilding completed.	
490	Darius I defeated by Greeks at Battle of Marathon.	
486–465	Xerxes	
480	Victory at Thermopyle, then forced from Europe; Xerxes assassinated.	
		ca. 460 The preaching of Malachi
465/4–424	Axtaxerxes I Longimanus	*458? Ezra's mission?*
449	The peace of Callas	
	During the fifth century: flourishing Jewish colonies throughout Fertile Crescent; some Jews continued to return to Palestine; Judah administered as a Persian province from Samaria; local affairs under supervision of the high priest.	
445–433	Nehemiah's first period as governor of Judah.	
432?–411?	Nehemiah's second period as governor of Judah	*428? Ezra's mission?*
		400 Final edition of the Chronicler's work *(II Chron., Ezra, Neh.)*

THE BOOK OF

Haggai

Introduction

> If we should consider the subject matter unsympathetically,
> the prophet will seem quite trivial on the surface, especially in
> our day. Everything about which he prophesies, especially
> about rebuilding the temple, has ceased. As a consequence, we
> must consider the subject matter correctly, so that we look not
> so much at it as at the Word of God (Martin Luther XVIII, 367).

In the prophetic writings, the word of God is spoken into
human history at definite times and places, in divine reaction
to particular situations. So it is with the word spoken by Haggai
the prophet. His entire book dates from the year 520 B.C. In that
year, the only remaining political entity left to Israel, the Chosen People of God, after the Babylonian exile of 587–538 B.C.
was Jerusalem and the small surrounding territory of Judah,
forming a sub-province of the Persian Empire. Subject to the
control of Samaria, Judah was nevertheless granted its own
somewhat independent leadership under the governor Zerubbabel, the grandson of the exiled Davidic Jehoiachin (II Kings
24:15; I Chron. 3:17 [Jeconiah], and the high priest Joshua, the
grandson of the exiled chief priest Seraiah (II Kings 25:18;
I Chron. 6:14). Both had returned to Judah from Babylonia,
after the 538 B.C. edict of Cyrus (Ezra 1:2–4; 6:2–5), either in the
party led by Sheshbazzar (Ezra 1:11), or sometime later.

Darius I, Hystaspes (521–485 B.C.), having quelled wide-
spread rebellion in the eastern part of his empire after the
death of his predecessor Cambyses, was firmly established on
the Persian throne. He sanctioned the rebuilding of the Jerusa-   93
lem temple and ordered the pro-Persian governors of Trans–
Euphrates to cease their opposition to the work and to pay for

its reconstruction and its sacrificial offerings (Ezra 5:3—6:12). It is with this rebuilding of the Jerusalem temple that Haggai is concerned.

We know nothing about Haggai other than that he was a prophet for five months in 520 B.C. The only other mentions of him and his contemporary I Zechariah are found in Ezra 5:1 and 6:14. He is identified by his editor simply as "the prophet" (1:1, 3; 2:1, 10) and as "the messenger of the Lord" (1:13), designations apparently sufficient in a time when prophecy was rare. There have been scholarly discussions about the significance of his name (festival), about whether or not he saw the temple of Solomon before the fall of Jerusalem and was therefore elderly when he was called to be a prophet (cf. 2:3), about whether he was a cult prophet or a priest (cf. 2:11–13); but none of these questions can be laid to rest with certainty, and none is of pressing theological importance.

Haggai's book stands in a carefully planned chronological order. It has five sections, each exactly dated in 520 according to the months and days of the Babylonian lunar calendar. Using the equivalent dates on the Julian calendar, these five sections and their dates are

> 1:1–11 from August 29,
> 1:12–15a from September 21,
> 1:15b—2:9 from October 17,
> 2:10–19 from December 18,
> 2:20–23 also from December 18.

Because the prophet is referred to in the third person in the dated introductions, in the report (1:12), and in the abbreviated introductions (2:13, 14), it is clear that the book was put together by an editorial hand. Most commentators assume the editor was a disciple of the prophet and that he recorded the prophet's words shortly after Haggai spoke them.

The principal message of the book can be summed up in the words of 1:8:

> "Go up to the hills and bring wood and build the house, that I may take pleasure in it and that I may appear in my glory, says the LORD."

Temple building! Among all the prophets of Israel, Haggai is unique for his insistence on temple building. When Haggai preached, the Jerusalem temple was still a fire-blackened ruin (cf. II Kings 25:9), and so the prophet concentrates almost single-mindedly on the necessity for the Judeans to restore their place of worship on Zion's hill. Even the zeal of his contemporary Zechariah for the temple pales before Haggai's ardor for the project, while the vision of the restored temple in Ezekiel 40—48 remains just that—a vision. But Haggai wants the temple rebuilt, and he wants the work on it to begin immediately —on August 29, according to the dating of his initial preaching (1:1).

A strange message that is for an Israelite prophet! Those spokesmen of God had opposed the temple as early as the time of Nathan (II Sam. 7:4–7) and as late as the time just before Haggai of Third Isaiah (66:1). Isaiah had proclaimed that the Lord of Hosts hated the superficial worship carried on in the temple (1:10–17, v. 14), and Jeremiah had labeled the sanctuary a "den (that is, a hiding place) of robbers" (7:1–15, v. 11), because the Judeans had thought they could worship God without reforming their lives. Ezekiel called the Judeans' idolatry in the temple an abomination before the Lord (chap. 8) and declared that God would take from them a worship center that had itself become a place of sin (24:15–24). To have Haggai turn around and urge the rebuilding of the temple therefore seems a contradiction of most of the prophecy that preceded him.

We do not know what to do with Haggai in the canon. He crops up in the midst of the goodly fellowship of the prophets like a misguided stranger from the wrong part of town. No cry for social justice escapes his lips, no assurance that God dwells with the humble and contrite. Instead, he reeks of something that smells very much like the external and superficial religion of which we would all like to be rid. The result is that the church has used Haggai 2:1–9 for a lesson at the dedication of a church, but otherwise the *Book of Common Prayer* relegates Haggai to a few services of evening prayer during the week, and many lectionaries ignore the book altogether.

Some scholars have speculated that we have in the Book of Haggai simply the evidences of the political struggles of his day. For example, some maintain that the Persian king Darius supported the temple reconstruction (cf. Ezra 5:3—6:12) in order to quiet and secure his Judean province as a buffer facing Egypt. Conversely, others have maintained that Haggai was a nationalist, taking advantage, if somewhat tardily, of unrest in the eastern part of the Persian empire and summoning his people to reconstruct the symbol of their national pride. That was the reason why, it is therefore argued, that Haggai at the end of his book dubbed Zerubbabel messianic king (2:20–23).

But are there theological motivations lying behind Haggai's call to temple building? Worship was still being carried on at the ruined temple site (cf. Jer. 41:5). Did the people of God then, and do they now, need always to localize their worship in a particular building? Cannot the God of the Bible be found anywhere at any time?

The testimony of the entire canon, and of Haggai in particular, is that the Lord of Hosts is not everywhere and at all times available to human beings. "Canst thou by searching find out God?" asks the Scripture (Job 11:7 KJV), and the answer is "No." Only when God draws near to human beings and lends the means of approaching him can he be known and his presence experienced. He must be sought "while he can be found," called upon "while he is near" (Isa. 55:6). He is not a servant of his worshipers, available at their beck and call, but transcendent and sovereign Lord over all of life—"the Lord of hosts," as Haggai has it (1:5, 7, 9)—who nevertheless in mercy and compassion desires to make himself known.

The God of the Bible further reveals himself as concretely present and personal. In contrast with the diffuse numina of the ancient Near East's fertility and nature gods, he is one (Deut. 6:4), manifesting himself in specific times and places through particular revelatory words and actions. He comes to his people in a rescue out of Egyptian slavery or in a birth at Bethlehem, and he thereby reveals himself to have a very particular character. When he promises Israel in the covenant, "I will be your God and you will be my people" (Gen. 17:7–8; Exod. 6:7), that gracious giving of himself is therefore symbolized in the cult of Israel by specific manifestations of his presence (Lev. 26:11–12).

According to the priestly writings, God's presence with his people in the desert was first marked by the descent of the shining light of his glory to the tabernacle (Exod. 40:34–38) and by his accompaniment with them in pillar of cloud and fire on their march through the wilderness. After the entrance into the land, God was enthroned above the Ark of the Covenant, whose mercy seat and cherubim formed the base of his dais (I Sam. 4:4; II Sam. 6:2). At first the primary cultic symbol at the central shrine of the tribal federation, the Ark was later brought to Jerusalem by David (II Sam. 6) and finally deposited in the Holy of Holies in the Temple of Solomon, lending to Jerusalem the title of God's chosen, everlasting "habitation" (Pss. 132:13–14; 78:68; 68:16).

For the Deuteronomists, God dwelt not above the Ark but in heaven (Deut. 4:36, 39 *et al.*), and the Ark was viewed as only a repository for the tablets of the law (10:2; 31:26). Nevertheless, God "chose" Jerusalem and "made his name dwell there" in the temple, and the sanctuary with its Ark remained the symbol of his presence in the midst of his people (Deut. 12:11 *et passim*).

When Jerusalem and the temple were destroyed by Nebuchadrezzar's troops in 587 B.C. and the Ark of the Covenant was lost (cf. Jer. 3:16), it was therefore a sure sign that God had abandoned his people because of their covenant faithlessness. Indeed, Ezekiel saw in prophetic vision God deserting his holy habitation (Ezek. 11:22–25), just as Jeremiah before him had prophesied the destruction of temple and city and land (cf. Jer. 7).

When God is present with his people, that presence is symbolized by concrete reminders of his actions among them: for Israel, by a temple with an Ark containing tablets of law, even by a pot of manna (cf. Exod. 16:32–34) and Aaron's rod (cf. Num 17:10); for us, by a cross, a Bible, and a table set with bread and wine. God is not bound by the symbols. In Israel, he destroyed them all. Nevertheless it should give us pause, when we become iconoclastic, to realize that when God incarnated himself in his Son, that One also gathered up and fulfilled Israel's symbolism. His body became the incarnate word (John 1:14) and temple (John 4:20–26); in him the glory and name of God were present and tabernacled among us (John 1:14; 2:19–21; 12:28; cf. Mark 15:29).

This God of the Bible localizes himself. In great condescension, the Lord of Hosts rends the heavens and comes down and dwells in the midst of his people. And he sets apart and makes holy the temple, the symbol of that dwelling; or he sets apart for his use Bible and cup and bread, in order that flesh and blood persons can see and remember and know that the holy God is in their company.

When Haggai, "the messenger of the Lord" (1:13), calls for temple rebuilding, it is therefore an announcement that the Lord of Hosts yearns to give himself again. That is what the Book of Haggai is about—God's yearning to enter into covenant fellowship with his Chosen People once more. Their years of abandonment under God's judgment are over. They should prepare themselves for the Lord's return: "Go up to the hills and bring wood and build the house, that I may take pleasure in it and that I may appear in my glory (1:8)."

Haggai 1:1–15

The Judeans have no stomach for construction work, and it seems doubtful that we would blame them. Their leaders, Zerubbabel and Joshua (1:1), may dwell in "paneled houses" (1:4), but most of the Judeans are desperately poor. Drought has led to crop failure (1:10–11), to hunger (1:6), and the encroachment of the desert into their farm lands. Inflation, always caused by shortages, eats holes in their purses (1:6). The enmity of Samaritan foreigners to the north and of quislings within the land several years earlier had discouraged them from any attempt at rebuilding their worship site (cf. Ezra 4:4–5). Why worry about the presence of God when reality is dictated by famine and fate and foreign power? After all, Persia rules the world and Judah is but its minor sub-province. Better to spend one's energies trying to stay alive than to bother with religious dreams! The harsh realities of life have to determine finally what one does in this world.

It is precisely the nature of reality that Haggai discusses in his initial preaching (1:1–11). His call is, "Consider how you have fared" (1:5, 7; cf. 2:16; literally, "put to heart the paths you have walked"); that is, stop in your busy efforts (1:9) to survive and ponder in your hearts what really is taking place. As the prophets who preceded him, Haggai knows that faith is a matter of the deepest recesses of the human heart (cf. Isa. 29:13; Jer. 4:4; 31:33; Ezek. 36:26 *et al.*), and Haggai wants his people to realize in their hearts that God is in control of their reality. They are suffering because God is keeping his covenant promises.

In the way covenant was made, first at Sinai and then renewed for each generation in the covenant renewal ceremony of Deuteronomy, the covenant requirements were followed by a series of blessings and curses (Lev. 26; Deut. 27—28), which the Lord of the covenant promised to bestow on those who, respectively, obeyed or disobeyed the command-

98

ments. Haggai sees the deprivations the Judeans suffer in his time as the effect of God's covenant curses. Haggai 1:6 echoes Deuteronomy 28:38–40; 1:10 recalls Deuteronomy 28:23–24 (cf. Deut. 11:13–17); 1:11 is similar to Deuteronomy 28:22. In recalling such covenant curses, Haggai follows in the footsteps of many of the earlier prophets (cf. Amos 4:6–11; Isa. 5:6; 65:13, 21–22; Jer. 14:3–4; Hos. 8:7; Micah 6:15), and he uses the curses much as they did: to point out that not foreigner nor fate nor workings of nature control the Judeans' lives, but God. Human life in its context in history and nature is in the hand of the Lord of Hosts. Therefore, beyond all other concerns, God's people should be concerned about the relation with him. "Seek first his kingdom and his righteousness, and all these things shall be yours as well" (Matt. 6:33). God's working shapes reality, and finally his people must shape their lives to that sovereign working if they want to live in the real world.

Haggai actually has no thought that God will reward the Judeans with prosperity if they build him a temple—a sort of "you-be-nice-to-me and I-will-be-nice-to-you" religion. Human beings cannot buy the favor of the Lord of the universe. Rather, God yearns to return to this people and to dwell in their midst. The temple is symbolic of that dwelling; and if the Judeans rebuild the temple, their efforts will signal that once more they have turned toward God as he has now turned toward them. The temple will be sign and seal of their renewed hearts' devotion—the evidence that they have finally come to terms with reality.

It may be that no prosperity whatsoever follows the return of the heart to God. The so-called "good things in life" remain only a future promise in the Book of Haggai; but somehow they fade in importance when the fellowship with God is renewed: ". . . I have learned, in whatever state I am, to be content. I know how to be abased, and I know how to abound; in any and all circumstances I have learned the secret of facing plenty and hunger, abundance and want. I can do all things in him who strengthens me" (Phil. 4:11–12).

The word of God spoken through his prophet Haggai brings about that of which it speaks (cf. Isa. 55:10–11; Ezek. 12:25–28). It stirs up Zerubbabel, Joshua, and the people, over a period of three weeks to clear the rubble from the temple site. On September 21, according to the report of the editor of Haggai in 1:12–15, the foundation of the building is laid.

99

Haggai 2:1–9

How can human hands build a house worthy of the glory of God? They cannot of course. Solomon, for all the magnificence of cedar and cypress and gold and carving in his temple (I Kings 6), had to pray before the Lord of glory, "Behold, heaven and the highest heaven cannot contain thee; how much less this house which I have built" (I Kings 8:27)! The 1928 *Book of Common Prayer* echoes those words in its prayer at the Consecration of a Church.

There is genuine piety that weeps at the inability to do worthily for God—to erect any earthly symbol adequate to express his presence, to live any life of devotion fully deserving of his love, to perform any service in the world commensurate with what he has done. Earth's temples—whether of stone or wood or formed by our own sinful lives—never adequately contain the presence of the living God.

But God comes to be with his people not because they deserve it, not because they live lives worthy of his fellowship, and certainly not because they erect mansions worthy to house his glory but because in his covenant faithfulness he simply gives himself to dwell among them. After all, what need has he of earthly splendor, when all silver and gold are his (2:8)? What sacrifice could earn his love (cf. Micah 6:7) or what offering praise his mercy (cf. Isa. 40:16)? All is his, and nothing can be added to him. Yet to a struggling and despondent people he comes and says, "I am with you" (Hag. 2:4). The covenant broken by Judah's faithlessness is renewed by God's steadfast love.

Nevertheless, the old people of Haggai's time who had seen the temple of Solomon in all its glory sixty-seven years before weep when they see the meager beginnings of the reconstructed sanctuary (cf. Ezra 3:12–13). On October 17 (Hag. 2:1), four weeks after the foundation has been laid, Haggai acknowledges their grief. The temple is nothing (literally: "Much more than nothing") in the old people's eyes, and it can never be the same as before. The Ark with its mercy seat and cherubim is gone; the tablets of stone, the pot of manna; Aaron's rod, the

Urim and Thummim, the eternal fire on the altar—all have been swept away in the Babylonian holocaust; and though substitutes may take their place, they have not the same significance. The old cultic treasures were reminders of the mighty acts of God among Israel's forebears. Now they are gone, and dim old eyes can only fill with tears at the remembrance of what used to be.

The old ones forget that it was not Solomon but God who filled the temple with glory, and so they mourn the past that can never return. Worse still, they obstruct the new glory that is arriving, for as long as God is on the scene his people may confidently expect things which eye has not seen nor ear heard. The Lord who has done so much in the past can establish new symbols of his presence in the future. The God who rules past, present, future can manifest himself in ways yet undreamed and unknown.

The future that Haggai holds out before his discouraged and sorrowing countrymen is nothing less than a universal reordering of all things and the establishment of the Kingdom of God on earth, and it is in this sense that Hebrews 12:26 quotes Haggai 2:6. As God shook the earth at the Exodus (cf. Ps. 114) and at Sinai (cf. Exod. 19:18; Ps. 68:8; Judg. 5:4–5), so now he will "once again" shake the cosmos and cause all the nations to bring their treasures to fill his house with splendor (cf. Isa. 60:4–7, 13; 61:6; 45:14; Rev. 21:24). There is, however, no reference made here in Haggai 2:7 to the coming of the Messiah. Jewish and early Christian translations, such as the Vulgate, read "the desire of all nations" instead of "the treasures of all nations" in that verse, interpreting "desire" as the figure of the Messiah; but the plural verb renders a singular subject impossible. Instead, Haggai is saying that all peoples will finally come with their offerings to the Lord of Hosts, just as Paul, using Isaiah 45:23, promised that every knee would bow and every tongue confess that Jesus Christ is Lord (Phil. 2:10–11). Further, Haggai proclaims that God will establish in Jerusalem his *shalom*, that is, his abundant life (v. 9; RSV: prosperity) for his people, and indeed for all that universal company that will flow toward Jerusalem (cf. Isa. 2:2–4).

In Haggai's phrase, such a final reordering of the cosmos and introduction of the Kingdom of God will take place in "a little while" (2:6). The phrase, like the similar indeterminate "in that day" (cf. 2:23) is used by the prophets to refer to events that

101

INTERPRETATION

are imminent (e.g., Isa. 10:25; Amos 8:3) or distantly future (e.g. Isa. 29:17–18; 2:11) or even in the past (e.g. Isa. 63:18; 22:8). Haggai refers not so much to the shortness of the interval as to the vastness of the powers involved (Macgregor). God moves on toward the future, and those who love God know that they are always within a step of undreamed-of changes. They have seen so much of God's working in the past: a word transforming a life, his power tumbling empires. Christians have even seen him overcome the bonds of sin and death, as Israel saw him transform their captivity into the glorious liberty of the children of God. Do not the people of God, then, walk always on the edge of discoveries, feeling that any day there may be new workings of divine power, unmeasured possibilities of transformation, the bursting in of new heavens and a new earth? Haggai prompts those who have known the past with God to realize what it means for the future. When God is with his people they can have great expectations.

Haggai further prompts those who have known the past with God to see what it means for the present. In view of the unmeasured possibility of the power of God, see that you yourself be found working! Three times Haggai says it: "Take courage . . . take courage . . . take courage . . . work! (v. 4). In short, be faithful in the present! "I am with you . . . My Spirit abides among you" (vv. 4, 5). Therefore, be found faithful and at work with all your might when this present God brings in the future yet unknown!

For the Christian, the temple of God is no longer a building, but a spiritual house, the church, "built upon the foundation of the apostles and prophets, Christ Jesus himself being the cornerstone, . . ." (Eph. 2:20). To the faithful building up of that temple we too are called by the words of Haggai (cf. Eph. 4:11–13).

Haggai 2:10–19

102 The ultimate danger of temple building, and indeed of all works of religion, is the temptation to become self-righteous: to believe that association with the things of God automatically

communicates moral purity, right judgment, unconquerable power—all those qualities associated with holiness, that is, with the total otherness of God. How many futile crusades have been launched on the basis of such blind assumptions! How many communities have been split by those claiming such rightness! How many smug presuppositions of such superiority have prevented the communication or the receipt of the gospel!

Haggai addresses this temptation with a parable and its explanation delivered almost nine weeks after 2:1–9, on December 18. The question is, Does the very act of rebuilding the temple make the Judeans a morally pure, acceptable community in the eyes of God? Having dealt with God's holy place, have they themselves become holy?

To answer the question, Haggai is commanded by God to ask the priests how holiness is communicated (for the relevant laws, see Exod. 29:37; Lev. 6:26, 27; 10:10; cf. Ezek. 44:19; Matt. 9:21; 14:36; 23:19). If holy meat, that is, meat set aside for sacrifice, is carried in a garment, does that garment communicate the holiness to other food that it touches? No. And if the holy meat of the sacrifice is touched by one who has been made ritually impure by some means, it itself becomes unholy and unfit for use in sacrifice. In short, sinfulness contaminates everything and everyone, and because the Judeans are sinful people, their sin contaminates even the temple and its worship. Just because they are handling the things of God, they have not become suddenly morally pure and acceptable in God's eyes.

Neither does our familiarity with the things of God's church—Bible, sacraments, doctrine, ritual—automatically make us into pure and righteous Christians. To speak often of the Lord, to quote the Scriptures, even to participate in worship and sacrament lend to us no magical claim to be sinless before our God and other people. Jesus told what he thought of such claims in the parable of the Pharisee and tax collector, just as Haggai here proclaims the same lesson in his parable of holiness. Indeed, to drive home the point Haggai once again recalls the sin of the past and God's covenant curses on it and the failure of the people to repent and return to their God (vv. 16–17; cf. Amos 4:6–11).

Yet nevertheless, despite the Judeans' sin, God works his stunning reversal (vv. 18, 19). From this day, December 18, on, he will accept them and forgive them and dwell in their temple and shower his favor on them. Verse 19*b* should be read as a

103

question about the future: "Will the vine . . . ?" There had been no new harvest of vine and fig, of pomegranate and olive since the foundation of the temple was laid. The autumn rains began in Judah in mid-October, and when the ground had softened, the seed was sown and then ploughed under. The Judeans do not know by the time of this parable whether their seeds and vines and trees will bear or not. But God, the Lord of nature and of their lives, promises that he will bless them. His forgiveness and mercy alone make human beings acceptable in his eyes. In Christian terms, it is not Bible or sacrament or any kind of religious work that automatically brings with it God's acceptance and favor. Those are given only by the grace of God in Jesus Christ.

Haggai 2:20–23

One question remained to be answered for the post–exilic Judeans: What about Zerubbabel? In the tenth century B.C., God promised David that there would never be lacking an heir to sit upon his throne (II Sam. 7:12–16). When the Davidic Jehoiachin was rejected by God and carried into Babylonian exile in the first deportation of 597 B.C. (Jer. 22:24–30; II Kings 24:10–17), it seemed as if this promise had come to nothing. Second Isaiah therefore preached that God's care for the Davidic house had been transferred to Israel as a whole (Isa. 55:3). But Jehoiachin was released from prison in Babylonia (II Kings 25:27–30), and Zerubbabel, his grandson, returned from Babylonia to Jerusalem after the 538 B.C. edict of Cyrus (Ezra 1:2–4; 6:2–5). Zerubbabel therefore was a walking question: What about Zerubbabel? Will God keep his promise to David? Will Zerubbabel resume the throne of David, and will Judah therefore be freed from her foreign overlords to become once again an independent nation?

Some interpretations maintain that Haggai here promises such independence and that Zerubbabel is then heard of no more because the Persians quickly removed him from power and put down the independence movement. But we have no evidence to support such a theory.

Haggai's vision of the future transcends the limits of such historical and political speculation. He speaks not of the overthrow of Persia but of the subjection of all nations to God—of the destruction of weapons of war and the establishment of universal peace. In short, Haggai speaks, as he spoke before (2:6–9), of the coming of the Kingdom of God "in that day." And Zerubbabel is addressed not as an individual but as the holder of the Davidic office.

God will keep his promise to David. God always keeps his promises. In a stunning reversal of the judgment on Jehoiachin, who is symbolized in Jeremiah 22:24 as God's signet ring, which he tore off his right hand and flung into exile, God will once again place that ring on his finger in the person of Zerubbabel, verse 23. God holds his Davidic king dear! The judgment on the house of David is over, as the judgment on the people of David has been reversed by God's mercy. When the Kingdom of God comes on earth, the Davidic ruler or "anointed"—(called the *masiah* in Hebrew, *christos* in Greek, Messiah in English)—will be God's chosen servant and regent over all the earth.

God always keeps his promises. And so, when the Kingdom of God began to come among us in the person of Jesus Christ (Mark 1:1, 14, 15), that One born of the house and lineage of David came as the descendant of Zerubbabel (Matt. 1:12; Luke 3:27) and as the beginning of the fulfillment of this word to Haggai the prophet. He introduced God's Kingdom which has no end (Luke 1:32–33), which will overthrow every rule and authority and power (I Cor. 15:24–26) and which cannot be shaken or ever pass away (Heb. 12:28). The word of God spoken by Haggai the prophet began to find its fulfillment in Jesus Christ our Lord. When the Lord returns to complete his Kingdom, may he find us working to build up his church.

THE BOOK OF

Zechariah

Introduction

At the end of the collection of the Minor Prophets, we find three blocks of material: Zechariah 9:1—11:17; 12:1—14:21, and Malachi 1:1–4:6. Each of these units is given the title, "An Oracle (or Burden) of the word of the Lord," and it seems probable that they were added to the corpus of the Minor Prophets to expand the number of the latter to Twelve, a holy number.

We shall deal with Malachi as a separate book, but it seems almost certain that Zechariah, chapters 9—11 and 12—14 could not have come from the author of Zechariah, chapters 1—8. As we shall see, the first eight chapters of Zechariah form a careful, well-ordered whole in themselves. Further, exhaustive studies have shown that the vocabulary, style, and content of Zechariah 9—11 and 12—14 differ markedly from those of Zechariah 1—8 (see Mitchell, pp. 232ff.). Even one who reads the three sections in English can sense such differences. It has therefore become customary to view Zechariah 9—11 and 12—14 as collections of miscellaneous oracles that were added to the original Book of Zechariah by an editor, and that is the division of the material that we shall use in the pages that follow, designating the separate sections as I Zechariah (1—8), II Zechariah (9—11), and III Zechariah (12—14).

I Zechariah

CHAPTERS 1—8

Introduction

In Zechariah 2:13 we find the words, "Be silent, all flesh, before the Lord; for he has roused himself from his holy dwelling." Certainly it is difficult to picture the action of such a text in any terms that make sense to our modern world. Yet this one sentence encompasses the message of I Zechariah: The Lord of Hosts, the ruler of the universe, has set out on a new course of action.

How should we imagine that? Second Isaiah could speak of the God who "sits above the circle of the earth, and its inhabitants are like grasshoppers" (Isa. 40:22). Is the picture one, then, of God on his throne in heaven, done with observation of his creatures, rising to his feet and issuing commands to his messengers? Perhaps. In the eight strange visions of 1:17—6:15, the prophet hears and sees those various messengers, pursuing God's errands on earth. Or is the picture so filled with mystery that, like Ezekiel's vision (chap. 1), it defies description and can deal only in approximations? Certainly that quality also comes through the bizarre portrayals in the book of I Zechariah. Who knows exactly what the prophet means when he says, "I saw in the night..." (1:8), or that he is "like a man that is wakened out of his sleep" (4:1)? We are dealing in I Zechariah with that which eye does not normally see and ear does not normally hear.

As a result, I Zechariah is one of those books of the Old Testament to which we usually give passing glance. Almost nothing is obvious in it, and it is significant that passages chosen from it for some lectionaries—2:10–13 and 8:3–12, 16–17—are not from the visions of the prophet, for it is precisely the dominating vision sections that give us the most trouble. They seem neither necessary nor profitable for the life of the church.

108 Nevertheless, God rises up, according to I Zechariah, to initiate new events on our earth; and that which he commands his angelic messengers to set in motion is the coming of the new age of his Kingdom. God has a purpose, according to this

prophet (and according to all of the prophets), and that purpose brackets Israel's life—past, present, and future. It was God's purpose which he worked out in the exile of Israel in the past (1:6). It is the same purpose which he will work out in her present and in her future (8:14–15). God rises up to complete his will on earth for human life, and because that completion is the goal for which the church also prays (Matt. 6:10) perhaps this strange book has relevance for us after all.

The first eight chapters of Zechariah are among the most carefully crafted of documents. Chapter 1:1–6 forms the introduction to the whole. The first section (1:7—2:13) announces the good news of the coming of the new age and begins and ends with the theme of God's re-election of Jerusalem (1:17 and 2:12). The second section (3:1—6:15) deals with the question of who will have authority in the new age and is bracketed at beginning (3:7) and end (6:15) by a call for obedience from those authorities. The third section (chaps. 7—8) is framed by the question about fasting (7:3 and 8:19) and describes the nature of Israel's life in the new age, while the closing oracle of 8:20–23 compliments the invitation of 1:3. Nothing is out of place in the text or needs to be rearranged.

OUTLINE OF I ZECHARIAH

Introductory Oracle	1:1–6
The Visions	
Section I	1:7—2:13
Vision One	1:7–17
Vision Two	1:18–21
Vision Three	2:1–5
An Oracle	2:6–9
An Oracle	2:10–12
Conclusion of the First Section	2:13
Section II	3:1—6:15
Vision Four	3:1–7
An Oracle	3:8–10
Vision Five	4:1–14
Vision Six	5:1–4
Vision Seven	5:5–11
Vision Eight	6:1–8
A Prophetic Symbolic Action	6:9–15
Section III	7:1—8:19
A Prophetic Torah	7:1–14
A Series of Oracles	8:1–2, 3, 4–5, 6, 7–8
Three Oracles	8:9–13, 14–17, 18–19
Concluding Oracle	8:20–23

109

Three characteristics of I Zechariah's prophecy have led to endless speculation: (1) the unaccustomed form of the revelation given to the prophet in his visions in that all have to be explained by an interpreting angel who stands between the prophet and God (1:9, 21; 2:3; 3:1; 4:1; 5:2, 5; 6:4)—a departure from the usual direct communication of God with his prophets; (2) the prophet's apparent anxiety to legitimate his word as word of God (2:9, 11; 4:9; 6:15); and (3) the emphasis on the fact in 3:1-7 that Joshua the high priest has to be cleansed from his sin. While all three characteristics have separate parallels in other Old Testament writings, it is strange to find them so prominent and grouped in I Zechariah.

All three characteristics stem from the historical situation of I Zechariah. His prophetic ministry overlaps by almost two months that of Haggai (cf. 1:1 and Hag. 2:10, 20) in 520 B.C. (cf. Ezra 5:1; 6:14). The final date given in I Zechariah's oracles is December 7, 518 B.C. (7:1). This probably means that his ministry also follows almost immediately, if indeed it does not overlap, that of the authors of Third Isaiah (Isa. 56—66), who were probably Levitical priests who remained in ruined Judah during the Babylonian exile of 587-538 B.C. Along with a group of reform prophets, they stood in the covenant reform traditions of Deuteronomy and Jeremiah, but they also joined cause with the Isaian school. They championed the legitimacy of the Levitical priesthood over against the claims of the Zadokites to be the only true priests.

The author of I Zechariah, on the other hand, was with the Zadokites in exile; and he fully supports the Zadokite high priest Joshua, as did Haggai. But Zechariah, unlike Haggai, also stands in the traditions of the Isaian-Jeremian school of prophecy. His call to prophesy, in the first vision of 1:7-17, is closely modeled after that of Second Isaiah in Isaiah 40:1-8, with its angelic beings as mediators of the word of comfort and its characteristic command to "Cry!" At the same time, there are numerous linguistic and theological parallels between I Zechariah's words and the Jeremian corpus, as we shall see. I Zechariah confirms Isaian and Jeremian tradition, and yet he is an advocate for the Zadokites—a strange combination after the scathing attacks that Third Isaiah made on the Zadokites and their followers.

110

I Zechariah therefore must prove that he has a right to his prophetic position; and he continually maintains, in the manner of Deuteronomy and Jeremiah, that the fulfillment of his words will be the confirmation of their legitimacy. But he must also deal with Third Isaiah's condemnation of the Zadokite priesthood; and this is done by the vision of chapter 3, in which Joshua's iniquity is removed and Joshua is confirmed by God in his high priestly office.

Thus I Zechariah is a unique document, not only because of its strange visions but also because of its peculiar combination of opposing Zadokite and Isaian-Jeremian positions. Yet, important above all else is I Zechariah's announcement that God has been stirred into new activity—that the great King has risen to his feet and issued new orders to his angelic agents. When that happens, it behooves all persons to sit up and take notice. "Be silent, all flesh, before the Lord; for he has roused himself from his holy dwelling" (2:18).

Zechariah 1:1-6

Introductory Oracle

God has a plan that he is working out in his people's history. That is the principal message that Zechariah, the grandson (contra Ezra 5:1; 6:14) of Iddo the priest (cf. Neh. 12:16), is called by his Lord to announce to Judah. But it is very difficult to believe that fact when apparently chance happenings and unlucky fortunes of everyday life obscure any perception of the divine design. Who can clearly discern God's purpose in the ravishment and destruction of a nation? Who sees a plan in the midst of poverty, crop failure, runaway inflation, and civic strife? Who believes in a goodly purpose when freedom has been lost and one's country has become a puppet province in the empire of a distant ruler? Such was the situation of the Judean populace to whom I Zechariah was sent to prophesy.

It is precisely among the ruins of Jerusalem, therefore, that the prophet is told to take his stand. "Here, here," it is said in so many words, "is the evidence of God's working among you —the ruined walls, the rubble in the streets, even that pitiful temple building that you are beginning to reconstruct on Zion's

111

hill (cf. Hag. 2:1–9). All this destruction and poverty has come upon you, because your fathers would not heed and obey God's words, spoken through his prophets."

As if to drive home the point, Zechariah 1:4 quotes the preaching of Jeremiah (cf. Jer. 25:5; 18:11; 35:15), that prophet who before the fall of Jerusalem had joined forces with a group of reformers to recall the Judeans to obedience to the Deuteronomic law. "But," says Zechariah, "none of your fathers took Jeremiah's preaching to heart, and so all the curses of God's covenant law came upon them and destroyed them (cf. Deut. 28:15–68). You stand now in the midst of the ruin caused by your fathers' disobedience. They realized too late that they should have heeded God's word. Your fathers have died, as have the earlier prophets—indeed, as I shall die—but God's word remains and comes to pass. He works his purpose out among you and fulfills his promises."

Such preaching poses the question as to whether or not the ruins of our lives are not also testimony to God's purposeful fulfillment of his word. Every generation is called to that return to God, to which I Zechariah called his compatriots (v. 3; cf. Mal. 3:7)—a return to be characterized not by legalistic obedience to an ethical or ritual code, or by intellectual assent to a dogma, but by heartfelt love and obedience and gratitude to the God who has created and sustained one's life. Such was the call of Deuteronomy and Jeremiah (cf. Jer. 4:3–4; 6:16–17) that Judah's fathers had failed to heed. When our generation also fails to heed the call, are sufferings we endure God's judgment upon us too? If so, then I Zechariah's call to return is still an urgent summons.

Yet, I Zechariah, unlike his pre-exilic prophetic predecessors, is sent to deal not so much with the behavior of Judean society as he is with the beliefs of her heart. Only three brief passages in his book treat what we often consider to be standard prophetic ethical concerns (5:3–4; 7:9–10; 8:16–17). Rather, the prophet is told to point to the evidence of God's work in Judah's past in order to inspire confidence in that work in the future, and the primary burden of Zechariah's message will deal with the new age that is coming.

112 The Visions

On February 15, 519 B.C., about three and one-half months after his initial preaching (cf. 1:1), and two months after Haggai's final oracle (Hag. 2:20–23) which announced the coming of the messianic kingdom, I Zechariah was granted eight separate prophetic visions. Whether they all were given him in one night is not said. When the prophet reports, "I saw (in) the night," in 1:8, he may be referring not to a time but to a prophetic ecstatic state (cf. 4:1) in which he is granted to see symbols and messengers at the gate of heaven and to talk with God's interpreting angel. His repeated phrase, "I lifted my eyes" (1:18; 2:1; 5:1, 9; 6:1; cf. 5:5) suggests that he looks up toward heaven from earth.

The series of visions is interrupted by prophetic oracles at three points: 2:6–9, 10–12, 13; 3:8–10; 4:6–10 and by the report of a symbolic action in 6:9–15. This arrangement, along with the carefully crafted order of the book and the third–person introductions (1:1, 7; 7:1, 8), suggests that its final form came from the hand of an editor. But I Zechariah's visions are not literary constructions but reports of genuine prophetic experiences.

Zechariah 1:7—2:13

Vision One (1:7–17)

While this first vision granted to I Zechariah is rather complex, and the reader has the task of distinguishing the man among the myrtle trees who is sometimes called the angel of the Lord (vv. 8, 10, 11, 12) from the Lord himself (vv. 10, 12, 13, 14, 16, 17) and from the angel who talks to Zechariah (vv. 9, 14), the visual details of the scene are not very important. The colors of the horses and the "glen" apparently have no known significance. Myrtle trees or, properly, shrubs may be indications of the eschatological nature of the vision (cf. Isa. 41:19; 55:13). The important fact is that God's angelic horsemen have scouted the earth and found it undisturbed and at rest (v. 11).

How ideal that may seem to a modern reader—to have a world rid of violence and of the clash of arms—to find a scene of tranquility where all appears in order!

Yet the tranquility of the earth in I Zechariah's time is an "accursed happiness," as John Calvin phrases it, because the order gained is not God's order and the tranquility won has

113

been at the expense of God's people and purpose. It is quite possible for humankind to create its own false peace in home or society or nation and to label it good, when God views it as thoroughly corrupt and evil—in the words of another prophet, to say "Peace, peace" when in reality there is no peace of God (Jer. 6:14; 8:11).

So it is that the angel of the Lord intercedes for the struggling people of Judah and appeals to God to remember his divine purpose and to upset the earth's false peace (v. 12). God had planned to send his disobedient people into Babylonian exile for seventy years (Jer. 25:11) and then not only to restore them to their land but also to do good to them and to give them "a future and a hope" (Jer. 29:10–11). If the seventy years were reckoned from the first deportation of 597 B.C., the time of judgment was up—though "seventy" may be just a round number to indicate a lifetime (cf. Ps. 90:10). The angel's intercession relies, nevertheless, on the expressed promise of God—surely a firm foundation on which to base a plea for mercy!

The Lord replies to his angel (v. 13) in words similar to those that Second Isaiah also heard God tell his heavenly beings: "Comfort, comfort . . ." (Isa. 40:1). Judah's evil fortunes will be changed to good, because the Lord of Hosts is jealous with a great jealousy for Jerusalem and its people. That is, God loves his people so tenderly, so fiercely, so zealously, that he will not allow others to injure them. He intended only to discipline his people and to bring them to their senses. But the foreign nations used by God to carry out his will subsequently thought that they were masters and conquerors and began to pursue their own purposes, devastating Judah far beyond her deserving and claiming for themselves the absolute authority of God. "I am," Babylonia boasted, "and there is no one besides me" (Isa. 47:8). Thus does all human power become corrupt and blasphemous when it forgets that it exists solely to serve the purposes of God (cf. Rom. 13:1).

The message given here to I Zechariah is that God is the ruler yet, and now the anger loosed on Israel's fathers (1:2) will be turned against Judah's secure and relaxed oppressors (1:15). The question of just what particular foreign nations the Lord has in mind should not be pressed, however, because the divine word is dealing here with the ultimate fulfillment of God's purpose. These words are spoken in 519 B.C., but they have also to do with the end of the age—with the time when all the enemies of God's people will be destroyed. Thus these words proclaim hope for Jerusalem in the sixth century B.C., but they also proclaim hope to God's suffering people in any century. The time is coming for the covenant people when all the earth will be quiet; but that tranquility will be the fruit not of the conqueror's oppressive hand but of "the peace of God which passes all understanding, . . ." (Phil. 4:7; cf. Isa. 2:2–4).

God intended such happy security from the beginning of Israel's history. He set out in her forebears to make for himself a new people, who knew how to live in justice and righteousness and peace under the protection and guidance of his lordship. Into that goodly community he intended to draw all the families of the earth—in short, to set up on the earth his Kingdom, his realm over which he ruled. But Israel subverted his plans with her sin and rebelled against his rule and refused to serve his purpose. God therefore pronounced her "Not my people" (Hos. 1:9; cf. Jer. 12:7–8) and abandoned her to her enemies.

Now, in this glad vision of the prophet's, God catches up once more the raveled threads of his purpose. Again . . . again . . . again . . . again—four times the word is repeated (v. 17). The temple and Jerusalem will be rebuilt (v. 16). Second Isaiah's cry of comfort (40:1) is raised anew. Abundant life will return to Judah because—and this is the important fact—God has re-elected his people ("chosen Jerusalem," v. 17). He has returned to them and forgiven them and taken them back as his own, to be guarded and guided by his love. Because of that fact, all the earth will in the future find true rest.

Vision Two (1:18–21)

The smiths of God. These are the instruments the Lord will use to bring down the proud nations that have scattered his people throughout the Near Eastern world and interrupted his purpose of bringing his Kingdom on earth.

The horn, the pride of the young bull, is often a metaphor for strength in the Old Testament and can symbolize the power of a nation. In this second vision, I Zechariah sees four single horns, which are indicative not of four specific enemies but of all those nations that have attacked Israel, perhaps from the four corners of the earth. God's response to these four horns, Zechariah is shown, will be four metal-workers or smiths who with their hammers will destroy the proud power of Israel's

115

mighty oppressors. It is a forceful image, born of the faith that God is stronger than any earthly power, and skillfully presented by the use of the contrasting verbs: "lifted up (RSV: raised) . . . cast down . . . lifted up," verse 21.

The fact that God brings low the pride and power of his enemies and exalts the lowly and oppressed is axiomatic throughout the Bible. But the interpreter well might ask, How does God accomplish such a reversal? Where do we see the smiths of God at work destroying the mighty foe?

Surely those smiths were supremely at work fashioning a cross on Golgotha. But just as surely, that victory is applied in the historical movements of nations. In our age, we might say that the smiths are those of providence that return the evil of the oppressor on his own head; that take advantage of the slightest error or miscalculation to undermine the ruthless' plans; that chip away a little here, a little there until the whole structure crumbles (cf. Isa. 28:13); that harden the wicked heart to bring upon it its own ruin. The smiths of God sometimes work slowly, but they are at work. And so the people of God still live "in spite of dungeon, fire, and sword"; and God triumphs over his enemies and presses forward with his plan for his earth.

Vision Three (2:1–5)

In this third vision, I Zechariah is shown a man who sets out to measure the dimensions of Jerusalem's ruined walls, preparatory to rebuilding them. It is a striking characterization, for the man is not an angel but a visionary symbol for human expectations. This man has believed the prophet's message that Jerusalem will be rebuilt, but he expects the new Jerusalem to be no different from the old; and he would therefore conform its measurements to those it had before its fall. The man has no vision of a greater city "whose builder and maker is God" (Heb. 11:10), no thought of a new Jerusalem, expanded and made glorious by the Lord (cf. Rev. 21:2). No, this is a practical and realistic man, who relies on what he has seen in the past and who never glimpses the dimensions of God's Kingdom that is coming.

But an angel quickly appears and tells Zechariah's interpreting angel to run after the young man and to inform him that God's new Jerusalem will spread out beyond all its former dimensions (cf. Isa. 49:20; 54:1–3; Mark 2:22). God's future bursts the limits and realities of the past, and the new Jerusalem will have to be like an unwalled village, so multitudinous will be her inhabitants and cattle.

This passage has often served in the preaching of the church as an admonition against despair over the seeming ineffectiveness of the word of God. So few seem to take the word to heart, and the body of Christ appears so weak over against the powers and propaganda of the world (cf. I Kings 19:14). But here is another picture: God's redeemed crowding the streets of the new Jerusalem, bursting out beyond the city limits and covering the surrounding hills as the sand covers the seashore in God's fulfillment of his promise to the fathers (cf. Gen. 22:17; 32:12; Hos. 1:10; Heb. 11:12).

This passage from I Zechariah has further been used by the Christian pulpit as a warning against drawing the limits of the Kingdom too narrowly. An amazing and motley multitude enters the Kingdom in the teaching of the Scriptures. ". . . I have other sheep, that are not of this fold," Jesus taught (John 10:16). Persons are not to be excluded from the new Jerusalem on the basis of narrow human judgments.

Yet, the new Jerusalem of the Kingdom does have dimensions. It has a cornerstone (cf. Isa. 28:16; Eph. 2:20; I Peter 2:6) and God defines its limits (cf. Rev. 22:15-19), and not everyone who says to him "Lord, Lord" can expect to enter into it (Matt. 7:21-23). God knows who are his, and the enemies of God find no place in the city, according to these visions of Zechariah.

The purpose of the young man in measuring the outlines of Jerusalem is to reconstruct her walls, in order to give her a defense against her enemies (cf. Ezra 4; Neh. 4; 6). What an ironic picture! Lying at the young man's feet are the stones and rubble of the old walls that furnished no protection. Zechariah projects that picture into a lesson for the future: The only sure defense for Israel is God himself, who will be like a wall of fire round about his people (cf. Isa. 26:1; 60:18; 4:5).

The figure of fire is associated with the presence of God throughout the Bible, and both Old and New Testaments describe the Lord as a devouring fire (Deut. 4:24; Heb. 12:29)— as one awful in judgment, burning in love, radiant in purity, all-consuming in power. Such a God will surround the people of his Kingdom, protecting them against all harm and barring the entrance of all who, for lack of faith and love, cannot "dwell with everlasting burnings" (Isa. 33:14).

117

In one sense, the necessity of God's wall of protecting fire contradicts the prophet's preceding vision. If all the people's enemies have been destroyed, from whom do they need to be protected? But Zechariah's visions encompass a scene that is "already" and "not yet." The Kingdom with its new Jerusalem is coming—that the prophet is given to see. But his message to his compatriots, in 519 B.C., is to live in the light of that coming —to live as if the Kingdom were already present and to trust God now for their protection and security.

God will be not only Jerusalem's protecting wall of fire, according to this vision, but also her "glory within." God's "glory" has two principal meanings in the Scriptures. First, it is the shining effulgence of his presence on earth. Therefore, throughout the Bible, it is said that the new Jerusalem will have no need of sun or moon or lamp, for the glory of God will be its light (cf. Isa. 60:19–20, 1–3; Rev. 21:23–27; John. 1:9; 8:12). Second, God's glory is the honor and esteem given to his person (cf. Pss. 8:1; 19:1; Luke 2:14; John 5:41; Rom. 11:36; Rev. 7:12).

When Zechariah says, then, that God will be the new Jerusalem's glory, he means that God will be the light within her. But he also means that Jerusalem's honor will depend solely on the presence of God. The people of God are to win esteem in the world not by their wealth or their wisdom or their influence, not by the magnificence of their architecture or the status and learning of their clergy, but solely by pointing to their God, who alone is glorious.

Such a message meant that even the struggling and impoverished Judean community of Zechariah's time would have a glory about it—namely, the presence of the God of glory in its midst. The church in our day should look to no other source for its own glorification.

An Oracle (2:6–9)

Reinforcing the message of the second vision (1:18–21), this prophetic oracle raises the cry to those still in exile to flee their captors and to return to their true home in Zion. Jews were dispersed throughout the ancient Near Eastern world after the fall of Jerusalem in 587 B.C., and only a small fraction of them returned to Judah after the liberating decree of Cyrus (cf. Ezra 2:2–64). This oracle urges, in the manner of Second Isaiah (cf. 48:20) and of Jeremiah (cf. 51:6), that God's people still abroad escape their foreign homes, before God, with just a wave of his hand, brings his destruction on Israel's enemies. Babylon is spe-

118

cifically referred to, but "the land of the north" is, as in Jeremiah's prophecies, symbolic of all Israel's foes.

Like Jeremiah (cf. 1:10), I Zechariah is here sent as a prophet to the nations, not by the Lord's "glory" (as the RSV reads in v. 8) but at God's "insistence" (reading "glory" in its sense of "heaviness"). And when Zechariah's words to the nations come to pass and Israel becomes master over those she formerly served, the prophet's calling will be confirmed.

The most important announcement in this oracle, however, is that Israel's enemies are God's enemies—a fact left rather unclear in the preceding visions. Whoever harms Israel has, in effect, harmed the Lord at his most sensitive point, the pupil of his eye (cf. Deut. 32:10; Ps. 17:8). No part of the human body is more carefully guarded than the eye. No threat brings a quicker defense than does a jab at that vulnerable and precious organ. Indeed, defense of the eye is instinctive, accomplished at a wink: God's protection of his people is part of his very nature. Whoever would attack Israel attacks the God who guards and loves them (cf. Matt. 25:41–45).

The covenant people have not earned such protecting favor, of course. In fact, by their apostasy from God's love and their disobedience to God's commandments, they have earned permanent exile, abandonment into the hands of their enemies, to disappear from history: "For the wages of sin is death" (Rom. 6:23*a*). And not only once have God's people deserved that death but over and over again. Yet this God of the Bible cannot and will not let go of his own (cf. Hos. 11:8).

Perhaps the only explanation for why God so cherishes his people is that he is working out his purpose through them for his world (cf. Deut. 7:6–8), and nothing and no one will deter him from accomplishing that purpose. Yet, the mystery still remains: Why us? Why these particular people? There is no answer that can be given. But this much is certain: There is nothing to fear. "If God is for us, who is against us" (Rom. 8:31 *b*)? He who keeps Israel, keeps his church too as the apple of his eye.

An Oracle (2:10–12)

This second oracle follows naturally on that in verses 6–9. But this is a separate cry addressed to Jerusalem that reinforces the content of the first (1:7–17) and third (2:1–5) visions.

119

The content of the visions is made explicit. God will return to Zion (cf. 1:16), and his glory will dwell once more in the Holy of Holies of the rebuilt temple, in the midst of his people (cf. 2:5). Jerusalem will therefore become holy, that is, reserved for God's purposes and pervaded by his power.

Such promises were probably understood by I Zechariah as fulfillment of the plan for a reconstructed Israel that the Zadokite priesthood had formulated while in Babylonian exile, and this oracle belongs firmly to Zadokite tradition. But a new note in this passage separates it from that exclusivism so characteristic of the Zadokites and joins their vision of the new temple and of God's returned glory with the universalism of Isaian tradition: God will deal with the foreign nations not only in judgment, as announced in Zechariah 1:18–21 and 2:6–9, but he will also accept many of the foreigners as members of his covenant people. When they see God's reversal of Israel's fortunes (1: 14–17; 2:9) and his glory shining forth in the midst of her (2:5), many foreigners will voluntarily "join themselves" to the covenant community and will be accepted along with Israel as members of God's Chosen People. The new Israel, like the new Jerusalem (2:1–5), will burst the limits of the old; and all peoples will be united in one universal fellowship.

Once again (cf. v. 9) the prophet states that when such an event comes to pass, his prophetic calling will be proved. Perhaps it is the Christian church, therefore, which should most firmly approve Zechariah's inclusion in the canon. This oracle is the stated Old Testament lesson for Christmas eve in some lectionaries, and it is the church which has known the dwelling of God in Jesus Christ in the midst of its universal fellowship, made up from all nations.

The oracle closes by repeating that God has re-elected Jerusalem, reiterating that glad announcement with which the visions began (see 1:17).

Conclusion to the First Section (2:13)

All of these things that have been revealed through chapters one and two, God has now roused himself to do: Such is the good news of the first section of the book. The heavenly plan has been set in motion. The new age will break in soon—the sure outcome of Judah's history. These glad tidings are the hope with which I Zechariah comforts his struggling compatriots in 520–519 B.C. These visions of salvation are the words he calls them (1:3) to believe with all their hearts. Surely the only possi-

120

ble response to that is to be silent (cf. Hab. 2:20; Zeph. 1:7)—
to catch one's breath and then to wait in hope and obedient
faith for the final fulfillment of the prophet's words.

Zechariah 3:1—6:15

Vision Four (3:1-7)

With this fourth vision (vv. 1–7) and its interpreting oracle
(vv. 8–10), we begin the second major section of I Zechariah.
This section is concerned with the question of who is to govern
the new people of God in the new age. It is framed by a call to
obedience in 3:7 and 6:15.

The scene has apparently now moved from the gate of
heaven into the courts of heaven itself (cf. v. 7), or at least the
prophet is allowed to see into those courts. "He" in verse 1
refers once again to the interpreting angel of chapters 1 and 2.
The angel lets Zechariah witness the tribunal where the high
priest Joshua is on trial before "the angel of the Lord" (cf. 1:8,
10, 11, 12). Joshua's accuser, standing at his right, is Satan, "the
adversary" (cf. Job 1:6), who is never a fully developed personification of evil in the Old Testament but who nevertheless has a
certain maliciousness about him.

There is no doubt that Joshua, here head and representa-
tive of the Zadokite priesthood, is guilty of failing to obey God's
ethical and ritual commandments (cf. v. 7). The priesthood's
sins are symbolized by Joshua's filthy garments (v. 3; cf. Isa. 4:4;
64:6), and their apostasy and injustice were severely chastised
by Third Isaiah, shortly before the time of Zechariah (cf. Isa. 57;
58:1–5; 59:1–15; 65:1–7; 66:3–4). Therefore, before Joshua can
be high priest in the new age, his sin must be dealt with.

God does away with the sin of his priest by forgiving him.
This is no usual court of law, where the accused receives his just
deserts. No. Satan, who knows only legalistic, tit-for-tat justice,
is rebuked by the Lord (cf. Jude 9). God speaks directly only in
verse 2 here, and when he rebukes, no one can reverse his
decision (cf. Ps. 9:5; Isa. 17:13). Hell is where a person receives
what he deserves, but heaven is where he is forgiven.

121

Joshua is "a brand plucked from the fire" of judgment, a dry stick who would have burned up and disappeared had God not delivered him from exile and reinstated him, guiltless, in his office. His grandfather had been taken captive by the Babylonian captain Nebuzaradan and slain by Nebuchadnezzar at Riblah (II Kings 25:18–21). His father, Jehozadak, was carried into Babylonian captivity (I Chron. 6:15), and there Joshua was born. And now Joshua has returned to Jerusalem with Zerubbabel (cf. Ezra 2:2), redeemed from captivity by the mercy of God. More than that, he is now robed in festive garments, symbolic of his cleansing from sin (cf. Isa. 52:1; 61:10; Job 29:14; Luke 15:22) and of his worthiness to be accepted before the presence of God (cf. Matt. 22:11–13; Rev. 19:8). God's priests, too, must be forgiven before they can approach the throne of grace (cf. Lev. 16:6–14), and all clergy serve only by the mercy of God.

Joshua further is given a role as high priest with powers far beyond those previously granted the Zadokites. Now he not only is to have sole charge over the rebuilt temple, with absolute authority to say who can be admitted to it, but he will also have free access to the courts of heaven and to communion with God. The way to the Father now lies through the mediation of Joshua. But Joshua must obey God's commandments given through *torah* and prophets.

An Oracle (3:8–10)

As the accompanying oracle interprets this vision (vv. 8–10), Joshua and the Zadokite priests over whom he will have charge in the temple are, however, also portents—"good omens" of a bright future that lies beyond them. Once again I Zechariah is speaking in terms of "now" and "not yet," and the future that is not yet is characterized by the three promises of verses 8 and 9, each beginning with "behold!"

First, in the fullness of the new age, the true ruler of the people of God will come—God's servant, the Branch (cf. Jer. 23:5; 33:14–15; Isa. 4:2; 11:1). Who this Branch is or what he will do are not explained. He remains a mysterious figure of the future.

Second, an enigmatic seven-faced stone will be set before Joshua. Commentators have speculated that the stone is intended as the topstone or cornerstone of the new temple or of the new Jerusalem (cf. Isa. 28:16). Others say it is a precious stone intended for Joshua or for the Branch. Some equate it with the plummet-stone of 4:10.

Third, however, the stone will be engraved by God; and this probably means that it is a precious jewel, equivalent to the gold plate which Aaron wore on his turban and which was engraved with the words, "Holy to the Lord," as a symbol of the priest's atonement for the people (Exod. 28:36–38). Thus the stone, too, emphasizes that the way to the Father lies through the high priest's office, and by his mediation the new Judah will be forgiven all its iniquity. Whether Joshua or the Branch will wear this stone is, however, not yet said.

These are promises for the future in I Zechariah—plans of God's which the prophet sees already taking shape in heaven. Zechariah wants his people to live in the certainty that such plans will be put into effect on earth.

No one who comprehends the obedience required of Joshua, the atoning authority invested in him, and his privileged access to God should interpret this chapter without seeing its New Testament parallel in the high priesthood of Jesus as set forth in The Letter to the Hebrews. In that book, Jesus is appointed high priest after the order of Melchizedek because of his perfect obedience (4:15; 5:8–10); he makes atonement for all sin once for all (7:26–27; 9:24–26); and he enjoys continual communion and intercession for us before the Father (4:14–16; 1:3; 8:1; 9:24; 10:12; 12:2). That role which the high priest was to have in the new age has found its fulfillment in Christ; and God has begun that Kingdom on earth in the person of his Son that he promised through his prophet Zechariah. (See the fuller discussion at 6:9–15.)

Vision Five (4:1–14)

Zechariah 4:6 was probably more frequently used in preaching in the past two centuries than were any other words from I Zechariah. Yet this fifth vision of the prophet's is so strange and difficult to understand that it is largely ignored today. Verse 6 is, however, the key to this passage; and it explains in words what Zechariah also sees in the vision.

In contrast to the first vision (1:7–17), every detail of what the prophet sees here is important. Awakened as if from a dream and shown reality, Zechariah is given to see a golden lampstand. This is not the well-known seven-branched Jewish

123

menorah, nor is it like the lampstand designed for the tabernacle (Exod. 25:31–40). It is not related to Solomon's ten temple lampstands (I Kings 7:49). Rather, as we know from similar lamps found by archaeologists, this is a cylindrical column, probably tapered upward, on top of which is an oil bowl. Around the rim of this bowl are seven smaller bowls, each with seven pinches in its rim to hold seven wicks, making a total of forty-nine lights. On each side of the main bowl is an olive tree with a branch overshadowing the bowl, to which it feeds oil directly through a gold pipe. The whole lampstand is distinguished by the fact that it is made of costly metal and receives its liquid fuel directly from the olive trees without the necessity of human processing of the oil from the olives: "Not by might, nor by power. . . ."

Obviously the prophet is as puzzled by the sight of this lampstand and of the olive trees as are we. Three times (vv. 4, 11, 12) he asks his interpreting angel to explain what the vision and specifically the olive trees signify. But the answer is not immediately given. Instead, the interpreting angel delivers the oracle found in verses 6 and 7, and Zechariah himself proclaims the divine words of verses 8–10. These are followed by a saying about the lights of the seven small bowls. Only then, at the very end of the passage, is there an explanation of the olive trees (v. 14).

What does all this mean? First, the lights of the lampstand represent Israel, the covenant people of God, who are to shine forth in all the world. In verse 10b these lights are also called "eyes," because it was thought that the eye was the source of light (cf. Matt. 6:22). The new Israel in the new age, then, is to be that light shining in the darkness which penetrates the gloom surrounding all peoples, which dispels the shadows from the valley of death, and which draws all nations to its worship of the God of light and life (cf. 2:11; Isa. 60:1–3; Matt. 5:14–16; John 1:4, 5, 9; Acts 13:47).

But God's people have no ability in themselves to give light to the peoples walking in darkness. They must be fueled by the Spirit of God, here represented by the oil of olives: "Not by might, nor by power, but by my Spirit. . . ."

124   "Might" is often translated "army," "force," "ability," "efficiency" of men or means. It can even bear the connotation of "wealth." It has to do with human resources, the provisions we use to fight our battles. "Power" on the other hand is purposeful

force, dynamic strength and resoluteness. Not by their own resources and strong resolve can the people of God bring light to the world. The resources may be plentiful, the resolve unshaken and never-ending, but we are talking about God's light here—the light that can hold back the evil of chaos (cf. Gen. 1:3–4); the light that shines in the darkness and the darkness cannot overcome it (cf. John 1:5); the light by which sorrow and sighing and pain are forever done away (cf. Rev. 21:4). That light is given only by the word of God. Speaking to an earlier England, G. Campbell Morgan put it this way:

> Not by resources, not by resoluteness. These may be high, pure, mighty; but in so far as they are human they cannot accomplish the work of God in the world. By might and by power, by resources and resoluteness, we may be able to legislate for England; . . . we can do much upon a human level; but by these things we cannot shine as lights in the world or bring in the Kingdom of God. . . . We are very far from believing that. If I were asked to-day to give what I think to be the reason for the comparative failure of the Church of God in missionary enterprise, I would say that we are terribly in danger of imagining that by our own splendid resources and resoluteness we can accomplish the work . . . ("The Divine Worker," pp. 53–54).

"I am the light of the world," Jesus said (John 8:12), and ". . . apart from me you can do nothing" (John 15:5). Thus, the lights of the golden candelabrum in this vision must be fed by the sacred oil—the enabling Spirit of God that makes it possible to do God's will and speak his word in the world.

The Spirit is not given to the covenant people directly, however. It is mediated to them by two "anointed," who are represented by the two olive trees and their branches. These two can only symbolize the high priest and the Davidic king of the New Israel. Kings and priests were the only ones anointed to office in Old Testament times, and the oil used in the ceremony symbolized the Spirit of God poured out upon them, by which alone they were enabled to rule (cf. Isa. 11:2; 42:1). "Not by might, nor by power, but by my Spirit. . . ." It is these two empowered ones, then, who will govern the new Israel in the new age. But because they "stand by the Lord" (v. 14), that is, because they themselves receive his Spirit, they will be able to mediate that Spirit to the people.

125

It is significant that the high priest and the Davidic king are not here named. I Zechariah has no hesitancy in elsewhere naming Joshua as high priest (3:1, 8; 6:11), but the name does not appear here. Neither is Zerubbabel identified with the Davidic king to come. Rather, Zechariah is speaking of a future for the people of God that stretches beyond the sixth century B.C. —a glorious future that will truly come but that is not yet.

The passage also deals with Zechariah's time, however, in the oracles given by the interpreting angel (vv. 6b–7) and by Zechariah himself (vv. 8–10a). The new age will not come without the completion of the temple building. Therefore the opposition to that project (cf. Ezra 4:2, 24), here symbolized by a great mountain, will be leveled by the Spirit of the Lord; and Zerubbabel will be enabled to put the topstone in place as the people shout with joy, "How beautiful it is! How much grace the Lord has shown us!" (vv. 7, 10: "plummet" in v. 10, RSV, should be translated "great stone"). That project too will be accomplished "not by might, nor by power," but only by God's powerful working in the midst of this people. Even enterprises as seemingly earthy as carpentry and stone masonry, even struggles as seemingly difficult as fighting enemies and finding resources and overcoming skepticism, owe their good outcome to the unseen Enabler, the Spirit of the living God.

But because of the presence of the Spirit, Zerubbabel's completed temple will become something grander than he initially envisions or even builds. We know from a passage in Haggai that the rebuilt temple began as a small and inglorious structure (Hag. 2:3), "despised" by many—in Zechariah's words, the evidence of a "day of small things" (v. 10). But the implication of this vision is that the temple in the new age will be neither small nor inglorious. By God's Spirit, it will be transformed into a graceful and magnificent center of worship.

That such glory came into our world cannot be denied by any who has believed the New Testament's story. "Destroy this temple, and in three days I will raise it up," Jesus said (John 2:19) —that One who in his glorious resurrected body became our incarnate temple, our place to worship the Father. Born of the Spirit, baptized of the Spirit, led of the Spirit into the wilderness, Jesus came in the power of the Spirit to proclaim the beginning of the Kingdom of God in his person.

But more! In final vindication of Zechariah's prophetic calling (v. 9), Christ poured out the Spirit on his church, mediating to his covenant people the power to shine forth in the world, to declare the wonderful deeds of him who called them out of

126

darkness into this marvelous light (I Peter 2:9). Christ became Zechariah's promised high priest and Davidic king, the mediator of the Spirit to the people—our means of grace and our sure guarantor of glory. (See also 6:9–15.)

Vision Six (5:1–4)

Corrupt leadership leads to a corrupted populace. There is ample evidence in the writings of Third Isaiah that the apostasy and injustice of the Zadokite priesthood infected their lay followers (cf. Isa. 58:1–5; 59:1–8; 65:1–7). It is therefore not enough, in this section dealing with the governance of the new people of God (3:1—6:15), that the Zadokite high priest is cleansed of sin (3:1–5). Those Judeans who have followed the Zadokites in their evil ways also must be dealt with, and precisely the twin evils of apostasy and injustice are the subjects of this sixth vision of the prophet. "Every one who steals" (v. 3) symbolizes all those who have injured a neighbor in any way. "Every one who swears falsely" (v. 3) stands for all who have dishonored God. The vision deals with the covenant law's comprehensive protection of the rights of God and of neighbor.

The interpreting angel shows Zechariah an enormous skin or parchment scroll, ten by five yards in dimension (a cubit equals about 18 inches), which descends from the heavenly court (cf. 3:1–10 for the setting) and which is emblazoned with words of judgment apparently written large enough for all to read (cf. Ezek. 2:9–10; Hab. 2:2). The words are God's curse upon the covenant lawbreakers in the land of Judah.

A modern reader needs to appreciate fully what it means in the Old Testament when God curses. Not only is the accursed cut off from all life and good, which come only from God, but a curse is active, evil power which brings destruction and wasting and death upon its object. As is always true of the word of God (cf. Isa. 55:10–11), this word works until it brings about a new and, in this case, evil situation in human life. The oracle of the Lord therefore, in verse 4, is that his curse will insinuate itself into the houses of unfaithful Judeans and eat away at their lives and property until they are destroyed. Thus will God cleanse the land of Judah in preparation for the new society of the Kingdom.

We modern students of the prophets sometimes recoil before such a portrayal of God because we have so sentimentalized the deity that we do not believe he would curse any one

127

or any lifestyle. But the prophets know better. God demands obedience to his commandments and he will settle for nothing less. Presented with less, he does indeed eat away at the structures of a disobedient life, like a leprous mold (Lev. 14:34–35) or an unseen moth or a penetrating dry rot (Hos. 5:12); and our illnesses and anxieties, our distorted relationships and broken homes, our servitudes and murderous societies are symptomatic of his unseen but judging presence.

Before God can bring his Kingdom upon earth, evil must be done away: That is the principal message of this sixth vision. There can be no compromise of God's final rule, no live-and-let-live acceptance of the status quo. The seed must fall in the ground and die before it can bring forth fruit (John 12:24–25). The old life must be crucified before it can be raised to newness (cf. Rom. 6:6). The evil ways of our society must be purged and destroyed by God before he can bring in his new order. Our personal decision about that outcome therefore involves searching our hearts to discover whether or not we truly want God's Kingdom to come. If we do, then we must welcome God's purging judgments, at the same time clinging to the one Hope who can save us from eternal death in that judgment.

Vision Seven (5:5–11)

The seventh vision (vv. 5–11) deepens the understanding of evil previously presented. Zechariah is shown the strange sight of an ephah, or large five to ten gallon barrel, used to measure grain, that has a leaden cover. Inside the ephah huddles a woman whom the prophet is told is the personification of wickedness in the land of Judah. He then sees two female beings, with long, strong wings like those of the unclean high-flying stork (Lev. 11:13, 19), bear the ephah away; and he is told that it will be taken to the God-defying land of Shinar between the Tigris and Euphrates Rivers in Babylon (cf. Gen. 10:10; 11:2; Dan. 1:2; Rev. 14:8), where it will become an idol in a temple for worshipers of evil.

The wicked woman in this ephah symbolizes the objective power of evil (cf. the female figure in Prov. 7:5–27; Rev. 17). That is, wickedness consists not merely in wrong–doing and the evil acts of human beings but is a power in itself, let loose upon the world and upon the people of God. In the images of the New Testament, it is "the principalities"; "the powers"; "the world rulers of this present darkness"; "the spiritual hosts of

128

wickedness in the heavenly places" (Eph. 6:12; cf. Rom. 8:38); the adversary who "prowls around like a roaring lion, seeking someone to devour" (I Peter 5:8). In our time, evil is the Big Lie, the corrupted ethos of an age, the overwhelming force for wrong which holds individuals and societies captive to its powers and turns human life into slavery to sin (cf. Rom. 6:16–17).

Such wickedness has awesome power; and when the cover is lifted on the ephah, the Evil One tries to escape. But God's interpreting angel is stronger and forces her back into the container. There can be no dallying with wickedness, no conditional countenancing of its ways. Let loose, wickedness spreads like gangrene (cf. II Tim. 2:17). It must be firmly rejected, and willful renunciation of it belongs always to the life of the people of God.

God alone removes evil from his people's lives for all times, according to this vision. In an act of pure grace, he takes it away as far as the East is from the West (cf. Ps. 103:12) and lets it run its course among those irretrievably lost who dwell always in the darkness of defiance of God (cf. Gen. 11:2). There, in the shadowy land of Shinar, it can work its destroying ways. But God's people will be delivered from it—not by their own efforts, not by their willful practice of morality, not by their resolute faith, but by God's merciful deed of cleansing that he performs in preparation for the coming of his Kingdom. Finally only God is able to "deliver us from evil."

Vision Eight (6:1–8)

In his first vision (1:7–17), to which this eighth vision corresponds, Zechariah was shown a false peace abroad on the earth, enforced by the oppressor's hand (1:11), and he was told to announce the glad news to Judah that God would destroy the oppressor's might (cf. 1:18–21) and bring the true *shalom* of his Kingdom to his covenant people and over all the earth. Now, in this final vision of the future, the prophet is shown the way fully prepared for the accomplishment of that purpose.

Once again various colored horses, this time pulling war chariots symbolic of God's sovereign might, come forth from the entrance to heaven, which is here symbolized by the two impregnable mountains of bronze (cf. Jer. 1:18). The horses and chariots are said to represent the four winds of heaven (v. 5, contra RSV; cf. Jer. 49:36; Dan. 7:2). That is, they are the messengers of God (cf. Ps. 104:4). Impatient to leave on their mis-

129

sion, they are dispatched by God over all the earth, symbolizing that his sovereignty is worldwide. This is explicitly stated in the oracle of the Lord in verse 8: God's Spirit is at rest in the north country; nothing further needs to be done before the Lord can bring in his Kingdom.

No chariot goes toward the east (v.6), but everything necessary is said in verse 8. The "north" in the Old Testament frequently represents all evil and all the enemies of God (cf. 2:6), probably because not only most of Israel's enemies came out of the north but also because the pagan gods of the Canaanites— Israel's most frequent temptations to apostasy—were believed to dwell on a sacred mountain in the north. There, all that was evil and sinister lurked, and when Zechariah heard that God's Spirit had been set at rest in the north country and no longer needed to be at work, he knew that the preparations for the new age were now complete. Evil had been conquered. All the earth could now receive the true peace that comes only when God's rule is acknowledged.

That this remains a vision of the future in Zechariah's time is shown by the report of the prophetic symbolic action that follows in verses 9–15. Nevertheless, the prophet knows that the blessedness promised in the vision will surely come, and that is the promise of comfort and hope that he proclaims to his struggling compatriots.

A Prophetic Symbolic Action (6:9–15)

In this conclusion to the second section of his book (3:1— 6:15), dealing with the governance of the new people of God in the new age, Zechariah is commanded to perform a prophetic symbolic action. Reports of such actions are found throughout the writings of the prophets, and they are to be interpreted in the same manner that we interpret prophetic words from God. That is, both prophetic actions and words begin an action of God within Israel's life. That which is spoken or symbolized is at the same time set in motion, and it works its effects in Israel's history until it is fully fulfilled. We are therefore dealing in this section, as in the others, with that about which Zechariah is absolutely sure; and he once again stakes the validity of his prophetic calling on the fulfillment of this sign (v. 15; cf. 2:9, 11; 4:9; Deut. 18:21–22).

The prophet is commanded to gather three witnesses from among recent returnees from Babylonian exile and to go with

130

them to the house of Josiah, who was perhaps a metal-worker but who also could serve as a fourth witness to the prophet's act. (The law required only two; Deut. 17:6; cf. II Cor. 13:1.) In Josiah's house, the prophet takes some of the silver and gold that the returnees have brought as gifts from the Persians (cf. Ezra 7:14–16; 8:26–30) and these are fashioned into a double-ringed crown.

There follows the most solemn ceremony. The company proceeds to Joshua the high priest. Joshua is symbolically crowned with the double-ringed royal tiara, and Zechariah pronounces a five-part oracle over him:

1) "Behold, the man whose name is the Branch:" This is clearly a promissory reference to the coming of the Davidic king or Messiah in the new age (cf. 3:8; Jer. 23:5; 33:15; Isa. 4:2; 11:1).

2) ". . . he shall grow up in his place, ..." That is, the Messiah (the anointed one or *mašiah*) will come from Israel and be elevated from among his own people (cf. II Sam. 23:1; Pss. 78:70–71; 89:19).

3) ". . . he shall build the temple of the Lord." While Zerubbabel will complete the temple in the sixth century B.C. (4:9; cf. Ezra 5:1–2; 6:14–15), that transformed and glorious place of worship at which the prophet hinted in 4:7–10 and which belongs to the new age that is coming will be built by God's chosen Messiah. Moreover, all nations, Gentiles as well as Jews, will be engaged in its construction (v. 15; cf. 2:11). The true temple, in which God will abide in the midst of his people for all time (cf. Ezek. 37:26–28; Rev. 21:3) remains a future reality.

4) "(He) shall sit and rule upon his throne." The Messiah, not Persia or any other master, will be ruler in the new age of the Kingdom (cf. Ezek. 37:24–25). God's regent, God's mandator over all the earth, will exercise his authority with the power of the Lord himself (cf. Pss. 2; 72:8–11; 110:2).

5) "And there shall be a priest by his throne, . . ." This is the most difficult part of the oracle. The Revised Standard Version, the Septuagint, and many commentators interpret this to mean that the high priest will assist the Messiah with his rule, that all ancient rivalry between throne and priesthood will be overcome, and that the two rulers together will know how to bring abundant life to the people.

However, the common Hebrew construction is probably better read, "And there shall be a priest *upon* his throne," and

131

this furnishes the proper meaning. In every other part of this oracle, Zechariah has set forth traditional understandings of the Messiah; and as we know from a royal psalm, the ideal Davidic anointed was also expected to exercise an eternal priesthood (see Ps. 110:4). Zechariah therefore envisions here the combining of the offices of Messiah and high priest in one wise counselor who will bring forth *shalom* to all peoples. The seven-faceted stone connected with the Branch, in 3:8–9, will be a jewel worn on the headdress of this priest-king, whose mediation will remove the iniquity of Judah in a single day.

After this symbolic ceremony, in which Joshua only stands in for the coming Branch, the crown is removed from his head and is set aside, to be placed in the rebuilt temple as a reminder of the new age of the Messiah that is coming. There the crown remains—in 515 B.C. when the temple building is completed and through four long centuries that follow. Its silver and gold glitter in the light of the candlelabra, piercing the shadows of the Holy Place, but the identity of the one who will wear it remains unknown. No one comes forward to don it. No one can rightly claim it. Though there are pretenders to its lustre, Israel waits and waits to crown her true King. Of each one who presents himself, she anxiously asks, "Are you he who is to come, or shall we look for another" (Matt. 11:3)? The crown cannot be worn "until he comes whose right it is" (Ezek. 21:27). It rests there in the temple—unused, unclaimed—until God keeps his word to his prophet.

Moreover, Zechariah's promise of the coming of the Messiah has a condition attached to it here: ". . . this shall come to pass, if you will diligently obey the voice of the Lord your God." These words are addressed to Joshua, and this section on the governance of the new people of God begins (3:6–7) and ends with the admonition to Israel's leaders to be faithful to the covenant law, which at its heart required, above all else, love for God and total dependence on him (cf. Deut. 6:4–9; 10: 12–22). The prophet rightly sees that the life of a people is largely determined by the faith of its leaders (cf. Hos. 4:4–6), a view consistent with that of the Deuteronomists from whose traditions Zechariah so frequently draws. He therefore charges the ruling priesthood to cultivate that faithful obedience that will prepare the Israelites' hearts to receive their Deliverer.

In the years that followed, the popular tradition grew up that Messiah would come if Israel for even a few brief moments

132

could perfectly fulfill the law. And priestly Sadducees and faithful Pharisees and those who looked for this promised redemption of Israel (cf. Luke 2:25, 37–38; 23:51; 24:21) strained heart and mind and strength to observe the last jot and tittle of the law and to cleave to their God with all their being.

We should not despise such efforts. God's deliverance comes only to those whose hearts are open to receive it. We sing that at every Christmas season: "Where meek souls will receive him, still the dear Christ enters in." Lacking such open hearts, we end up crucifying the Lord of glory.

But Israel's own efforts fully to keep the law led her into pride and formalism and endless legalism (cf. Matt. 23). God therefore had to raise up in Israel that One who could, by the power of the Spirit at work in him, perfectly fulfill all righteousness (cf. Matt. 3:13–17); that One who could become the obedient Son that Israel had been intended to be (Matt. 2:15; 4:1–11) —that One who could perfectly fulfill the law of God by steadfastly loving and clinging to the Father (cf. Matt. 5:17–20). Indeed, to change the New Testament references, there had to come that high priest after the order of Melchizedek "who in every respect" was "tempted as we are, yet without sinning" (Heb. 4:15). He rendered to God on Israel's and our behalf that perfect faithfulness that we can never give and so removed our sin on the day of his victory and prepared us to receive God's deliverance.

At the same time, he came preaching that the Kingdom of God had broken into human life in his person (Mark 1:14–15; Luke 11:20), and at his death even Pontius Pilate had finally to acknowledge that he was Israel's awaited King (John 19:19–22). When he was raised three days later from the dead, his followers also understood: This crucified One had been exalted and had become the Messiah (Acts 2:36) who could bring abundant life to all peoples.

Moreover, he now builds the true temple of God from those of every nation (cf. Eph. 2:17–22; I Cor. 3:16–17; II Cor. 6:16); and thus, though Zerubbabel's temple has been destroyed, the crown that Joshua deposited in it has endured. In some Christian churches, the replica of it is symbolically suspended or emblazoned above the altar table as sign of the fact that the crown now rests on the head of Jesus Christ.

133

Zechariah 7:1—8:23

A Prophetic Torah (7:1–14)

Zechariah now turns in this third and final section of his book to the implications of the coming of the new age for Judah's life in the meantime. The immediate occasion for these prophecies is the arrival in Jerusalem on December 7, 518 B.C., of a delegation from the northern city of Bethel. The delegates are returnees from Babylonian exile (cf. Ezra 2:1, 28), and Regemmelech's name *(friend of the king)* may indicate that he was a high-placed Persian who converted to Judaism.

The delegation has come to Jerusalem not only to offer sacrifices and to worship in the temple (entreat, v. 2; cf. Mal. 1:9) but also to ask a *torah (teaching, instruction, direction)* from a priest or prophet. Since Jerusalem fell to the Babylonians in 587 B.C., the Israelites have been observing, first in Babylonia and now in Palestine, four yearly fasts (cf. 8:19): (1) on the ninth day of the fourth month, commemorating the breaching of the city's walls (Jer. 39:2); (2) on the seventh day of the fifth month, remembering the destruction of the temple (II Kings 25:8); (3) in the seventh month, marking the murder of the governor, Gedaliah (II Kings 25:25; Jer. 41:1–2); and (4) on the tenth day of the tenth month, commemorating the beginning of the siege of Jerusalem (II Kings 25:1–2; Jer. 39:1). But now the temple is being rebuilt, and it no longer seems appropriate to remember its destruction. Should the fast of the fifth month, which the Israelites have held for over sixty years, be continued? Since worship practices in Israel were legislated by God, the answer must be sought from God through an oracular *torah.*

This concern of the delegation is narrow and specific, but the Lord has broader and deeper concerns. His forgiveness and comfort and saving presence are going to be given to his people. The pressing question which the Jews should be asking therefore is, What should they be doing in the meantime? How should a person live when he or she knows that the Kingdom of God is coming?

134

Biblical faith is always oriented toward the future. Its gaze lifts up from the sufferings of the present to see the glory breaking over the distant horizon (cf. Rom. 8:18). Its immediate circumstances are always understood in the context of God's future. But that does not mean that biblical faith is otherworldly, caring nothing for this life. Unlike every other nonbiblical religion, the Judaic-Christian faith sees salvation to consist, not in an escape from this world, but in a transformation of it. No other religion is so concerned with the everyday decisions and actions of human beings. No other religion so squarely faces and deals with evil and suffering and death in human existence.

God's Kingdom comes. And precisely because that is true, the people of God have tasks to do. They are to live in the light of that coming. They are to cast aside their despair and live in certain hope, to forego their resigned inactivity and make preparations to receive their Lord (cf. 8:9, 13), to reform their indifferent morals and fit themselves to live with God. That is why this third section of I Zechariah turns to those ethical admonitions so reminiscent of earlier prophetic and Deuteronomic literature (7:8–10; 8:16–17).

Zechariah's prophetic predecessors used ethical teaching in two ways: first, to call the people to repent, lest the Lord should come in judgment (e.g., cf. Isa. 1:16–20); second, to indict the people for the sin for which the Lord was in fact coming in judgment (e.g., cf. Isa. 1:21–25). Now, according to Zechariah, the judgment has taken place (7:12–14; cf. 1:4–6; 8:10, 13; Hag. 1:5–6); and the Lord is returning to his people in mercy and forgiveness and jealous love (8:1; cf. 1:14). In the light of that final coming, Zechariah teaches ethics.

Zechariah goes right to the heart of the matter, drawing on the traditions of Isaiah and Jeremiah. Instead of replying directly to the delegation's question about the fast of the fifth month, he teaches that external religious observances are useless if the relationship with God has been lost (vv. 5–6; cf. Isa. 58). God takes no notice of piety that does not issue out of a listening and obedient heart (vv. 8–12; cf. Jer. 5:3, 21; 7:26; 8:5; 11:10; 17:1, 23). As had Third Isaiah (65:1, 12), he points out that the Lord was ready to answer a sincere people, but that they had not truly turned to him (v. 13). Therefore, they were sent into exile (v. 14)—a reiteration of the lesson the prophet gave in his initial oracle (1:1–6).

135

Now, however, through the mercy of God the Israelites have another chance. Their Lord is returning to do them good (cf. 8:15). But his commandments to love him and their neighbors still stand. God's grace never removes the demand for true worship and hearty obedience (cf. Mark 12:28–31 and par.), but it does give to the people new motive and power for complying with that demand. Now the Israelites are to love God and their fellows, not *in order* that God will bring his salvation to them, but *because* God is in fact bringing that salvation. Surely the grateful response of God's people to such deliverance can only be overflowing love for their Lord and faithful obedience to his word. That response is what Zechariah seeks to prompt by his preaching.

A Series of Oracles (8:1–8)

Zechariah is a man intoxicated with the vision of the coming Kingdom. He therefore quickly leaves behind the ethical exhortations of 7:1–14 to rhapsodize once more over what God is going to do for his people. If Israel can be made to see what Zechariah has seen in his visions, then they will respond with that obedient love appropriate to life under God's rule.

Much in this series of brief salvation oracles has already been said, but there are also some new announcements. First, Zechariah proclaims what life will be like in the coming Kingdom and what we need do to enter into it, and the picture he presents is one of the most profound and poetic to be found in the Old Testament. The Kingdom of God, says verses 4–5, will be like a public park, where the elderly can sit together and talk and bask in the sun, and little children can play in contentment and safety with nothing to threaten them—no pervert lurking in the shadows to lure one of them away with candy; no drug dealer waiting to peddle his poison to innocents; no child bruised or warped by abusive parents or stunted by poor nutrition or inadequate education; not even a bully among the group to terrorize the younger and weaker.

Children peacefully at play in a park—of such is the Kingdom of God! The picture explodes all our mythology and other-worldly misconceptions of the Kingdom as an ethereal never-never land, divorced from earthy realities. This is a picture of this world made new by the coming of God—its goodness confirmed and restored to that wholeness that its Creator intended for it from the beginning (cf. Gen. 1:31).

136

The Bible, throughout, pictures that goodness for us in terms of a little child: "Let the children come to me, and do not hinder them," Jesus said, "for to such belongs the kingdom of heaven" (Matt. 19:14). The Kingdom a playground for children! —and unless we turn and become like children in our humility, we will never enter into it (Matt. 18:3–4). There the child "shall play over the hole of the asp, and the weaned child shall put his hand on the adder's den" (Isa. 11:8)—the serpent of our sinfulness (Gen. 3:15) turned to harmlessness and a plaything for children!

The little child leads us (Isa. 11:6) in the Bible's conceptions of God's future; and when we think to join cause with God's purpose for his earth, we need ask ourselves if we are constructing a place where little children may play. Perhaps Prime Minister Golda Meier fleetingly caught that vision when she welcomed Anwar Sadat of Egypt on his historic peace-mission to Israel, not with the silver bowl or other art object so often exchanged between heads of state but with a simple present for his grandchildren.

God's Kingdom will not have come on this earth until its streets are fit for its children. But by the same token, it will not have come until its children are fit for its streets. Zechariah has given us a standard here for all our planned utopias, and set up against a little child, none of them measures up. But there came a child—there came God's child—who was fit for the Kingdom. And because he came, God's playground for all children surely comes.

Three Oracles (8:9–19)

Three salvation oracles follow Zechariah's magnificent vision of life in the Kingdom of God, and all of them add further promises. Originally, each was a separate pronouncement, but all have the same theme: the description of how Israel is to live because the Kingdom of God is coming (see also 7:1–14). "Cling to the promises!" is their cry, "Live in the light of their advent!" The prophet vividly describes God's promised future.

First, paralleling the preaching of his contemporary Haggai (see Hag. 1:1–11; 2:15–19), Zechariah announces that the covenant curses (v. 10; cf. 1:4; Deut. 28:15–68; Lev. 26:14–39) God laid upon Israel for her faithlessness to the covenant relation will be replaced with blessings. The results will be immediate. The drought and crop failures and famine that the Israelites

137

have suffered at the hands of God will no longer occur. Instead, God will send the dew and the rain, and the earth will bear a bountiful harvest—the result of "peace" with God (v. 12; cf. Hos. 2:21–23).

Most of us in the twentieth century do not believe that God has anything to do with the processes of nature. We have a totally secularized worldview in which our universe is a closed system, operating according to natural laws, unaffected by the power and actions of its Creator and Sustainer. But Old and New Testaments alike give a different witness which we should not simply attribute to pre-scientific thinking. God is Lord of nature as well as of history. He alone sustains nature in its course, and he makes it serve his sovereign will. It can therefore be an instrument of his judgment or of his blessing.

This does not mean that every natural phenomenon is a clear witness of God's grace or wrath. We no longer have the prophets of biblical times who made that witness clear. But it does mean that we should view the natural world as a whole in the context of our relation with God and always ask ourselves how we stand with our Lord and what he may be doing about it. Zechariah is quite sure of the answer: The Lord of nature who judged his people will now, in forgiveness, shower them with blessing.

The response of the Israelites to that mercy should therefore be rededication to the work of rebuilding the temple. Zechariah and Haggai, and perhaps other prophets as well, have continually urged on the work in the face of great difficulties (v. 10) ever since the foundation was laid on September 21, 520 B.C. (v. 9). Now once again, Zechariah exhorts, "Let your hands be strong!" (vv. 9 and 13, which bracket the oracle). But he exhorts his countrymen, not because the temple's completion will insure that God's blessings will come, but because a house worthy of God's dwelling in their midst will be a proper response of gratitude to his promised mercy toward them. "Cling to the promises, and respond to them!"—that is the theme.

Second, Zechariah assures his compatriots that God will keep his word (v. 11; see also 1:7–17). At the beginning of Israel's history, when God first called Abram out of Haran in Mesopotamia, he made the patriarch a promise: ". . . in you all the families of the earth shall be blessed" (RSV margin, Gen. 12:3). Through Abraham and his descendants, the curses of death and drudgery, of pain and slavery, of broken family and

lost community so vividly portrayed in the stories of Genesis 3
—11 would be done away and replaced by God's blessings of
abundant life, equitable and meaningful and whole. Israel was
to have been the mediator of that promised blessing. By trusting her God, who would bring all peoples into her righteous
fellowship, she would become the cornerstone of a universal
community under God. But Israel did not trust God, and so,
instead of being a mediator of the Lord's blessing upon the
earth, she became a "byword of cursing" (v. 13) and peoples
swore against one another, "May you be cursed as Israel was
cursed by her God!"

God never fails to keep his word, however, and the promise
to Abraham still stands (cf. Isa. 40:8). Therefore, despite her
rebellions against her Lord and her present feebleness of faith,
God will bring his word to fulfillment by making Israel a me-
dium of blessing for all the families of earth.

In other words, the struggling sixth century B.C. Judean
community is told that its life and labors have meaning far
beyond their immediate results—that they have a universal
effect, influencing the course of every nation's history. Judah's
work, its sufferings, its defeats and triumphs are not in vain, but
will be used by God to complete his purpose for all humankind
(cf. I Cor. 15:58; I Thess. 3:5; cf. II Chron. 15:7, which echoes
Zech. 8:9–13 and Jer. 31:16).

No reassurance is more needed by human beings. To know
that our labors will bear fruit, that our lives serve some larger
purpose, that their good does not just trickle out and become
lost in the sands of time or the smelly bogs of evil—that knowledge gives reason and purpose and joy to living. So Zechariah
can end his proclamation with the exhortation: "Fear not! Let
your hands be strong" (v. 13)! In short, "Do not fear futility!
Cling to the promise!"

Further, verses 14–17 point out that God purposed evil
against the Judeans in the past for their sins against him and did
not turn from that purpose until it had found its fulfillment in
the judgment of the Babylonian exile (cf. 1:6). God's purpose
never remains simply inner desire or intention on his part; it is
always worked out in resulting events. But if God turns from
anger against us and announces, as he here announces through
Zechariah, that he is coming to do us nothing but good (v. 15;
cf. Jer. 31:28), the response of faith therefore is a glad clinging
to his commandments in preparation for his coming.

139

God hates quite specific sins. He hates lies and deceit, guile and smooth talk that mask an inner selfishness or fear that bend the truth to one's own purposes, that make the spoken word unreliable and break the trust so necessary for community, that deny that human beings are members one of another (v. 16; cf. Jer. 9:5; Micah 6:12; Eph. 4:25; James 3:6–12). Only those can truly worship God who speak the truth from their hearts (cf. Ps. 15:2).

Then, too, God hates corruption of the structures of justice. (The reference of v. 16 is to the lay courts, held in the plazas of village or city gates by the elders of the community.) Human communities cannot exist without common agreement, written or unwritten, about the behavior acceptable within them. But Israel's legal structure was unique. Her laws were given her by God and intended to establish her as a community of equity and peace into which God could draw all peoples of the earth. To corrupt Israel's court procedures was therefore to corrupt God's purpose for his world, and the prophets of Israel emphasized the sanctity of her justice and the necessity of keeping it unstained by human corruption.

Keep your heart true! (v. 17; cf. 7:10)—Zechariah focuses on the center of morality, "For out of the heart comes evil thoughts, murder, adultery, fornication, theft, false witness, slander" (Matt. 15:19). The inner disposition determines the outer action, and if the heart is turned against a neighbor or loves not God but falsehood (cf. 5:3–4), the inner disposition of the heart will corrupt the outer action. Persons of faith are never sinless, but they do long to do the will of God (cf. Ps. 51); they want to do the right; their motivation is sound; their attention is directed toward God and not toward themselves or evil. They do not rejoice at wrong, but rejoice in the right (I Cor. 13:6); and they desire to do the right with all their heart and soul and might. Above all else, they do not wish to grieve their Lord (cf. Eph. 4:30), and they long after fellowship with him "as a hart longs for flowing streams" (Ps. 42:1; cf. Pss. 73:25; 84:1–2).

This is the behavior that Zechariah seeks to inspire in his compatriots by setting forth God's promise: "I [have] purposed in these days to do good to Jerusalem and to the house of Judah (v. 14)." Therefore, respond in love to that love is the message of the prophet. Love neighbor and God with true hearts because God has first loved you (cf. I John 4:19).

Finally, in verses 18–19, Zechariah turns to that question of the delegation from Bethel (7:3) which prompted this series of salvation oracles; and his oracular answer to their inquiry is presupposed: "No." They should not keep the fast of the fifth month commemorating the destruction of the temple. Neither should they observe the other three fasts that remember Jerusalem's fall, for their past sorrows will be forgotten and their fasts replaced by cheerful feasts, full of that revelry and joy appropriate to a rescued people (cf. Jer. 31:10–14).

As in the two preceding oracles, God's gift of salvation is, however, to call forth a response from Judah. God comes to change her despair for delight, her suffering for singing, her poverty for plenty, her ruin for restoration, her abandonment for his abiding presence. Therefore! "Therefore," exhorts the prophet, "love truth and peace" (v. 19)! God's love requires a response, not of duty but of love, flowing out of hearts overwhelmed with the experience of his mercy. "Love so amazing, so divine, demands my life, my love, my all."

Three further points should be noted. First, Zechariah has now left behind completely that conditional proclamation of salvation with which he began his preaching. His first words were, "Return to me, says the Lord of hosts, and I will return to you, says the Lord of hosts" (1:3). But in these oracles of the third section, we do not find a God who waits for his people to repent before he comes to them. Zechariah's God—the same God who is found throughout the pages of Scripture—takes the initiative. He comes "with healing in his wings" (Mal. 4:2) before his people repent and turn, before they deserve his salvation, before they have earned his love (cf. Rom. 5:8). God promises undeserved redemption, and it is to such grace that Judah and Jerusalem are asked to respond.

Second, the love with which Israel is asked to respond to the unmerited love of God is to be acted out in the love of neighbor. This God, it seems, is always giving away that which belongs to him. "If you want to love me," he says, "then love your neighbor in my place." ". . . as you did it to one of the least of these my brethren, you did it to me" (Matt. 25:40).

This leads directly into the third point: God's love requires the response of love for neighbor because God's final purpose for his world is to make a new community. This was his purpose in Israel, as it is also his purpose in the church. I Zechariah

141

begins (1:6) and ends (8:15) with concern for that purpose; and as we shall see in the following, concluding oracle, Zechariah envisions that purpose fulfilled.

Concluding Oracle (8:20–23)

Zechariah now lifts up his eyes from Judah's immediate circumstances ("in these days," vv. 9, 15) to envision the outcome of the people's faith and work ("in those days," v. 23), and his is a universal vision (cf. 2:11; 8:13).

God's kingdom on earth is coming not to the Jews alone. To be sure, Zechariah, like the prophets before him, understands Jerusalem to be the center of the earth (v. 22). But Jerusalem and Judah serve a divine purpose that encompasses all nations. God wishes to establish on earth a new community—that is the goal of God's action in history—a community in which human divisions and hatreds have been overcome, in which family relations have been restored and work has again become meaningful, in which peoples can understand one another and dwell together in peace, in which human beings live in harmony with the natural world and partake of its bounty and beauty (cf. Gen. 3–11), in which God and his creatures are bound together in an unbreakable covenant of love. God intends to establish that community, moreover, by creating it first within Israel and then by drawing all peoples into her covenant fellowship. Israel does not exist for her own sake. She is loved by God because he wishes to bestow his love on all peoples through her. She will be blessed by God because he wishes to pour out his blessing on all humankind by means of her (cf. Gen. 12:3; Zech. 8:13).

How, then, will God draw all peoples into Israel's covenant community? This oracle answers that question. When other races and nationalities ("peoples," v. 20) see the new life of Israel—when they see wholeness and peace within her community, when they see her "seasons of joy and gladness" (v. 19), her fertile fields (v. 12), her children at play in her squares (v. 5), her population restored (v. 7), and her temple rebuilt as a dwelling place for her God (vv. 9–13)—then they will know that her God is truly God, because he has power to do such wonders and in mercy has accomplished them.

142

Nowhere in the Old Testament is there an active missionary enterprise involved in Israel's witness to the world, not even in the Book of Jonah, which has other purposes. In this respect, the Old Testament differs radically from the New. Rather,

Israel's lure to the nations is the salvation wrought in her by the power and compassion of her God. Her new life, shining like a beacon in the darkness of the nations, will draw all peoples to her Lord.

Indeed, Zechariah here envisions foreign peoples urgently spreading the news of what God has done in Israel (v. 21). One has heard and urges others to go with him to worship ("entreat") in the temple and to "seek" God's presence—gentiles turned missionaries! Ten foreigners grasp the sleeve of one Jew (the term is used to distinguish Israelites from other nationals for the first time in Jer. 34:9, for the second time here, and then frequently in Ezra-Nehemiah) and ask to accompany him on his pilgrimage to Jerusalem, so that the number of travelers to the holy city swells into thousands: The number "ten" signifies completeness, the fullness of the covenant community.

When all peoples are thus drawn to Mount Zion to join Israel in her worship and service of her Lord, God's rule over all the earth will have been acknowledged and all the families of the earth will partake of that new and abundant life which God will give to his covenant people. Then peoples "shall beat their swords into plowshares, and their spears into pruning hooks" (Isa. 2:4); then "the earth shall be full of the knowledge of the Lord as the waters cover the sea" (Isa. 11:9). The Kingdom of God will have come on earth even as it is in heaven.

To that end and for the accomplishment of that divine purpose Israel has been called "from the ends of the earth" (Isa. 41:9) and will be forgiven and re-elected and given that new life by her God which Zechariah has so vividly set before her eyes. Until the Kingdom comes, she therefore is to live for that purpose and structure her society and prepare her heart to foster and to receive its completion.

Any Christian interpreter of this passage cannot help but note the similarity of Israel's role in Zechariah with that of the Suffering Servant in Second Isaiah. It is when the Servant Israel is saved and exalted and lifted up, in Isaiah 52:13—53:12, that he prompts all nations to confess that God has acted in Israel for their sake and is therefore God alone. That in turn leads the interpreter to concentrate on the final Suffering Servant who, in the Gospel according to John, proclaims, "I, when I am lifted up from the earth, will draw all men to myself" (John 12:32). Jesus Christ has become that true Israel (cf. John 15:1), promised by Zechariah, who draws all peoples to him.

143

Further, the Christian church is the body of Christ, and we need always remember that it is by the exaltation of Jesus Christ in us that God will convert the world. God is with us as he was with Israel (v. 23)—for us, in the person and Spirit of his Son (John 14:16–20). Only if we hold up Emmanuel (Matt. 1:23) and manifest his transforming presence in our fellowship will nations be drawn to our light (cf. Matt. 5:14–16). People will not say, "We will go with you because you are the friendliest church in town" or "you run a progressive Sunday school" or "you have a marvelous choir" or "your preacher is a regular fellow" or "you are pushing the best liberal programs in society." They will come only when they have heard that God is with us in Jesus Christ.

Paul wrote, ". . . how are they to hear without a preacher" (Rom. 10:14)? The church's good news, that God has come to us in his Son and triumphed over sin and death and given us the power to walk in newness of life, must be proclaimed throughout the world. This final oracle of Zechariah's reminds us what we must preach: God with us in Jesus Christ our Lord.

This final sermon by the prophet also reminds us how we must live: as the new covenant people whose lives have been transformed by the mercy and power of God with them.

God with us, in his Son—that is all we have to offer. But it is enough to convert and save the world.

II Zechariah

CHAPTERS 9—11

Introduction to Chapters 9—11; 12—14

As we have seen in the introduction to Zechariah (chapters 1
—8), chapters 9—11 and 12—14 are later additions to that first
corpus, have long been regarded by scholars as separate works,
and have been given the titles of II Zechariah and III Zechariah.
As to the dates of these later additions, however, no one pro-
posal has ever solved all of the problems connected with them,
and it is probably correct to conclude that we cannot pinpoint
their historical references. Rather, we are dealing in these collections with traditional materials from Israel's theology. Actual
events once lay behind such traditions, but such events have
become obscured and lost as the traditions have been passed on
and the historical background of the traditions can no longer be
recovered.

The proper questions to be asked about II—III Zechariah,
therefore, are, Why were these materials added to I Zechariah
and When were they added and by whom? Among these questions, the first is by far the most important: What function do
these additions now serve in the Book of Zechariah?

I Zechariah announced to his struggling countrymen the
certain and effortless coming of the Kingdom of God. God's
opponents will be defeated without a struggle, according to
Zechariah 1—8, and evil banished from the earth. But Israel
knew and Zechariah's compatriots knew and we know, as does
the New Testament, that the coming of the Kingdom of God on
earth is not an easy triumph. Evil is too woven into the fabric
of human society to be easily disentangled. For this reason, the
apocalypticism of the Bible, in Daniel, Revelation, Mark 13,
Matthew 24, and Luke 21, portray God throwing away the
garment of the world, as it were, and just starting over. Evil is
banished from the old world by the creation of new heavens
and a new earth. 145

The Book of Zechariah, as a whole, however, is not apocalyptic. The Kingdom comes on this earth, which has been trans-

formed by the power of God. It therefore is the function of II—III Zechariah to remind the people of God in every age that the coming victory of the Lord will be achieved only through the suffering of the faithful and the war of the Lord against evil. Human sin has real power to resist God's purposes. That is the sobering message of II—III Zechariah; and because chapters 9 —14 have been added to I Zechariah, they bestow upon it a certain realism. The initial vision of Zechariah is tempered in down-to-earth fashion by the struggles pictured in its later chapters, just as in the New Testament the announcement of the arrival of the Kingdom in the person of Jesus of Nazareth is tempered by the cross.

As to who added chapters 9—14 to Zechariah 1—8 and when, there is no reason to assign them to a period other than the last half of the sixth century B.C. The authors of chapters 9 —14—and there are several authors—probably belong to that community of reform prophets reflected in Third Isaiah, who favored Isaian and Jeremian-Deuteronomic-Levitical tradition (see the Introduction to I Zech.). There are therefore many parallels between Zechariah 9—11 and the prophecies of Jeremiah, just as many Isaian traditions are also preserved in II—III Zechariah.

These are not supporters of the Zadokite priestly party, nor have they been in exile, as was the author of I Zechariah. These are members of the prophetic reform group who remained in the land during the time of exile and who fought the battle of purifying Israelite religious life and leadership after the return of the exiles to Jerusalem and Judah.

Some of the oracles found in II—III Zechariah may therefore actually pre-date by a few years the prophecies of I Zechariah, but they have been placed in their present position by an editor. Originally they were intended to remind the community of its continuing sin, but now they testify to the fact that the Kingdom's coming is frought with the desperate struggles occasioned by that sin.

Zechariah 9:1–17

I Zechariah announced that God would destroy the enemies of Israel (1:18–21; 2:9; 6:1–8). This chapter now pictures that destruction, but it does so using traditional terminology borrowed from earlier historians and prophets. The conquest of the cities to the north of Palestine (vv. 1–4) gives to the Jews the borders of the ideal kingdom surpassing even that of David. The conquest of Philistia and its cities (vv. 5–6) subdues people traditionally named as enemies in the preaching of the prophets. Indeed, even the reference in verse 13 to "Greece" is a traditional symbol for unknown peoples on the edge of civilization. These are not historical battles pictured here, but the final battle preceding the coming of the Kingdom to Jerusalem, when Israel's age-old enemies—and all enemies—are subdued by the Lord.

As in the traditions of Isaiah and of I Zechariah (see the comment on Zech. 2:11 and 8:20–23), some of those conquered enemies will be incorporated into Israel to form a universal people of God on earth (v. 7). The guard for his people will be none other than the Lord himself (v. 8; cf. Zech. 2:5), who will so strengthen them that they will be like invincible weapons in his hand, never again to be attacked by foreign nations.

In this connection, the Revised Standard Version of verse 15 is incorrect. There is no battle pictured in that verse, but rather it depicts the victory celebration after the battle that was portrayed in verses 1–8. The verse should therefore read: "The Lord of hosts will be a shield over them/ and they shall eat (the victory banquet), and they shall tread over the stones of slinging (which are no longer needed in battle)/ And they shall drink, they shall be noisy as with wine/ and they shall be full like a bowl, drenched like the corners of the altar." The bloody conflict that the Revised Standard rendering of verse 15 yields would be quite incongruous with the coming of the messianic peace portrayed in verses 9–10. From verse 9 on, the Kingdom of God is portrayed as having come on this earth, and "how good and how fair it shall be" (v. 17)!

147

God the Divine Warrior (9:1–8, 11–17)

The God who is depicted coming to join his people in their victory celebration, chapter 9, is a warrior God, and perhaps especially in our time we need to ask what to make of such a witness to God. Faced as we are with the constant threat of nuclear annihilation we shun such militaristic language, and the horror of war is incompatible in our minds with the personhood of God.

God is, however, throughout the Bible described as a Divine Warrior. From the time of the Exodus on, "The Lord is a man of war; the Lord is his name" (Exod. 15:3; cf. 14:14), and it is as the Divine Warrior that he conquers the promised land for his people (cf. Josh. 3:10–11; 5:13–14) and defends them from their enemies in the time of the Judges (cf. Judg. 5:4–5, 19–21) and of the early monarchy (I Sam. 5). Faced with the apostasy and injustice of Israel herself in the time of the monarchy, however, God turns to fight against his own people, according to the prophets (cf. Jer. 4 or Ezek. 13); and it is not until Second Isaiah announces that Israel's "warfare is ended" (Isa. 40:2) that God ceases his onslaught against his people. Then in Second and Third Isaiah (cf. Isa. 42:10–13; 59:15–20), he arms himself once more to put down his enemies and to bring in his kingdom among the faithful. This language is then picked up by the New Testament (cf. Mark 13:24–27) and culminates in the final battle of Armageddon (Rev. 16–19). The life of the Christian is therefore described in the New Testament as participation in God's battle (cf. Eph. 6:10–17), and the church militant in every age has waged God's warfare against evil.

What is being said with such language? First of all, the biblical faith is testifying to the fact that on the stage of human history, where force of arms has always determined the ownership of wealth and territory and the power of authority, God's is the supreme force, the final ownership, and the ultimate authority. In general terms we might say in our day that the threat of nuclear holocaust is as nothing before the might of God; but the Bible is very specific: The war chariots and swords of the Egyptians or Assyrians or Babylonians or Persians are as nothing before the hosts or armies of the Lord. We may object to such language and refuse to use it, but the witness to God which it conveys is not to be discarded. If God has no power against the principalities and powers of this world, he cannot fulfill his purpose of love. Love without power is ineffective in a world such as ours, and the marvelous fact is that God is both supreme power and supreme love. If that be not true, then there is no hope for our evil history.

Second, the Bible is testifying to the fact that evil must be actively resisted and done away. It does not disappear by itself. Hitlers must be made to cease their holocausts; civil rights must be guaranteed with the force of law. Someone has got to break the swords and fashion the spears into pruning hooks. But by testifying that God is the Divine Warrior, the Bible is saying that the ultimate destruction of evil belongs to him.

There are a few causes in society where good and evil are clearly distinguishable, and there are times when the Christian must take a stand and actively work against the forces of wrong. There are even times when sincere Christians have believed that they must take up weapons. Writing in 1971 of the struggle of Africans against their white overlords, Colin Morris expressed such belief:

> ... there are certain situations where the only hinge that moves great weights is force. And insofar as Christians wish to identify themselves with freedom struggles in Africa, Asia, and Latin America, this is one nettle they will have to grasp.... Violence, to put it in Dantean terms, may well not establish a Paradise, but it can destroy an Inferno ... Christians ... have an obligation to formulate a theology of violence which will lay down the conditions under which its use is permissible (pp. 38–39).

Precisely "the conditions" under which the use of violence is "permissible" are dealt with by the biblical testimony to God as the Divine Warrior, because it recognizes that we human beings err terribly in our decisions about those conditions. How many have been slaughtered with the sword of some so-called religious crusade! And the use of the language of warfare with reference to God points to him as the final judge of good and evil. Thus, far from promoting our warring tendencies, the biblical typology of the Divine Warrior is designed to lay a check upon them (cf. Matt. 13:24–30). God is ultimate judge and destroyer of all evil, and while that does not solve all the problems, it cautions us about our positions concerning them.

The comfort which this chapter of II Zechariah offers the struggling sixth century B.C. province of Judah, therefore, is based entirely on faith in the actions of God; and it is for that reason that the inhabitants of Judah—and indeed, all Israel—

149

are called "prisoners of hope" (v. 12). They dwell as those in a "waterless pit," which is a symbol of sheol or death in the Old Testament. But God remembers his covenant at Sinai with them (v. 11), sealed by the blood of the sacrifice. He therefore promises that he will set them free from all that threatens their life (v. 11) and restore to them a double prosperity (v. 12). In God's actions, Israel has her comfort and promise; he is her "stronghold" against the forces of evil and death and her "hope."

In similar fashion, Christ is the Christian's "hope," and Christians struggling with the vicissitudes and evils of our present world are "prisoners of hope."

That is very different from being prisoners of despair, who rely on themselves and their own feeble efforts to find security and joy, and who find to their sorrow that the night comes and that there is nothing to be done about it. But that is also different from being prisoners of optimism, who do not recognize the presence of evil and death in the world, and who learn too late that human history does not automatically evolve ever upward.

"Return to your stronghold, O prisoners of hope!" Israel is bidden by II Zechariah to put her trust in the promises of God because it is the fulfillment of those promises that will give the future its shape. What God has pledged will come to pass. That is the nature of his providence. His sovereign will works in and through and under the events of human history and uses and shapes them to his purpose. His faithfulness will not fail, nor his love languish, but will bring Israel's life to his desired outcome.

The Coming of the Messianic King (9:9–10)

> Rejoice greatly, O daughter of Zion!
> Shout aloud, O daughter of Jerusalem!
> Lo, your king comes to you;
> righteous and saved is he . . . (Zech. 9:9 [Hebr.]).

At the center of Zechariah 9 stands this famous announcement of the coming of the messianic king. Perhaps verses 9–10 once formed an independent oracle. They now continue the poetic structure of verses 1–8 and reveal how the Kingdom of God, announced in verses 1–8 and 11–17, is to be governed:— by the Messiah, earlier promised in 3:8 and 6:9–15.

150
It should be noted in the above translation of verse 9 that the messianic king is "righteous" and "saved" (or delivered) by God. That is, only the victory of the Divine Warrior, God, allows

the Messiah to rule over a peaceable and universal Kingdom; and in verse 10 God himself does away with chariot and war horse and battle bow.

II Zechariah here fleshes out the picture of the coming Branch who was promised in I Zechariah 3:8; 6:12. The Revised Standard Version has translated the two adjectives of verse 9*d* with "triumphant" and "victorious," to connote the coming king's victory in war, but probably neither is a proper rendering of the text. The Messiah is first of all "righteous," which means that he rules as a king should rule over his subjects. "Righteousness" is throughout the Bible the fulfillment of the demands of a relationship. Thus, the coming king will properly fulfill his role as king of his people and as judge over all the earth (cf. Jer. 23:5–6; Isa. 32:1).

> He shall not judge by what his eyes see,
>   or decide by what his ears hear;
> but with righteousness he shall judge the poor,
>   and decide with equity for the meek of the earth; . . . (Isa. 11:
>   3*b*–4*a*).

He will protect the weak and prosper the good and be like "the shadow of a mighty rock within a weary land" (Isa. 32:2). But he will do such things because he will be enabled to do them by God. In every one of these passages in the Old Testament dealing with the "righteousness" of the Messiah, he has that character as a gift from God (cf. also Ps. 72:1).

Similarly, the Davidic Messiah will be "saved" or "delivered" from his enemies by God; but once again, there is no hint of victory in war here (cf. Ps. 33:16), and it may be that the thought is more of "vindication"—of being "declared right," like the Suffering Servant in Second Isaiah (Isa. 49:4; 50:8–9; cf. 53:11–12). The Messiah's manner and cause are now those that have God's approval, and therefore his realm is one that will endure.

The Messiah, then, is also "humble" because he is the recipient of God's saving action (cf. Ps. 18:27–28). His life and rule and interests rest solely in the hand of God, upon whom he is totally dependent for the success of his reign. He has no glory in himself, but is given his majesty by God. He has no authority except that bestowed on him by his Lord (cf. Pss. 110:1–5; 2:6–9). The picture is consonant with the traditions of the Messiah found in both Psalms and prophetic writings.

There is a real question, however, if the fact that the Mes-

151

siah rides on an ass is intended to contrast that peaceable beast
of burden with the war horse of other rulers. There is evidence
from the time of the Judges that Israel's princes rode on asses
(cf. Judg. 5:10; 10:4; 12:14), as does David when he flees Jerusalem before Absalom (II Sam. 16:2). Most telling, the promise of
the Davidic ruler in Genesis 49:10–11 foretells that he will be
mounted on an ass, and Zechariah 9:9d is certainly patterned
after verse 11 of that prophecy. Thus, the ass is a mark of
identification of the Messiah, who rides on an ass's colt, that is,
on an adult, purebred ass, born not of a mule but of an ass. Also,
contrary to Matthew 21:7 and Mark 11:2 (Luke 19:30 par.),
which misunderstand the Hebrew poetic parallelism in Zechariah 9:9d, only one animal is involved, and there is no reason
to think that it has never been ridden before. It is true, however, that the prophetic diatribes against trust in war horses and
chariots (cf. Isa. 2:7; 31:1; Micah 5:10; Hag. 2:22) may have
influenced this portrayal of the Messiah (see also Zech. 10:5, but
cf. Jer. 22:4).

God speaks in verse 10, and it is he who abolishes all
weapons of war. The Messiah then rules over a reunited kingdom of Ephraim and Judah, whose ideal boundaries stretch
from the Reed Sea to the Mediterranean and from the wilderness of Sinai to the Euphrates. He commands "peace to
the nations" because the justice of his righteous decrees
makes the appeal to arms unnecessary (cf. Isa. 42:1–4). Thus,
from its center in Jerusalem the dominion of God extends
over all the known world.

Certainly this picture of the coming Davidic king is intended to contrast with that of the faithless "shepherds" or
leaders that follows in 10:2–3; 11:4–17. Much of human misery
comes because there is no one who rules (cf. Judg. 21:25) or
because rulers are corrupt. Only by a righteous rule are the
weak protected and the strong enabled to serve beyond their
own self-interest. Only by a caring rule are we delivered from
the tyranny of ourselves or of the mob or of outrageous fortune.
We need a power, a wisdom, a shepherding beyond our own
temptations and limitations; and it is the coming of such a wise
and powerful and peaceful shepherd that is announced here to
Israel.

152

She therefore is bidden to cry out in exultation—to celebrate the entrance of this King into the midst of her community. "YOUR king comes to you," reads the text: A king comes

who fits her case, on whom she has claim, in subjection to whom there is no longer fear or humiliation. For her deliverance, her honor, her consummated bliss he comes. He makes Jerusalem his abode and his people's welfare his task. God has seen with his own eyes now (9:8) the need and suffering of his people and sends his shepherd to gather together and to rule and to prosper his flock (cf. v. 16). That is always the source of Israel's highest joy—the care of God for his sheep—as, amazingly, such care too is God's greatest joy (cf. Luke 15:3–7). So people and God rejoice together here and shout in exultation.

There is more to the story, however:

> Ride on! ride on in majesty! In lowly pomp
> ride on to die . . . (Henry H. Milman, 1827).

There is a somber note introduced into the scene when Jesus of Nazareth takes this oracle of II Zechariah's as a model for his entrance into Jerusalem (Mark 11:1–10 and pars; John 12:12–16), because unlike the setting in II Zechariah, the Divine Warrior's conquest of evil and the establishment of his rule over all the earth have not yet taken place. Sin and death still reign, and there is still that cross at the end of the road. The Gospel writers all therefore appropriately omit the fact that the king is "righteous" and "saved." His fulfillment of his covenant with his people is yet to be tested, and he has not been saved or delivered from his enemies. He will instead suffer at their hands and be subject to the rule of death. Indeed, so prominent is the thought of the cross in Mark that Jesus is not even celebrated as the Messiah: The Kingdom of David is yet to come (Mark 11:10). But the other evangelists use the title of "King" or "Son of David"; and Matthew, following its usual bent, sees the entrance into Jerusalem as a fulfillment of Zechariah 9:9. The Gospel writers all are careful, however, to precede the entry with a prediction of the passion (Matt. 20:17–19; Mark 10:32–34; Luke 18:31–33; John 12:1–8).

How should we interpret the use of this prophecy by Jesus? Certainly Matthew, Luke, and John understand our Lord to be claiming the title of Messiah and that is therefore a legitimate use of the passage for us: as a witness to the identity of Jesus of Nazareth and as the glad announcement that our King now comes to us—for our redemption, to make his abode in our midst, in answer to our pleas of "Save us, O Lord!"

One writer has suggested that by receiving the acclaim of

153

the disciples (in Luke) or of the crowd (in the other Gospels), Jesus was fully identifying with our human condition:

> That triumphant entry into Jerusalem . . . so lovely! Our Lord deigned to taste of human triumph, as of other things, as of death. He rejected none of our joys, He only rejected sin (Bernanos, p. 183).

There is nothing in Scripture to suggest, however, this particular interpretation.

Zechariah 9:9–13 is the stated lesson in some lectionaries for Palm Sunday and for the seventh Sunday in Pentecost, and most sermons on 9:9–10 and its Gospel parallels have emphasized the humility of the scene: the peaceful ass, and borrowed at that, the small company of disciples, the poor but spontaneous offering of a few cloaks and some tree branches. This then, has been contrasted with the pomp of earthly rulers.

The exegesis of the text has shown, however, that the emphasis on the ass and the humility of its rider may not really capture what was intended by Zechariah 9:9–10 and its use by the Gospel writers. The figure in the prophet's oracle is described as "humble," but not because he rides on an ass. Rather he is "humble" because he is totally dependent on God for his defense and office and reign. His is a kingship of total powerlessness, upheld by an unseen but Divine Warrior, who possesses all power. Thus, the use of this oracle in the Gospels carries with it its context in Zechariah 9, and the entrance into Jerusalem does not contrast but rather fits with all those predictions of the passion that have preceded it.

William Malcolm Macgregor has written of the consequences for us. He asks us if we really want such a King:

> . . . We nearly all trust in some degree in an arm of flesh, and find our comfort in a Church which is a kind of second-rate world, with supporters amongst the learned and the mighty. . . . Jesus of Nazareth, on His borrowed farm-beast, with His wayworn company of poor men, and yet offering Himself to His nation as the King of prophecy, is the speaking reminder of the powers which lie behind our sight. I wonder when we, in the Church of Jesus, will learn from Him to trust these powers and to cease from man ("The Prince of Peace," pp. 88, 89).

Zechariah 10:1—11:17

It is clear that we are presented with oracles in II—III Zechariah that are not in order with regard either to their time of composition or to their content. Zechariah 9 depicted the Divine Warrior's final battle with the nations, the establishment of the Kingdom of God, and the entrance of the messianic king to reign over that Kingdom from Jerusalem. In these following chapters, however, there is by no means an ideal realm in existence in the holy land. Instead, they picture the idolatry (10:2), the confusion of the population (10:2), the injustice (11:5), the lack of community (11:14) occasioned in Israel because of the corruption of her leaders or "shepherds." The picture is certainly intended to contrast with that of the messianic rule of justice and peace in 9:9–10, and it shows the difficulties attendant upon the coming of the righteous society.

Chapter 10 opens with the arresting thought that fertility in nature is connected with the faithfulness of human beings and of their leaders to God (vv. 1–2)—a thought found frequently in the Old Testament and especially in passages having to do with Israel's king (cf. Ps. 72:1, 3, 16; Isa. 32:1, 12–18): God grants a righteous king material prosperity for his people.

Chapter 10 then continues with the promise of God's judgment upon Judah's faithless leaders (v. 3), but it is not until chapter 11 that that judgment is pictured as carried out. Instead, the passage changes to a salvation oracle, prompted by the assurance that the Lord cares for his flock, the house of Judah (10:3c; cf. 9:16). This is then developed at length and a series of saving actions by God are promised (10:4–12).

God will replace the faithless leaders of Judah with strong and reliable men: The "cornerstone," "tent peg," and "battle bow" are symbols of the steadfastness and strength that the new leaders will have (10:4). Because the Lord will be with such leaders, they will be invincible warriors against every foe (10:5; cf. 9:13).

155

Verse 10:6b then turns to the "ten lost tribes" of the Northern Kingdom, who were dispersed in the Near East by the

Assyrian conquest of Samaria in 722/1 B.C. (II Kings 17:6). God will bring them back to Palestine (cf. 8:7–8), and the judgment on their sin, carried out in the Assyrian victory over them, will be a thing of the past. "The ten lost tribes are not lost in God's purposes" (Calvin). Now God will have compassion on them and answer them when they call to him (10:6; cf. 13:9). Indeed, that which is pictured in the return of the northern tribes is a new exodus-redemption, paralleling the first redemption out of Egypt (10:8, 11), and the metaphors used are much like those used in Isaian (cf. Isa. 11:11–15; 51:9–10) and Jeremian tradition (cf. Jer. 31:10–14). So many will be the returnees that even Gilead in Transjordania and Lebanon to the north will be insufficient to accommodate their renewed population. The judgment on Assyria, promised in Isaiah 10:12–19, will be carried out; that is, the world powers, symbolized here by Assyria and Egypt will fall (10:11). Reunited Israel and Judah will live anew, vigorous and strong in the Lord, and will walk in his name (v. 12); that is, they will obey his covenant commandments.

The judgment of God promised against the faithless shepherds of Judah in 10:3 is not forgotten, however, in this intoxication with such lyrical visions of the future. Chapter 11 pictures that judgment.

The chapter opens with a brief oracle of doom (11:1–3), which has been put in its present place by an editor but which serves as an appropriate introduction to what follows.

In pictures reminiscent of Jeremiah's foe from the north (cf. Jer. 1:13–14) and Isaiah's Day of the Lord (cf. Isa. 2:12–19), the Lord sweeps down from the north—the site of the mount of the gods in Canaanite mythology—leveling all human pride before him. Lebanon, its majestic cedars, the oaks of Bashan, and impregnable forests are all prophetic symbols of pride. In verse 3, then, which is modeled after Jeremiah 25:34–38, God's destruction falls on the faithless shepherds of Judah who, like lions deprived of their lair, roar in dismay. Such will be God's future judgment on Judah's unfaithful leaders.

But the question now treated by II Zechariah is, What will happen to the faithful shepherd from the Davidic house, the messianic king of 9:9–10? Verses 4–14 supply the answer and verses 15–16 depict its consequences.

As in the prophetic symbolic action of Zechariah 6:9–14, here the prophet symbolizes the fate of that coming Messiah or King by simulating his role in the community. Judah's other greedy leaders have simply been using the people for their own ends, like sheep-dealers buying meat or selling breeding stock (v. 5); so the Davidic shepherd deposes the evil leaders (v. 8), tends the sheep with graciousness (v. 7), and brings back the scattered flock to form a reunited nation (v. 7). All of this is apparently acted out by the prophet in symbolic form, using two staffs that recall the earlier prophecy of Ezekiel 37:15–25, where the action was also linked with the Davidic ruler.

The amazing fact is, however, that the people hate this "ruler" (cf. 12:10–14; 13:3–6), and the "king" grows impatient with their obstinancy (v. 8). He therefore annuls his covenant with them (v. 10; for such covenants between king and people, cf. Deut. 17:14–20, and the Davidic covenants of II Sam. 5:3; II Kings 11:17) and breaks the symbolic staffs (vv. 10, 14), as sign that graciousness and community are now removed from the people. This is noted by the deposed leaders, who are indifferent to the fact that it symbolizes God's judgments on them (v. 11). They simply pay off the "king" for his trouble, with thirty shekels of silver—the compensatory price for the death of a slave (Exod. 21:32)—and bluntly dismiss him. These actions were apparently all dramatized in some fashion by the prophet.

Verse 13 is obviously meant to be ironic, with its reference to the "lordly price" with which the "king" is paid; but the irony comes not from the mean sum—thirty shekels of silver represented considerable money—rather the irony consists in the fact that the leaders are actually paying their Messiah!—as if he were their servant and they were not his subjects! They want a Messiah who can be bought, whom they can hire or dismiss at will. In short, they want to run their own community. Once again, this is a drama that the prophet is acting out.

The Lord therefore commands the "king," represented by the figure of the prophet, to "cast" (the verb is quite strong, indicating the hurling of a vile and rejected thing) the shekels to the potter (RSV margin). As the rest of verse 13 shows, this is a potter in the temple. The money was probably thrown to him because he too was a minor functionary employed by the Zadokite leaders, and that was the status they wanted to give their Messiah also.

Matthew 26:15 recalls this verse by indicating that Judas was paid thirty pieces of silver for betraying Jesus and 27:3–10 then recalls that the money was given to the potter; but it emends the latter to make the money the price that the chief

157

priests paid for "the potter's field, to bury strangers in." When Judas returns the money and goes out and hangs himself, the chief priests realize that they cannot put the money into the temple treasury because it is "blood money," and so they buy the potter's field instead.

In Zechariah 11:15–16 the prophet then is commanded by God to "take" the implements of a worthless shepherd—probably the shepherd's usual staff and pouch, in contrast to the two staffs which he held before (v. 7) and which he broke. Or perhaps he simply carries the two broken staffs as a sign of his ineffectualness. This is then explained as the sign that God himself is raising up a worthless shepherd or leader, who will care nothing for the people, but who will seek only his own gain, sucking out the life of the people like a wolf or a lion so ravenous that it licks and gnaws at even the slain sheep's hooves. Such will be the fate of a flock that has rejected God's chosen messianic shepherd.

In short, the prophet is acting out the fact in this simulation that Judah and its leaders do not really want their promised Messiah to come. But the reader should note that this acted prophecy is concerned with the future. "You have heard all the prophets' promises about the messianic king," II Zechariah is saying to his compatriots, "and while you say you yearn for his coming, you do not really want your King to come. If he did appear, you would reject him and the good life God wants to bring to you by his rule."

The passage uncovers the mysterious depths of human sin, for it is almost inconceivable that Israel would reject the One who would bring peace and security and kindness and the reunification of her scattered community—all those qualities of life for which the human heart so hungers. Why would she do such a thing? Why would she reject her Messiah, as she did reject him in the person of Jesus of Nazareth? And why do we reject him, when he can bring us the good life for which we daily pray and for which we say we always long? The questions reflect the same mystery as does Genesis 3, where our propensity to sin is similarly symbolized in our rejection of God's paradise. Why do we so willfully and continually turn away from the good that God would do us?

158

Surely the answer can only be that which our exegesis has uncovered, and that which is similarly symbolized in Genesis 3: We do not want God to rule over our lives. We do not want a king. We want to be our own kings and run our own lives. The Messiah brings God's sovereignty with him and subjects us to his commandments, and we do not want to live by a rule other than our own. So in our supposed freedom, we reject the service of a gracious Christ for slavery to our selfish selves and for the deadly wages of sin.

The consequences of the rejection of the Messiah are chillingly set forth by II Zechariah in verse 9: "What is to die, let it die; what is to be destroyed, let it be destroyed; and let those that are left devour the flesh of one another." That is a picture of every era or society that rejects God's sovereignty over it. We devour the flesh of one another, by hatred or crime or warfare, by poverty and injustice and greed. Our works and monuments rot and pass, our lives disappear in death. When we rebel against the Good, our only inheritance is evil—pettiness, putrefaction, passing of our wasting and wasted lives. Such is God's judgment on our rejection of his Messiah, says this passage: He lets us have what we want (cf. Rom. 1:24–32)! In short, the judgment of God is to give us over to our freedom, to let us wander and flounder as we will, apart from the guiding and sustaining rule of his Messiah. To be free, according to the teaching of these Scriptures, is to be free to be destroyed and die. Paradise is not unbridled freedom but obedience and service to our King. With this stunning message of judgment, II Zechariah ends.

III Zechariah

CHAPTERS 12—14

Zechariah 12:1—13:6

Judgment is not the last word in the Book of Zechariah, any more than it is God's last word in his work in history. This God of the Bible is working to bless his world, not to curse it (cf. Gen. 12:3); he enters into time and space to save his world, not to condemn it (cf. John 3:17). The editors of the Book of Zechariah have therefore appropriately added on to the collection of Chapters 9—11 the second "Burden of the word of the Lord concerning Israel" in chapters 12—14. In the first section (12:1 —13:6) of this collection three promises are given: God will deliver Jerusalem and Judah from all their enemies (12:1–9); he will pour out on Jerusalem a spirit of repentance (12:10–14); he will cleanse the land of its idolatry and false prophecy (13:1–6).

Much in the manner of Second Isaiah (cf. Isa. 40:12–31), these promises are secured by the hymnic introduction to the whole in 12:1: God is the almighty Creator who has stretched out the immensity of the heavens like a tent, who has secured the foundations of the earth so that it cannot be moved, who has breathed the breath of life into humankind and made them living beings. Such a God can therefore guarantee the fulfillment of the promises that follow.

The first promissory section (12:1–9) utilizes several longstanding Judean traditions, the most prominent being that of the inviolability of Zion. In both the Psalms (46:4–7; 48:4–8; 68; 76:1–3, 5–6) and Isaiah (10:27b–34; 17:12–14; 29:1–8; 30:27–28; 31:4–5) is found a picture of the attack of all nations against Jerusalem and of the salvation of that holy city by its divine Warrior-God. Especially in Isaiah, God saves Jerusalem because of his promise to preserve the Davidic throne (cf. Isa. 7; II Sam. 7). But Zechariah 12:1–9 also utilizes the traditional figure of the cup of reeling (cf. Isa. 51:17–23; Jer. 25:15–29), the symbol of

God's wrath. The section is a skillful reworking of God's past words to Judah.

In the section, all nations lay siege to the holy city and even Judah is caught up in the siege, either by choice or compulsion. But Jerusalem is made the instrument of God's wrath, the cup of reeling which makes the nations stagger, or in the parallel figure, the enormous stone which they cannot lift. God the Warrior strikes the foreign cavalry troops with madness and blindness. Judah then throws in her lot with Jerusalem, and because she is in the midst of the besieging troops, she can devour them like a torch among sheaves. In fact, Judah does the fighting for God while the inhabitants of Jerusalem remain uninvolved, and thus Judah shares a glory equal to that of the citizens of the city. The secured capital is then ruled by a Davidic king who has the wisdom and moral purity of an angel of God.

The second promissory section (12:10–14) does contain something of the pessimistic outlook of II Zechariah. The people, who are so clearly shown in chapter 11 rejecting their Davidic king in favor of ruling their own lives, will finally kill him. There is not further mention of his reign in Zechariah's pictures of the future Kingdom that follow.

The awful fact is that in piercing the heart of its Messiah Jerusalem will destroy its future. It will wipe out that wise and pure one of 12:8 who is like an "angel of God." It will snuff out its own lamp (cf. II Sam. 21:17) by which it may walk through darkness (cf. Isa. 9:2). It will extinguish the breath of its own nostrils (Lam. 4:20) by which it has life. It will abolish its own protecting shade and rock (Lam. 4:20; Isa. 32:2), its own life-giving streams in the desert (Isa. 32:2), for through his chosen Davidic king, God promised life and love and security to Israel (cf. II Sam. 7:24–26). And so like a father weeping over the death of the one son, in whose name and person his own immortality, his own dreams, his own joys of his old age were guaranteed, Jerusalem will weep over the murder of her Messiah.

But the witness of this passage is that of herself Jerusalem will not so weep. Sin blinds human beings to their own wrong (cf. Jer. 8:6). Pride and self-rule never let us see when we have destroyed our one best, last hope. Our hearts are stone and can only be enlightened by the Spirit of God (cf. Ezek. 36:26). Therefore, this section promises that God's Spirit will be poured out. God will, in his mercy, transform the proud and stony

161

hearts of his people so that they will realize what they have done by killing their Messiah, and they will turn to God in true repentance and supplication. In short, repentance is a gift of God prompted by the action of his Spirit.

The sincerity of Jerusalem's future repentance is underlined in this passage by the description of her mourning, which will be comparable to the mourning of the nation pictured in II Chronicles 35:24–25 over the death of the good Davidide Josiah at the city of Hadadrimmon near Jezreel in the valley of Megiddo in 609 B.C. (contrary to the interpretation of the RSV, which takes Hadadrimmon as a personal name). But the depth of the coming lamentation is underscored by the privacy of it, unmarked by public display. The royal house (Nathan, v. 12, is a son of David, II Sam. 5:14) and the priestly house (the Shimeites, v. 13, stem from Gershom, eldest son of Levi, Num. 3:21) are but typical of the whole land. Each family will mourn in seclusion, closeted in its grief.

Judah's future mourning over her Messiah's death will not, moreover, be occasioned only by the realization that she has wiped out her own good future. The third clause of 12:10 should probably read, ". . . so that, when they look on *me* whom they have pierced, they shall mourn for him," following the Septuagint, Syriac, Aramaic, and Latin versions. In slaying God's Messiah, Judah will wound God to his heart, and her weeping repentance will stem from her grief over her injury to her Lord. "Against thee, thee only, have I sinned, and done that which is evil in thy sight" (Ps. 51:4). "Father, I have sinned against heaven and before you; . . ." (Luke 15:21). Selfishness grieves because it is sorry that it will suffer punishment for sin, but true repentance grieves that it has injured the Father. It is that sincere grief for sin against God which will mark Judah's future repentance.

Zechariah 12:10–11 forms a portion of the reading for the fifth Sunday in Pentecost in some lectionaries and is paired with Luke 9:18–24, a prediction of the passion of Jesus. And John 19:37 directly applies Zechariah 12:10 to the death of Jesus by understanding the spear thrust in Jesus' side as the fulfillment of Zechariah's words. The second stanza of the great passion hymn of Bernard of Clairvaux, "O Sacred Head Now Wounded," therefore quite appropriately mirrors the grief of the original Zechariah setting:

162

What Thou, my Lord, hast suffered
Was all for sinners' gain:
Mine, mine was the transgression,
But thine the deadly pain . . .

We weep before the cross of Christ because we have slain our one best, last hope of life: All that is worth having is gone when Jesus is gone. But we weep most of all because in piercing his Christ we have pierced the Father to his heart. It is that last, awful realization of our own heinous ingratitude and wrong toward the Father who loves us that marks our truest repentance; and it is that rueful gaze into the depths of our own barren lovelessness that the Spirit of God alone can inspire. Perhaps that is at least part of the power that is loosed when "we preach Christ crucified"—the power to see our wrong against the Father's love; the power to realize that Christ was guilty only of excess love and that we would have none of him; the power to confess that we are at heart deicides.

So, then, what is to be done? If Judah will destroy her future and her hope by murdering her Messiah—if we have put to death the only One who could finally redeem and save us—what is left but the mourning and the despair and the bitter, bitter weeping?

The amazing fact, according to Zechariah, is that God will be undeterred. The promise of the coming of the Kingdom continues. God works steadily on toward the goal of being all in all (see 14:20–21), as if Judah's very repentance will open up new possibilities for her. So too, our repentance at the foot of the cross opens up for us an amazing future: participation in the Easter victory of the God who cannot be defeated by our sin.

In the third promissory section (13:1–6), God therefore declares that he will open a foundation for the cleansing of the royal house and of the inhabitants of Jerusalem. This cleansing will be done not just by sprinkling, as in the past (cf. Num. 8:7; 19:9–22; Heb. 9:13–14), but by a veritable fountain of water. Further, the cleansing is not for the murder of their Messiah (that will be dealt with in 13:7–9) but for idolatry: 13:1 belongs not with 12:10–14 but with 13:2–6, and "uncleanness" here refers to the worship of idols, as in Ezekiel 36:25 and 37:23. It is for this reason that the passage also mentions prophets. The reference is to those false prophets who have urged the people to go after other gods. As in Deuteronomy 13:1–5, such proph-

163

ets will be slain. Therefore, false prophets who escape the sentence of death will give up their prophetic office and even try to hide the fact of their former occupation. Some may escape execution and their wounds may show that they are prophets, but they will try to hide the fact and will never prophesy again. Thus will God cleanse out the evil of idolatry and false prophecy from his coming Kingdom.

Zechariah 13:7–9

This section concerns not the false shepherds of 11:1–3 and 15–17 but the messianic shepherd of 11:7–14 and 12:10–14; its message is that God will not allow the murder of his Messiah (12:10–14) to go unpunished. Rather, he will use that very death as an instrument of his judgment on his sinful people (cf. John 3:19; 12:3–32). By their act of smiting God's anointed, the people will loose upon themselves the sword of God's wrath, destining themselves to be scattered, their young and tender ones to fall prey to the strong, and their own populace to stand helpless and leaderless before its enemies. Thus, the nations who come against Jerusalem (12:1–9; 14:1–5) will be able to slaughter two-thirds of the populace, and the remaining third will be purified by adversity, as precious metals have their impurities removed from them by fire. Sin against the purpose of God always brings its evil consequences.

Jesus applies the second half of verse 7 to his own death and the falling away of his disciples (Mark 14:27//Matt. 26:31), who, likewise, in betraying him leave themselves helpless before the powers of this world.

But the outcome of God's judgment here too is a work of mercy. Purified by his judgment of them, Judah's remnant will turn to seek God, calling on his name in prayer and supplication (cf. 12:10). And God in mercy will hear their prayer and answer them and restore his covenant with them, naming them once again "My people" (cf. Hos. 2:23), to which Judah will reply, "My God!" (cf. John 20:28).

Zechariah 14:1–21

Zechariah 14 is essentially an explication of 13:9 with its covenant formula. The fourteenth chapter explains how that renewed relationship between God and his people will come about, what the nature of the covenant relationship will be, and what consequences it will have for all the nations of the earth. As such, it has many similarities in thought with the closing chapter (chap. 8) of I Zechariah, but II—III Zechariah's somber note is not abandoned here.

The Kingdom comes only after God's conquest of evil and only after his thorough-going purgation of his people's sin. Thus, the first half of 13:9 is also spelled out more fully in 14:1–2. On a day reserved specifically for the Lord, in the battle of all nations against Jerusalem (cf. 12:1–9), there will first be a defeat before there will be a victory—a testing, a trial by fire, a further purging of the population (cf. 13:8). Jerusalem's conquerors will so thoroughly subdue her that they will be able to divide up their spoil in Jerusalem's streets in perfect security. The conquerors will plunder and ravish and send half of the populace into exile. (If this is added to the depopulation mentioned in 13:8, now only one-sixth of the inhabitants of Jerusalem remain.) In such a manner, God will cleanse out the faithless from the midst of his faithful remnant.

Then in a cataclysmic final battle, the Divine Warrior will come down to fight against the foe, standing on the Mount of Olives to the east of the city. As Lord over his creation (12:1), he will split the ridge that makes up Olivet. Half of the ridge will move to the north and half to the south, thus blocking up the Kidron Valley that lies between Mount Zion and the Mount of Olives. This will have the effect of forming on the east of the city a level plain stretching into the desert. As the text now stands, there is a gloss designating the plain as an escape route for the Jerusalemites, but it really is no such thing: The inhabitants have no reason to flee the city now. Instead, the plain is a way provided for God to enter into his holy city (cf. Isa. 40:3–5) —a royal processional way on which the Lord with his retinue

165

of heavenly attendants and servants comes to take up his abode in the midst of Jerusalem.

The effects of God's presence in the midst of his people are then described in verses 6–8 in traditional terms that picture a veritable new creation: The polarities of the original creation (day and night, cold and heat, summer and winter) are done away, and there is "one day" (Hebr., v. 7) with no night there (cf. Isa. 30:26; 60:19–20; Rev. 21:25; 22:5)—a symbol of the banishment of the darkness of evil chaos. The waters of life, always symbolic of the life-giving power of God, will flow down from the elevated city (cf. v. 10) to vivify east and west (cf. Ezek. 47:1–12; Joel 3:18; Ps. 46:4; Rev. 22:1–2; John 7:38), never to fail in the drought of summer and independent of the rain.

Then in the act that forms the goal of all human history God will take his throne as king over all the earth (v. 9; cf. Pss. 47; 93; 95—99), acknowledged by all the faithful as the only God, having but one name: Yahweh (the Hebrew name for the Lord). Verse 9 is a reference to Deuteronomy 6:4, and the Lord is enthroned here as covenant King and as the only King over the earth. No longer is he confused with any other god. Deuteronomy's concern was that he not be identified with the baals, the nature gods worshiped throughout Canaan, or with the gods of Mesopotamia. In our time he shares nothing with Allah or Buddha; nothing with some earthly despot like a Hitler or a Sun Myung Moon; nothing with some mythical Om or some great Soul of Nature or some Unity permeating all; nothing with a birthing, baalistic mother-goddess. No, for the Christian he is one God—the God and Father of our Lord Jesus Christ, and whoever knows Jesus Christ knows also the Father (John 14:7).

Further, the God whom Zechariah sees enthroned as sole King over the earth is also the covenant God—one who enters into relationship with his faithful people and one who gives that people covenant commandments by which they are to direct and practice their lives. The results of that covenant follow therefore in verses 10–21.

Isaiah had proclaimed that Zion's hill would become the center and highest peak of the earth, with all nations flowing to it to hear and practice God's *torah* (Isa. 2:2–3). Such a vision was passed down in the Isaianic school for more than two centuries. III Zechariah here picks up that tradition, but he puts it in a unique framework.

As in Isaiah 2:2, Zion will be elevated above the surrounding plain and the landmarks listed in verses 10–11 are located in all four directions, to show that the whole city will be included. As in Isaian tradition, the depopulated city will grow in the number of its citizenry (cf. Isa. 49:19–21; 54:1–3; 60:22; Zech. 8:4–5). The curse of God that rested upon Jerusalem and that was worked out in the destruction of the city and the deportation into exile (Isa. 43:28) will now be lifted (see the comment on Zech. 8:13), and Jerusalem will in the future dwell always in security (cf. Zech. 2:5, 8; 8:11–13; 9:8, 15). Noticeable is the fact, in contrast to Jeremiah 23:5–6 or Ezekiel 34:20–31, however, that such security will be given apart from the presence of any Davidic Messiah. While III Zechariah freely utilizes Isaianic tradition here, he sets that tradition in the context of a more ancient one—namely, the tradition of the tribal league as represented in Deuteronomy with its Mosaic covenant, its centralization of worship in Jerusalem, its covenant commands and curses, its covenant renewal ceremony at the autumn feast, and its lack of a Davidic king. The Lord was the only King over Israel in the tribal federation, during the period of the Judges. And while the seventh century B.C. homilies of Deuteronomy had to take notice of the presence of a king in Judah, they nevertheless made that ruler subservient to the covenant law (cf. Deut. 17:14–20). That is the context with which III Zechariah is working here in chapter 14.

In verses 12–15, the traditional covenant curses are therefore pronounced on those enemies who attack Jerusalem (cf. Deut. 28:15–68; Lev. 26:14–26). No longer are these curses pronounced on the people of Israel: The unfaithful among God's people have now been purged out, and the curse on Jerusalem has been lifted, falling instead on those who have attacked and entered the holy city: Verse 14 means that Judah fights not against the inhabitants of Jerusalem but against those enemy soldiers who have come into her streets. The details that Zechariah gives of the plague sent by God upon Jerusalem's enemies are horrible in their vividness, but the prophet wishes to portray the sudden and total defeat of Jerusalem's foes: They experience the decay of death instantaneously, while they are still on their feet. This covenant God is Lord over life and death and can bring sudden death to those who oppose him.

In the last scene of the chapter, verses 16–21, the remnant that is left from all the nations is pictured going up to Jerusalem, first to worship the one King, the Lord of all the hosts of heaven

167

and of earth, and second to take part in the covenant ceremony which was an integral part of the Feast of Tabernacles. In that ceremony, God's covenant commandments were read anew, the people took renewed vows to obey the commandments, and the covenant sacrifice was offered. It is this latter act with which verses 20–21 are concerned. So large will be the throng that will come to Jerusalem to enter into the covenant with God that there will not be enough sacred bowls in the temple to prepare the sacrificial meat. Therefore ordinary pots in the temple and indeed in every kitchen will be suitable for use in the temple, for God will have made all things pure and holy for himself. In fact, there will be nothing unclean and alien remaining in Jerusalem and its temple. The very harnesses on the horses that the foreign peoples ride into Jerusalem will be holy, as will be every foreign worshiper: "There shall no longer be a Canaanite in the house of the Lord of Hosts" (v. 21, Hebrew) —that is, there shall no longer be one person considered alien or profane, not one worshiper considered an outsider, not one man or woman excluded on the grounds of being unfit for the worship of the Lord of Hosts (contrast Ezek. 44:9; Neh. 13:1–3; Acts 21:27–29). All, all will have been made faithful by God and fit for his service. All, all will therefore be drawn into covenant relationship with him and become members of his people.

Despite the gruesomeness of some of the details that the prophet presents to us in this chapter, it nevertheless portrays for us a magnificent vision—of the whole earth cleansed and made faithful and obedient to God; of every people included in the covenant relationship with the Lord; of all nations worshiping at his throne, proclaiming him sole King over their lives for all time. In short, we are presented in this chapter with the picture of the Kingdom of God come on earth, and III Zechariah has arrived at that glorious vision given us also by I Zechariah. But in realistic fashion, II—III Zechariah have shown us that the Kingdom comes through travail and struggle and blood. They picture the death of the Messiah, the winnowing of God's people, and the warfare of God against his enemies.

The New Testament too portrays the death of the Davidic king and part of its final vision is of God's battle against his enemies (cf. Revelation). But the New Testament knows, because its writers experienced, the resurrection of the Messiah. In that triumph it sees the promise of God's final kingship and victory. The future coming of the Kingdom of God is no longer

168

only prophetic hope. Now it is guaranteed by the resurrection of Jesus Christ—his victory over human evil and death. When we sit down at the table of the Lord's Supper, therefore, and renew our allegiance to God and his commandments, we not only participate in our festival of covenant renewal and we not only remember the Messiah's death. Much more! We look forward to victory. We look forward in certain hope and anticipation to the glad day when the Lord will be acknowledged as King over all the earth and all nations will worship him as their one God, through the one name of Jesus Christ our Lord.

THE BOOK OF
Malachi

A New Look at Introductory Matters

Throughout the history of its interpretation, the Book of Malachi has given historical critics little trouble. There is broad consensus that Malachi dates from the first half of the fifth century, shortly before the reforms of Ezra and Nehemiah. The essential unity of the book is generally affirmed, though most scholars believe verses 4–6 of chapter 4 to be later additions to the work. It has been said to be made up largely of disputations in the form of questions and answers between the prophet and his contemporary Israelites. And most modern critics maintain that it is the work of an anonymous prophet, the title of Malachi ("my messenger") having been taken from 3:1 and put at the head of the work by an editor. In addition, many hold that because its superscription in 1:1 is identical with that of Zechariah 9:1 and 12:1, the book once circulated in a collection with II—III Zechariah, though it may always have been understood as a work independent of the Zechariah school.

Nevertheless, questions about Malachi continue to plague thoughtful interpreters. Has the title "Malachi" actually been borrowed from 3:1, and if so, does that not destroy the message of 3:1–4? Are verses 4–6 in chapter 4 really later additions to the work? What is the setting of these disputations that make up so much of the book, and why does the form suddenly switch to narrative in 3:16, followed by prophetic oracle in 3:17—4:3? I believe all of these questions can be answered if the form of the book is understood in the setting which its prophet has envisioned for it. Let me detail the argument.

It is almost universally acknowledged by scholars that Malachi reflects Deuteronomic law rather than the Priestly

171

Code that was brought back to Palestine by Ezra. In Deuteronomy 17:8–13, we find the stipulation that legal cases which are too difficult for the law courts in the town gates to decide shall be brought before the Levitical priests in the Jerusalem temple. We also read in Malachi 2:7 that the priest is "the messenger of the Lord of hosts." These facts furnish the key to the form of the book. The title of the book, "my messenger," is not borrowed from 3:1; rather, it is a reference to the function of the priest in 2:7, and the Book of Malachi has been cast by its anonymous prophet in the form of a court case, tried before the priest in the temple, with the prophet playing the role of the priest in his imagination.

Many details support this conclusion. The book is primarily concerned with the fulfillment of the duties of the covenant relationship, and initially the Lord is the defendant in the case, with the Israelites bringing two charges against him: You have not loved us (1:2), and you have not acted as the God of justice should act in fulfillment of your covenant duties (2:17). Israel is quickly put on the defensive, however, by the countering accusations of God against the people; and the roles of defendant and plaintiff are reversed. In 3:16 the jury therefore agrees that the Lord is innocent of the charges against him and that Israel is guilty. This is then followed by the court's verdict (3:17—4:3), by a final remonstrance by the priest-judge (the prophet) to obey the law of Moses (cf. Deut. 17:10–13), and by a concluding promise of mercy and love on God's part (4:5–6), paralleling the evidence of love offered in 1:2–5.

The form of the book with its questions and answers is therefore determined by this court setting, and its principle genres are two—those of the prophetic disputation (e.g., see Jer. 3:1–5; 2:29–37 and cf. Mal. 2:10–12) and of the prophetic *torah* (e.g., see Isa. 1:10–17 and cf. Mal. 1:2–5), both of which can have a legal setting. In much of the book, the two forms are combined; but the point is that the questions found in the book are not hurled at the prophet on the street, in some Socratic setting, and they are not scholastic questions characteristic of the scribes. Rather, they are questions asked in a court of law.

Malachi 1:1–5

Nations and individuals have often called God to account for his actions, hurling questions of bitter anger or plaintive lament in his face. Certainly Israel did: "How long, O God, is the foe to scoff?" (Ps. 74:10); "Rouse thyself! Why sleepest thou, O Lord? . . . / Why dost thou hide thy face? / Why dost thou forget our affliction and oppression?" (Ps. 44:23–24); "How long, O Lord? Wilt thou be angry for ever?" (Ps. 79:5); "Why should the nations say, / 'Where is their God'?" (Ps. 79:10)—all queries tumbling out from a distressed and suffering people. Within that people her greatest leaders also examined God: *Abraham* —"Shall not the Judge of all the earth do right?" (Gen. 18:25); *Moses*—"O Lord, why hast thou done evil to this people? Why didst thou ever send me?" (Exod. 5:22); *Jeremiah*—"Wilt thou be to me like a deceitful brook, / like waters that fail?" (Jer. 15:18). Everywhere throughout the Old Testament, the Israelites question God, as did that final Israelite suffering on his cross, "My God, my God, why hast thou forsaken me?" (Mark 15:34).

Nor has time and the perspective of the biblical history silenced the complaints. We still cry out from our pain or loss, "God, how could you do this to me?" Or weary with our struggles with the ways of the world, we ask, "O Lord, when wilt thou bring peace on the earth?"

It does little good to hear, in the midst of our suffering, the tales of God's love in the past. A vanquished Israel knew all about God's mighty past deeds of grace and that made her defeat more painful (cf. Pss. 44:1, 9; 80:8, 12). Job remembered the love of God and that rendered his suffering more incomprehensible (cf. Job 10:8–9)—just as our Lord on the cross must have remembered those words he had heard at the beginning of his ministry: "Thou art my beloved Son; with thee I am well pleased" (Mark 1:11). The truth is that the love of God in the past makes the taste of present suffering more bitter, because it contradicts what we have previously had from the hands of our Lord. It gives little comfort to remember past mercy when one is experiencing present agony.

So it is too with Israel, in the time of the prophet Malachi, about 460 B.C. Once more she calls her God to account for his actions, this time in the prophetic imagination summoning him to court for trial. And her accusations against him are fierce. Judah yet remains a struggling and impoverished little province within the Persian empire. None of Haggai's and Zechariah's promises of a glorious messianic kingdom have come to pass, despite the fact that the temple—inglorious as it is—has been rebuilt for over fifty years. The promised blessings from heaven have not been poured out: Locusts and drought still ravage Judah's crops; existence is still a desperate struggle. And so when God on trial defends himself, "I have loved you, and I love you still" (which is the sense of the verb in Mal. 1:2), Israel replies with a cynical sneer, "How hast thou loved us?" One can almost hear her angry retort: "Oh, do not recite the past for us! We know all about those marvelous things you did for our people in the past. All we want to know is, What have you done for us lately that could possibly show us that you in any manner love us in the present?"

In many respects, faith, according to the Bible, consists in waiting for God to act—waiting with the expectation that he will act; acting with the assurance that he will keep his word; trusting that the future will indeed bring that which he has promised. Faith is going out, not knowing where one is going, because a new land has been promised. It is preparing oneself for flight from slavery because the promise of deliverance has been given. It is entering battle with a seemingly overwhelming foe because God has guaranteed victory. It is obeying a command because one has been told that obedience leads to fullness of life. It is accepting a cross with the assurance of a resurrection. It is discounting suffering for the certainty of a glory that is coming. Faith in the Bible strains out toward a future that it knows God is bringing, and it acts in trust and obedience and certain hope in accord with that future.

Such was always Israel's role in the covenant relationship: She was to trust and obey her God. He had called her fathers and set his love upon them and made them his special people —set apart to be the means through which he would bring his blessing on all the families of the earth (Gen. 12:3). God had elected Israel (cf. Deut. 4:37; 7:7–8; 10:15), adopted him like a

174

son (cf. Deut. 8:5; Hos. 11:1), married her like a wife (cf. Hos. 2:15; Jer. 2:2), raised and nurtured her like a beloved child (cf. Ezek. 16), and all because he had a purpose to work out and promises to keep. And Israel, in return, was to trust that purpose and obey God's word and love him as he loved her. That was the nature of the covenant relation between Israel and her God.

But Israel in Malachi's time had grown tired of waiting and obeying and loving, because nothing—apparently nothing at all —was happening in her world. She was suffering under no persecutions that would fire up or steel her commitment. She had no nation attacking her, other than the pestiferous Samaritans, to prompt her to concerted defense of faith and life. Indeed, she was not even noticed on the landscape of the earth. The wave of great sea changes in history had rolled to the west of her, with the Greeks battling at Marathon and then Thermopyle. Nothing faced Israel but "the dailiness of life," obeying God's commandments in daily relations with neighbors and friends; spending money to pay tithes for the support of the priests; giving up prized lambs and calves to be burnt on the altar; learning religious traditions that seemed as distant as the God they portrayed; praying prayers that disappeared, unanswered, into the blue. God apparently was doing nothing at all in Judah's life, and all his promises for the future seemed hollow mockeries of her service to him.

Indeed, Israel in Malachi's time had begun to wonder if she really was God's Chosen People after all and if there ever was a covenant of love between her and her God. Certainly God did not seem to be honoring the relationship, if it ever existed. He had chosen Jacob over Esau, went the ancient story (cf. Gen. 25:21-26; 27—28), and yet Jacob/Israel had suffered the total devastation of his country under the Babylonians in 587 B.C. and long years of exile, while Esau/Edom had simply profited from Israel's loss. Edom had aided the Babylonian invaders, acting as informers, looting, cutting off escape routes (cf. Obad. 10-14), and then had gleefully taken over parts of Judah's abandoned territory (cf. Lam. 4:21-22; Ps. 17:7) in violation of his brotherly covenant with Jacob/Israel (cf. Deut. 23:7). Was that not proof that God had never chosen Jacob over Esau, that there was no election of Israel, and that God had no universal 175 purpose that he was working out through his elected people? Israel's questions to God on trial in Malachi's time concern the very heart of her faith, namely the validity of the covenant relationship. If there was no covenant, Israel's life had no purpose and God was not acting to save his world.

The reply God gives to these all-important questions is described in the superscription to the book as a "burden" (RSV: oracle; the word should be separated from the rest of v. 1, as in Zech. 9:1 and 12:1). The word is the most severe term used to designate prophecy, and it usually heads an oracle of unrelieved judgment (cf. Isa. 13:1; 14:28; Jer. 23:33–40). But the "burden" of God here to Israel is his covenant love: "I have loved you, and I love you still."

Certainly that love has been a burden, in our sense of the term, to God from the very first. When we read the sacred story his love for us seems to have given him nothing but sorrow and grief—grief in his heart over human wrong (Gen. 6:6); grief in the wilderness over disbelief (Ps. 78:40); grief over the rebellion of his children (cf. Hos. 11:8; Jer. 31:20); grief in his Holy Spirit (Isa. 63:10) over his beloved Jerusalem (Luke 19:41) and over the hardness of his people's hearts (Mark 3:5), until finally that grief is all gathered up, as it must have been, in his weeping at the sight of a cross. And yet, before a cynical people who have hauled him into court, God defends himself with only that word of compassion, "I have loved you, and I love you still."

But this people of Malachi's decade demand a proof of present love; and the divine Lover, in infinite patience, points to his work with Edom. Edom has not gone unpunished for his violation of his brotherly covenant with Israel: such is the meaning of the divine hatred in verse 3. Rather, Nabataean invaders from the desert have ransacked Edomite territory and the once gloating Edomites have themselves been forced to abandon their territory and to move into the Negeb, south of Judah. Such a defeat, God says, has been his work. Moreover, if the Edomites try to rebuild their ruined cities, they will suffer further defeat at God's hands, until they become synonymous with a people permanently subject to the wrath of God (vv. 3–4).

Historically, the prophecy seems to have come true. Edom never recovered its lost territory, but rather established the kingdom of Idumea in southern Palestine, with a capital at Hebron; and then in the time of John Hyrcanus (135–104 B.C.), was incorporated forcefully into the Jewish commonwealth, according to Josephus (Antiquities XIII.9). In addition, in Israelite prophecy, Edom was understood as the type of all those who oppose God; and her downfall was seen as an indispensable part of the picture of the messianic age (cf. Isa. 34:5–6; 63:1–6; Jer. 49:13, 17, 18).

Jacob/Israel on the other hand, the beloved, chosen ones of God, have been restored to their land, despite the deserved punishment of their sin in the destruction of Judah and in the exile. God has not remained angry with them forever. God has forgiven them and brought them home, and their return and rebuilding are the concrete historical results of his love for them. Judah has only to look at the fate of nations to see God's work in them (v. 5) and to realize that God hovers over her still with his encircling love (cf. Deut. 32:10).

This opening passage furnishes the leading motif for the Book of Malachi. The Lord of Hosts (v. 4)—that is, the Lord of all powers, seen and unseen, in heaven and on earth—never abandons the burden of his love for his people.

Malachi 1:6—2:9

The God of Israel has promises to keep. He restlessly, constantly marches forward through the Old Testament history, as he does through the New, toward the goal of his Kingdom established on earth—shaping, turning, subverting, and fostering human events and lives to aid the realization of that goal. He looks forward over time to that glad day when "from the rising of the sun to its setting" his name will be "great among the nations," when "in every place" men and women will worship him with a "pure offering" of all their devotion (cf. Rom. 15:16) and will bow before him as sole "King" (1:11, 14). Israel, in her finest moments, ecstatically glimpsed the same goal (cf. Pss. 47; 93; 96—99), and Malachi here in this court case preserves the same vision. Verses 11 and 14 of chapter 1 refer neither to the worship of the dispersed Jews nor to that of pagans but to the purpose that underlies every prophetic book: The future establishment of the kingship of God over all the earth.

Israel was the people called to be the special instrument through which God would realize his universal kingship, and

177

her priests were those who were especially responsible for mediating the knowledge of her great God to her (cf. 2:4–7). They were to preserve all the traditions of God's mighty acts in Israel's past and recount them in the cultic festivals that Israel might know the power and love of the God she worshiped. They were to instruct the people in proper reverence and awe before such a King of glory and to insist on the worthy worship of him (cf. Ps. 15; 24). They were to mediate God's instructions concerning ethics and morals and ritual when persons came to them for *torah*, teaching out of a knowledge of God gained in intimate prophetic-like communion with him (2:7). They were to "walk with" God (2:6; only elsewhere in Gen. 5:22; 6:9) in such a privileged fellowship that the King of glory was reflected in their lives and words and cultic ministrations. From them Israel too would learn how to walk in the ways of her God and to render unto him the glory due his holy name. No higher estimation of the priesthood is found in the Old Testament than this one given in Malachi 2:4–7.

Corruption of the priesthood leads to corruption of the people, however, as most of the prophets preached, and this whole section in Malachi concerns the failure of the priests (cf. 1:6; 2:1; Matt. 18:5–6). This is recognized in those lectionaries which pair Malachi 2:1–10 with I Thessalonians 2:7–13 and Matthew 23:1–12: All of those readings concern the nature of worthy ministry, and in the Protestant tradition in which we share in a priesthood of all believers, Malachi's words on the priesthood concern every believer.

Malachi's central charge against the priesthood is that they have "despised" the Lord's name (1:6), and in the indictment in this court case, in 1:6–14, the particulars of that charge are spelled out. God has authority over Israel as both the Father who has adopted her as his own in the covenant relation (cf. Exod. 4:22–23; Deut. 8:5; Hos. 11:1; Isa. 1:2; 43:6; 63:16; 64:8; Jer. 3:4; 31:9, 20) and as the Master or Suzerain whom she is called to serve (cf. 3:14; Exod. 3:12; 9:1; Ezra 5:11; Zeph. 3:9). It is the authority rather than the love connected with fatherhood that the prophet here emphasizes. The priests, above all others, as those who have "walked with God" and among whom he has shown himself "holy" (cf. Lev. 10:3), should honor that authority of God the Father and Master and know him as the great King before whom proper reverence and awe are due (cf. 2:5). Instead, the priests do not even think the Lord is as impor-

178

tant as a human governor (1:8)! They accept blemished animals for sacrifice in violation of the law (1:8, 14; cf. Deut. 15:21; Exod. 12:5; also Lev. 1:3, 10), offering to the Lord even that which has been mauled or killed by a wild animal (v. 13, "by violence;" cf. Exod. 22:31; Lev. 17:15). Such "gifts" could not be eaten or sold or even given to anyone else, they are totally worthless; and yet the priests accept such sacrifices as gifts good enough for God (cf. Rom. 2:24). Even when a worshiper voluntarily promises in a vow to make a sacrifice to the Lord as a token of gratitude for divine help (1:14; cf. Num. 30:2; Lev. 22:17–20), the priests allow the worshiper to break his promise (cf. Acts 5:1–4) and to substitute a blemished animal (1:14), because the priests really "despise" (1:6) or count worship before God as of little importance. Indeed, they deem the whole sacrificial system a mechanical routine and their service in it a tiresome duty (1:13; cf. Isa. 43:22).

One can view the worship of God in such a manner only when one has no ongoing, intimate fellowship with God and no understanding of his nature, and both types of knowledge of God are mediated through the sacred history of God's words and deeds—that is, for us, through the Scriptures. Through the recounting of the "old, old story" in the preaching and sacraments, the music and teaching, the speech and deeds of the church, God reveals himself to our hearts and minds as truly the great King over all the earth—as the Father who has created us and redeemed us and circled us with his electing love in Jesus Christ and as the Master who guides and empowers and commands our lives. Such a God demands our life, our love, our all. But when the church fails to tell its gospel story, its worshipers bring blemished gifts to God—the coins in the offering plate that cost them nothing, their discards for the poor, the remnants of their time, and the grudging gifts of their talents. Worship becomes a perfunctory, sometimes tiresome service, or at best a sleepy duty, ineffective to change or touch anything in the worshipers' hearts and lives.

Malachi here in this indictment is not interested in the mechanics of ritual. His concern is with the glorious nature of God, with the priests' intimate fellowship with him and therefore with the heartfelt responses of reverence and honor, of obedience and love, which should issue from that fellowship. The priests' hearts are corrupted (2:2; cf. Matt. 12:33–37; Luke 6:45) because they no longer walk with God in the ongoing

179

fellowship with him intended in the covenant with the priestly house of Levi (2:6). They accept unworthy worship of the Lord of Hosts because they no longer know him. They have broken their covenant fellowship with their Lord (2:8); they have therefore forfeited their right to be priests—a word which should make every minister and lay person in the priesthood of believers tremble in self-examination (cf. Matt. 21:43).

The judgment in this court case is therefore leveled against the priests, in 2:1–9, and the verdict fits the crime (cf. Matt. 7:2): Because the priests have "polluted" the worship of God (1:7) by considering it of no importance, they themselves will be cursed and polluted (2:2–3), making them unfit for service at the altar. The "dung" mentioned in 2:3 is that taken from the sacrificial animals, and it was supposed to be removed from the sanctuary and burned (cf. Exod. 29:14; Lev. 4:11–12). Because the priests will be contaminated by it, they too will be ejected from the sanctuary. Verse 3 in chapter 2 should probably be read as the New English Bible has it: "I will cut off your arm, fling offal in your faces . . ." (similarly JB; cf. Nah. 3:6), the former phrase indicating that the priests will no longer be able to raise their arm to bless the people (cf. Num. 6:22–27). Additionally, because the priests have "despised" God's name (1:6), the Lord will make them "despised and abased" among the people (2:9), for they have not guarded God's way and respected *torah*. (Such is the way the last phrase should be read.)

We might well ask, Are these the words of a God of love? The court case which started out to put God on trial, in 1:1–5, has here turned the tables and put Israel's priests on trial; and the most stringent verdict of punishment has been pronounced against them by God, who has become both prosecutor and judge. Is that an exercise of a God of love?

Yes it is. It is only when God leaves us alone that he no longer loves us. It is only when he abandons us to our sin that we have fallen from his mercy (cf. Rom. 1:24, 26, 28). Our highest good is fellowship with God (cf. Ps. 73:28) and obedience to his will, for his loving purpose is that we have life and have it more abundantly. His goal is that all shall know that life in his Kingdom of good (cf. 2:5). If God ever gives up on that purpose, if he decides to accept our sin as of no importance and to leave us as we are, then he has abandoned us to our evil and death and he no longer cares about us. But God does care: "I have loved you, and I love you still" (1:2). Therefore Israel's

180

priests are condemned, because the God of love, the Lord of Hosts, will not allow their sin to destroy either them or his beloved people.

Malachi 2:10–16

Because the God of love will not leave his people to be destroyed by their sin, his prophet now turns in this court case to give voice to God's covenant indictment against the populace of Judah, lay and clergy. The charge is twofold: First, some in the community have broken the Sinai covenant with the Lord by turning to the idolatrous worship of their wives' heathen gods (vv. 10–12); second, some have broken their marriage covenants by divorcing their wives of many years (vv. 13–16).

The text of this passage is exceedingly difficult, and the Revised Standard translations of verses 12, 15, and 16 are all conjectural, though probably as satisfactory as any. Verses 10–12 and 13–16 deal with different covenants, and the former is a disputation while the latter is a mixture of disputation and prophetic *torah*. But the whole passage is held together by its key word "faithless" (vv. 10, 11, 14, 15, 16) and by its concentration on covenant violations. It can therefore be assumed that the wives (vv. 13–16) have been divorced in order that the husbands may marry non-Israelite women (vv. 10–12). Though polygamy was lawful in Israel throughout her history, monogamy was the ideal in post-exilic times and the actual condition in most families (cf. Gen. 2:18–25; Prov. 5:18–20; 31:10–31).

Verse 10 is sometimes used as a text for sermons dealing with the universal family of humankind or with race relations or with individual rights, but Malachi is not speaking here of all peoples; he is speaking of Israel and of the Lord's creation of her in the exodus from Egypt and at the covenant ceremony at Mount Sinai. It is in those events that Israel was elected as God's own and made a people for the first time in history. Therefore God was the Creator of Israel and her Father. As the fatherhood of God was defined in terms of authority in 2:6, so here it is defined in terms of God's creation of his people. It is against the backdrop of Israel's special role in the world, as instrument of

181

God's kingship, that Malachi views the heinousness of her sin (cf. Amos 3:2, and see the comment on Mal. 1:6—2:9). Such a nation, chosen for such an exalted purpose, should surely be expected to be faithful to its covenant God! But tempted by whatever allure (youth? beauty? wealth? daring?) of the foreign women in their midst, some men in the community have divorced their wives of many years, married the foreigners (cf. Ezra 9—10; Neh. 13:23-27 and then in easy compromise slid into the worship of the gods of their wives alongside of or in place of their worship of the Lord of Hosts. An "abomination," that is, hateful to God, such idolatry profanes the whole body of the people, which is termed God's "sanctuary" in verse 11. The verdict against such idolators is therefore announced in verse 12: They will be excommunicated or cast out from the community. The Revised Standard reading, "to witness," is correct and refers to those taking part in the court case pictured in Malachi as well as to any who take part in other court cases or who worship in the temple (v. 12d), in short, any citizen.

The prophet then goes on to give such persons and the other Judeans present instruction about marriage and divorce (vv. 13-16). The passage constitutes one of the most sublime understandings of the marital relation to be found in the Old Testament—an understanding consonant with the view of both Genesis 2:18-25 and of the New Testament (cf. Mark 10:1-12; Eph. 5:21-33).

Marriage, in this passage, is not a strictly private or civil or secular matter, but a covenant ordained and protected by God. Its violation therefore affects the relation with God, and verse 13 makes it clear that the Judeans' worship and pleas for help are unacceptable to God because their marital practices are unacceptable—a view which, if applied to modern society, would call into question the prayers and petitions of millions of American churchgoers. Further, the marital relation is of the highest order: a companionship (v. 14), a mutual helpfulness (Gen. 2:18), mutual service (Eph. 5:21), and the establishment of a family in which parent passes on to child true faith and trust in God (v. 15). Israelites married very early, before the age of twenty, and therefore verse 14 speaks of "the wife of your youth" (cf. Prov. 2:17). The thought is that these men have spent years of mutual companionship with their spouses— building their homes, raising their children, facing life's vicissitudes together—and then they have abandoned their wives for the sake of other women. It is little wonder that the act is called "violence" (v. 16), for it violently injures the well-being, the dreams, the securities of all involved. (The reference to the "garment" is to the man's symbolic act of spreading his garment over the woman as a sign of his choice of her, cf. Ruth 3:9; Ezek. 16:8.) Malachi knows all about the desolation that accompanies the breakup of a family.

He also is quite certain about God's attitude: The Lord hates divorce. It is an attitude that God never gets over, according to the Bible, and yet it is a fact rarely considered by divorcing persons. Usually they ask all the wrong questions. When a couple is considering a separation, they are likely to ask, "Will I be happier?" "Can I make it on my own?" "Will it be better for the children?" rather than, "What is God's attitude toward the dissolution of this marriage?" Here in this prophetic *torah,* as the "messenger of the Lord of Hosts" (2:7), the prophet Malachi furnishes the reply.

Malachi 2:17—3:6

Verses 1–4 in chapter 3 of this passage are used more frequently in the church than any other portion of Malachi. Many sermons have been written on them, and in some lectionaries they form a stated reading for Advent (along with Phil. 1:3–11 and Luke 3:1–6), for the Nativity of John the Baptist (along with Acts 13:13–26 and Luke 1:57–67, 68–80), and for the Presentation of Our Lord (along with Heb. 2:14–18 and Luke 2:22–40). In addition, at least two well-known hymns have reference to these verses: "On Jordan's Bank" to 3:4, and "The God of Abraham Praise" to 3:6 (". . . who was and is and is to be, For aye the same").

We need to be clear about the situation of the Judeans to which these verses are addressed. Many commentators have written that the compatriots of Malachi are raising the familiar problem of theodicy in 2:17; that is, if God is just, then why do the wicked prosper and the righteous suffer? But that is a question that presents itself to the faithful in times of distress, and we have seen in what has gone before that the Judeans of

183

Malachi's time are anything but faithful. They are not living obedient lives and are not therefore perplexed by their suffering. They are living disobedient lives, and they do not think that matters one way or another—because God is totally absent from the scene and does nothing! When they ask, "Where is the God of justice?" they are expressing their doubt that he is anywhere, that he even cares for them, or that he has anything whatsoever to do with their lives. This is once again the expression of doubt in the existence of the covenant relationship and of its God that we saw in 1:1–5. The complaint or legal indictment therefore of 2:17 against the Judeans in this court case is that they have totally corrupted the language of faith. They call "good" that which they should call "evil" and say that God delights in it (cf. Isa. 5:20). For example, they call a divorce and remarriage a "good thing" or "the will of God," when in reality God hates divorce (2:16). Their sin is a total indifference toward the will of the Lord, rising out of their loss of intimate fellowship with God in the covenant bond.

It is therefore the God of the covenant whose coming is foretold in this passage. This is the only place in the Old Testament where God is called "the messenger of the covenant" (3:1), and he is identical with "the Lord" (Hebr: *Adon*) in 3:1. The phrases "whom you seek" and "in whom you delight" are ironical in the verse. The coming of the Lord of the covenant is to be preceded by the appearance of his "messenger," whose identity is not given but who is then identified with Elijah in 4:5 —an identification which may be a later interpretation of 3:1 and yet which is just as valid as any of the many others that have been proposed. The important point, however, is that to a people who think that the covenant relationship and its God are non-existent or merely memories from the past, the Lord of the covenant will himself come. That is a frightening prospect for any age that thinks God to be absent from the world.

Though God's coming will be prepared and foresignaled by the appearance of his preceding messenger, nevertheless he will suddenly appear in his temple. It is no accident therefore that Jesus constantly admonished his disciples to watch and be prepared for the coming (cf. Mark. 13:37; Matt. 25:1–13) and that Paul was, above all, concerned that his churches would be found pure and blameless through faith in "the day of Christ" (Phil. 1:6, 10; I Cor. 1:8; I Thess. 5:24; cf. Eph. 6:13). Such interpretations, prompted by the pairing of Malachi 3:1–4 with

Philippians 1:3–11 for the Second Sunday in Advent in some lectionaries, view the second coming of our Lord as the fulfillment of this Malachi passage. The lessons for the Nativity of John the Baptist, on the other hand, see the fulfillment of this Malachi passage in the appearance of the Baptist as the "messenger" and of the earthly Jesus as the "Lord" suddenly come to his people. That latter is the same interpretation as is found in the Gospels which quote Malachi 3:1 (Matt. 11:10; Mark. 1:2; Luke 1:76; 7:27). The Malachi passage admits a fluidity of interpretation in the church.

That which is pictured in the passage is Malachi's version of the Day of the Lord—that day so often mentioned in the prophetic writings which was apparently anticipated by the Israelites as the day when God would usher in his reign over all the earth and exalt Israel as his chosen folk (cf. Amos 5:18), and yet which was consistently pictured by the prophets as a day of awful judgment (Amos 5:18–20; Isa. 2:6–21; Ezek. 7:5–13; Zeph. 1; Joel 1:15–20). The question therefore is, Who can endure such a day and stand his or her ground when God appears? (The metaphor is taken from battle.) We may see in a glass darkly now, but then it is face to face, with a Lord before whom "the mountains will melt . . . / and the valleys will be cleft, / like wax before the fire, / like waters poured down a steep place" (Micah 1:4). All our feeble claims to righteousness and faith, much less excuses for indifference and unbelief, will be unavailing before that fire. Unless God himself saves his people, they cannot endure his coming.

The marvel in this prophetic promise is that God will save. He comes in awful, destroying judgment, to be sure. His people have doubted that there is a God of justice (2:17); he therefore comes to establish justice (3:5; the words for "justice" and "judgment" here are the same in the Hebrew: *mishpat*). In his court case against his people, which Malachi understands as an ongoing event, God expertly testifies (such is the meaning of "swift witness," 3:5) against all those who have broken his covenant commandments: against "sorcerers" who trust in evil spirits, necromancy, witchcraft, and magic and for whom the law's penalty is death (Exod. 22:18; cf. Lev. 20:27); against the adulterers mentioned in 2:10–16 and any others (Exod. 20:14; cf. Matt. 5:27–30); against perjurers (Exod. 20:16; Deut. 19:16–21); against those who withhold a worker's wages or do not recompense him justly (Deut. 24:14–15); against those who do not

185

protect the poor and weak (Exod. 22:22–24; Deut. 24:17–18) or who do not defend the rights of an alien (Exod. 20:10; 23:12; Deut. 14:29; 24:14, 17; 26:12–13; 27:19). All are covenant violators, lacking that relationship with the Lord that would lead them to obey his commandments in holy awe and responsive love. They will be condemned when God comes to establish his justice, his order, his universal reign in the earth (cf. 1:11, 14). There is no cheap grace, and the Lord of Hosts does not countenance evil in his realm.

The amazing fact, however, is that all in Judah are not already consumed by the fire of God's wrath, nor will they be consumed (3:6b), for this is the God of covenant love who will come (3:6 belongs with vv. 1–5, as the climax of the thought). God has loved his people, and he loves them still (1:2). He does not change (3:6a). The covenant still stands; his purpose still is to use Israel as his instrument in bringing all peoples to acknowledge his universal reign over the earth, which will be characterized by his just order and unstained by human sin. He still presses forward through Israel's history to fulfill his purpose of love for his world.

This covenant God therefore will come to his people, not as a consuming fire but as a refining flame and a cleansing lye that will remove the dross of Judah's evil from her and bleach white her dark stains of sin. And because Judah has been corrupted by her priests (cf. 2:8), it is with them that the separation of the dross and the cleansing of sin's blots will begin (3:3). The figures of speech imply not only that the wicked will be removed from the community, as in 2:3, but also that the remaining priests will be so transformed in their characters that they will be able to worship the Lord rightly with all their hearts (cf. 2:2), distinguishing between the clean and the unclean, the holy and the profane, and glorifying God's great name before all the people (cf. Lev. 10:3, 10–11; Ezek. 22:26). Being thus rightly taught and led, the people too will know God and enter into right relationship with him. Their offerings will therefore become acceptable to their covenant Lord, as they were in the beginning under Moses when the covenant was first established (3:4).

By pairing Malachi 3:1–4 with Hebrews 2:14–18 and Luke 2:22–32 for the Feast of the Presentation of our Lord, in some lectionaries, the Roman Catholic and Episcopalian churches interpret Jesus Christ as the faithful priest of Malachi 3:3, who has been made perfect through suffering and who therefore is able to save his people. Once again, we have an example of the fluidity to be found in the church's interpretation of this Malachi passage.

The passage has, however, importance also for the priesthood of all believers, for it serves as an interpretation of the suffering and affliction of the covenant people. In one of the great sermons on Malachi 3:3, Spurgeon pointed to the fact that the Lord will "sit" as a refiner—apparently an attitude of indifference. But no, said Spurgeon, the divine refiner is all attention, and he will not desert us in his fires of affliction until he has delivered us from our faults—"until He can survey every one of us, 'without spot, or wrinkle, or any such thing,'—pure lumps of gold and silver, brought home by Himself, without a speck of dross about us" ("The Sitting of the Refiner," p. 833). Such is the love of this God of Malachi for his people Israel and for us, his new covenant people. And such also is the assurance of this message from the prophet.

Malachi 3:7–12

The expression of the love of the covenant Lord for his people continues in this brief passage, which is one of the most theologically rich in the Book of Malachi. That love which we heard voiced in the preceding passage is reiterated here for the whole people of Israel, and in a sense, they are here given one last chance to repent.

Israel has broken the covenant law ever since her earliest days as a people. Yet, the invitation of her covenant God is still, in words borrowed from Zechariah 1:3, "Return to me, . . . and I will return to you, . . ." (v. 7). This is still the God who says, "I have loved you, and I love you still" (1:2). He still holds open the door for Israel to repent and to come in to his presence— an amazing invitation to a folk who has been so scornful of him (cf. 1:13), and seen to be even more amazing in the light of Israel's response: They see no necessity for the invitation! They feel themselves to be quite innocent and acceptable as they are and quite accustomed to being in God's presence. What more therefore should they do?

The court case must consequently continue, with God lay-

187

ing further charges against his sinful people (cf. 1:6–7, 13; 2:8, 14, 17). This time the indictment is that Israel is robbing God, contrary to the custom of every other religious people. (Such is the force of 8a.) Israel denies the charge, and so the Lord must be specific: They are robbing him by bringing only a portion of their tithes and offerings to the temple.

Here Malachi is apparently insisting on the custom, later codified in the Priestly law, of giving the whole tithe to the temple Levites, who in turn gave the best portion of it to the Zadokite priests for a sacrifice to the Lord (Num. 18:21–32). Offerings, on the other hand, were those portions of the sacrifices which were set apart for the sustenance of the priests and Levites (Exod. 29:27–28; Lev. 7:32–36; Num. 5:9) as well as gifts given to God for special purposes (cf. Exod. 30:14; Num. 15: 19–21; Deut. 12:6, 11, 17). The Lord here charges the Judeans with stinginess, with cheating, by failing to bring the whole tithe and the required offerings to the temple (cf. 1:14). Considering the accusations against the priests in 2:1–9, they may also have been withholding the best portions of the tithes from God.

We see such selfish grasping still in existence in the time of Nehemiah (cf. Neh. 13:10–13), but in the light of Judah's economic circumstances, it is here not too surprising. She has suffered under drought and crop failure and locust plague and blight (cf. Mal. 3:10–11), and when one has little, one is tempted to guard jealously one's meager stores. The difficulty is that one does not thereby show one's love for God by liberality toward him and needy neighbor. God loves the cheerful giver, we are told by Paul (II Cor. 9:7); we are to give with open hand and heart, says Deuteronomy (15:7–11); do not be anxious about what you shall eat or drink, nor about what you shall put on, teaches Jesus (Matt. 6:25). And the reason for all of that is trust —trust in the God whom we are to know and love with all our heart in the intimate fellowship of every day; trust that we are precious in his sight and that he will not abandon his care of us; trust that his love pours out with it more provision for all our needs than we could ever imagine—blessings given to us in ". . . good measure, . . . shaken together, running over, . . ." (Luke 6:38). "I have been young, and now am old," says the psalmist. "Yet I have not seen the righteous forsaken or his children begging bread. He is ever giving liberally and lending, and his children become a blessing" (Ps. 37:26). "I have never had to worry about my congregation providing for me," said a

188

faithful pastor. "I know how to be abased, and I know how to abound; . . ." wrote Paul. "I can do all things in him who strengthens me" (Phil. 4:12, 13). The motive-power that overcomes all our selfish and miserly tendencies is trust in our God of love.

It is to that trust that Malachi here calls his penurious people. "Prove me!" exhorts the Lord of Hosts, "Put me to the test" (v. 10)! Though we are not to test the Lord our God (Deut. 6:16; Matt. 4:7), he here is willing to allow that freedom to his unbelieving people. "Respond in love to my love," is the exhortation, "and see if I do not open the windows of heaven for you and pour down fructifying rain, and rid your crops of devouring locust and protect your vines from blight (vv. 10–11)! See if you do not become a land so delightful in every way that all the nations of the earth will call you blessed" (v. 12; cf. Isa. 60:3–14; 61:9; 62:1–4, 10–12)! Judah has suffered the effects of the covenant curses because she has broken the covenant (v. 9); here her God offers her the blessings that accompany covenant love and trust. But it is not a tit-for-tat arrangement, not a vending machine concept of God, not a bargain by which Judah makes an investment and receives a reward in return. To find in this passage any such legalistic or automatic or materialistic understanding is a complete distortion of the covenant relation with our God.

There is a true story of a man in Dade County, Florida, who sued his church for the return of the money which he had contributed to it. "I delivered $800 of my savings to the . . . Church," said the man in his court suit, "in response to the pastor's promise that blessings, benefits and rewards would come to the person who did tithe 10 per cent of his wealth. I did not and have not received these benefits." That crude bargain is not what is involved here when Judah is admonished to "bring the full tithe" (v. 10). Motivating and accompanying all true gifts to God is the pouring out of our life, our love, our all. And when we so present ourselves, a living sacrifice, holy and acceptable to God, it is surely true that heaven's richest bounties are heaped upon us. "Heaven's windows . . . swing upon love's hinges" (Morgan, p. 77). We find ourselves given graces anew every morning, too numerous to count—the glories of a good creation; joy in daily work; patience, kindness, self-control in the fellowship we have with one another; release from guilt and anxiety and dread of death; and above all, peace with God,

189

who winds us round and round with mercy, as if with air. The Kingdom's goal—the glory of God—becomes our chief occupation, and we find all these other things added to us as well. As G. Campbell Morgan once preached, "When men come and say, 'Here we are, our interests, ourselves, our business—everything,' then the windows of heaven are never shut—never" (p. 78)! On that promise, Judah is here asked to found her love, her trust, her life.

Lying behind it all, further, is the purpose of God—to establish his reign over all human hearts. The promise to Abraham in Genesis 12:3 echoes through Malachi 3:12—the promise to bring blessing on all the families of the earth through Israel, God's chosen people. Judah is loved because God loves all peoples and wishes to open the windows of heaven's blessings for them also. But God can use his elected folk for that purpose only if they love and trust him and let him have his way with their life (cf. Exod. 19:5–6). Thus, that for which the Father pleads in this passage is his purpose of love for the earth, and he calls Judah to be the instrument of that loving purpose. So too does he call the new Israel, the church. "Give me . . . a hundred men who love God with all their hearts, and fear nothing but sin," wrote John Wesley, "and I will move the world" (quoted in Morgan, p. 80). Give God a church that loves and trusts him, and all nations will be brought to praise his holy name in fulfillment of Malachi's vision of the Kingdom that is coming (1:11, 14).

Having set the context of these verses in the discussion above, we now can deal with the specific charge and command of verses 8 and 10.

"Will man rob God (v. 8)?" The prophet asks the question in utter astonishment, for stinginess toward God is a denial of the very nature of human life. Even the most backward tribes of the world have fashioned cults for themselves that approach their stone and wood deities with meticulous care and wonder before the sphere of the holy. Even pagan powers have hesitated to violate the sanctity of an altar or church, occasioning shocked cries of blasphemy when they have trampled some holy place. Every people on earth has realized that there is Something or Someone beyond them which demands their devotion. To mar that commitment with grasping self-interest is therefore a denial of the basic nature of religion. But to mar the worship of the God of the Bible with such selfishness is even more heinous, for the biblical confession is that he is Creator and Sustainer and Redeemer. To him we owe the order of the world and our very breath of life. To him we are indebted for unsleeping love and daily guiding sustenance and costly redemption of our lives. To slight such a God is therefore ingratitude at its most callous and stubborn level.

It is also dangerous, because as Paul pointed out, ". . . God is not mocked, for whatever a man sows, that he will also reap" (Gal. 6:7), as Malachi too will shortly announce. To rob the biblical God is to rob the One who sees the hearts of all persons and who can reward them according to their deserts. Robbers of such a God prepare for themselves their own rewards.

In addition, such thieves deny to themselves their highest good. This God of the Bible desires above all else that we have life and have it more abundantly in a blessed community guided and sustained by his lordship. In his service is perfect freedom; in loving response to his love are joy and goodness and eternal life. To turn our backs on that is to miss the Kingdom of God on earth and that eternal citizenship for which ultimately we were created.

But we can rob God in all sorts of ways. We can rob him doctrinally by watering down or distorting those great affirmations of the biblical faith that have been distilled into the primary creeds of the Christian church, thus denying the words and work that God has done in the sacred history. We can rob him morally by ignoring or softening his commands and letting the situation of the moment determine our compliance. We can rob him cultically by failure to pray and praise and petition. We can rob him evangelically by silence about his deeds or by failure to act according to his justice and mercy before other persons and in our communities. This God of the Bible is Lord, King, Master, Father, Judge, Savior, Redeemer over our lives and world. If in the conduct of our daily existence we try to make him less than that, we most assuredly rob him, as Judah was robbing him of the glory and honor due him.

It is nevertheless specifically with tithes that Malachi has to do—with the offering to God of the products and earnings of one's labor, and that raises in the mind of every church leader the subjects of giving and church budgets. Tithing was stipulated in Jewish law, and Christians have been freed from that law. There is no comparable duty to tithe laid upon us in the New Testament, though the Book of the New Covenant is full

191

of urgings to charity and giving as appropriate responses or gratitude and service to God. In addition, our Lord approves of tithing in his words to the scribes and Pharisees (Matt. 23:23// Luke 11:42), though he judges it insufficient of itself. But there is no New Testament commandment to tithe. Faithful Christians who practice tithing therefore usually do so as a convenient way of judging how much they should give in relation to their income, although they often distribute that tithe to community charities as well as to the church. Is the practice of tithing to be encouraged, therefore, on the basis of this passage in Malachi and the rest of the Scriptures? Or is this a remnant of Jewish law from which we have been delivered?

To answer these questions, we must consider the purpose of the law in the Bible. The covenant commandments in Judaism, and especially in Deuteronomy, were intended to furnish Israel with examples of what it meant to love and trust God. ". . . you shall love the Lord your God with all your heart, and with all your soul, and with all your might," preached Deuteronomy (6:5). Then in commandment after commandment, it spelled out how to love God that way. To love God, it said, was to show mercy toward the helpless (24:17–22) and honesty in commercial dealings (25:13–16) and "justice, and only justice . . . " in courts of law (16:20). To love God was to exercise responsible care toward God's creation (22:6–7) and to honor God's sovereignty over life (12:23–25) and to worship him and him only (5:7). And to love God was also to acknowledge his ownership of all things by giving him a tithe of all produce (14:22–29). In the New Testament, then, this same understanding of the commandments prevailed. "If you love me, Jesus said, "you will keep my commandments" (John 14:15). His instructions to us were intended as concrete examples of how to live out our love for him in the world, empowered by his Spirit in the new life given us by his death and resurrection. Thus, God's commandments in the Bible are means of grace for us—God's merciful guidance in how to live and what to do in the new life he has given us, in order that we not wander from his way of life and lose his gifts.

Our Lord gives no command in his teachings about tithing, but countless generations of faithful Christians have found that their gifts of money and time and talents, poured out from hearts full of love for Christ, have returned to them riches beyond all measure in their fellowship with God. Giving, in the

192

Christian life, is a means of grace—one manner by which we appropriate ever more fully the love our God has for us—that love that is "forever full, forever flowing free." We respond in love to his love and the windows of heaven are opened.

Malachi 3:13–15

In the final section of this court case, verses 13–15, it is therefore this grace of God which is rejected (see above)—that grace that pours out heaven's blessings upon those who love God with all their heart in response to his love. The Judeans, in their conversation with one another (such is the force of "spoken") have agreed that it is futile and foolish to keep God's commandments because they gain nothing from such practice; and it is ridiculous to petition God's help in rituals of penitence and fasting because that help never comes. "You have said, 'Put me to the test' " (3:10), they blurt out in court to God. "Well," they continue, "the test has been carried on every day, and it is only those who defy all your commandments who are blessed with the good things in life. Their sins never find them out" (cf. Job 21:7–10, 12–13; Ps. 73:1–14). The Judeans, with hearts closed to the love of God, reject the blessing God wants to give them. Because they seek first themselves and not his Kingdom, they will lose all other things as well. God rests his case. He has completed his prosecution. The court proceeding awaits the verdict.

Malachi 3:16—4:3

God has never left himself without witnesses, according to the biblical history. Within faithless, indifferent, rebellious Judah in the time of Malachi, there is also an obedient little group who recognize the divine Kingship, not merely as theory or as something of which they may boast to other people, but as the power in which they live their lives and spend all their

193

days. They are "Not the great heterogeneous crowd that bow
the head, and say 'Thy Kingdom come, Thy will be done'; but
the saintly souls in whose life the Kingdom *is* come, and the will
is being done" (Morgan, p. 105). Such are the little group described in verse 16 in this passage. They "fear" the Lord and
they "think on" his name. The latter verb has the meaning "to
esteem," "to give value to," "to treasure" (cf. Isa. 53:3; Phil. 4:8).
So this group in verse 16 are those who treasure and hold valu-
able and esteem the kingship of God. Where their treasure is
—with God—there is their heart also; and so they "fear" God,
that is, they spend their lives in trust and obedience and reverence and service to God the King. It is the attitude which the
Lord will find among all nations when the Kingdom of God
comes on earth, according to Malachi (1:11, 14), but here we
find the first-fruits of that kingdom already among the faithful
of Judea.

This group serves as the jury in this court case that Malachi
is presenting—a notable fact, for it implies that only those who
are faithful to God the King can see the situation as it really is.
Only those who in faith perceive the reign of God are free of
the distortions, the cynicism, the despair, the unbelief that defeat the rest of society and that loose upon it the anarchy of
human will freed from God's direction. Thus, in contrast to
what the faithless say to one another (v. 13), this faithful jury also
confers together (v. 16) and judges God aright—as faithful to his
covenant folk and overflowing with love, despite that people's
constant neglect of him.

We therefore find in this passage a separation between the
righteous and the wicked in Israel—a separation begun already
in the time of Third Isaiah (cf., e.g., 65:13–16) and continued on
into the New Testament (cf., e.g., Rom. 11:5–6). God hears the
words of those who fear him and esteem his name, and their
names are inscribed in his "book of remembrance" to be eter-
nally before his eyes and never forgotten. A book by which God
remembers the deeds of human beings is a familiar concept in
the Bible, but it bears the title "book of remembrance" only
here. God inscribes the names of the faithful or righteous in the
book in order that he may remember them on that Day of the
Lord, pictured already in 3:1–5, when he comes to set up his
kingdom over all the earth. The faithful remnant will be spared
in that Day, as a father (cf. 1:6) would spare an obedient son (v.
17; cf. Ps. 103:13)—an allusion perhaps to Deuteronomy 21:

194

18–21 (with echoes of the sparing of Isaac, Gen. 22, behind it).
The faithful will be, on that Day, God's *segullah,* his own
possession (cf. Deut. 7:6; Isa. 43:1, 21; I Peter 2:9), his "peculiar
treasure" (KJV, Exod. 19:5). The word *segullah* is taken from
the covenant preface in Exodus 19:4–6, and the thought is that
on the Day of the Lord the true Israel will stand forth and God's
covenant promise will be fulfilled. Israel, embodied in its remnant, will become as she was intended to be, a holy and faithful
community, living under the reign of God.

The verbs used of the coming Day, in 3:17 and 4:3, are
noteworthy for being participles, and the Hebrew literally says,
"on the day that I am making." Malachi understands this Day
to have begun already. Those who fear God and esteem his
name are evidences of it, and they already, in their court decision, have distinguished between the righteous and the wicked
(3:18), between a faithful God and his faithless people.

But there is more yet to be revealed, more still to come on
that Day—namely, the final separation of those who serve God
from those who do not (v. 18) and the recompense of each group
accordingly. The last, decisive great assize waits just outside
time's door, when the sheep will be separated from the goats
—those who love God from those who do not (cf. Matt. 25:
31–46). Thus, the final effecting of Deuteronomy's covenant
blessings and curses is projected into the future; and this passage finally defines, as 3:1–5 did not, who will be purified to live
in the Kingdom—who will stand in the Day of the great King's
coming—and who will be destroyed. The decision will be based
upon that love and trust in God, or lack of them, present in the
human heart (cf. Luke 18:8).

Malachi 3:16—4:2 is a stated Old Testament lesson for Pentecost in some lectionaries, where it is often joined with II
Thessalonians 3:6–13 and Luke 21:5–19, both of which are set
in this context of God's final Day. "Behold! the day comes consuming . . ." reads the Hebrew of 4:1. As in 3:5, the Day is a time
of judgment. But whereas the former passage did not say what
the punishment would be for all those who broke the covenant
commandments, here the sentence is spelled out clearly: They
will be burned up as the stubble in a field is dried out and
scorched and finally ignited by a furnace-hot, blazing, unrelent-
ing summer sun. (Those who live in southern climates can appreciate the metaphor.) Their sin is principally pride (cf. 3:15)
and self-will (4:1)—the failure of the heart to bow before and

195

to cleave to the covenant will and sovereign mercy of the divine King. All covenant breach finally consists, according to the Bible, in failure to trust and love our God. So thoroughly will the faithless be consumed that their very roots will be destroyed, with no possibility of renewal or propagation from their seed or shoots.

On the other hand, the very sun and its rays ("wings") that will burn up the wicked will prove to be healing warmth and light and morning joy (cf. II Sam. 23:4) to the righteous—to all those who have learned to place their lives in the hands of their King (4:2). "The sun of righteousness" here is not a personal name but a metaphor of God's salvation of his faithful remnant (cf. Isa. 60:1), and "righteousness" has the meaning—as it has in so much of the Old Testament and especially in Second Isaiah —of God's salvation or rescue and gift of abundant life to his own. Thus, like calves leaping and scampering about after being released from the confinements of a cold night's dark stall (cf. Isa. 35:6), the righteous remnant will luxuriate in the freedom and warmth and sheer joy of the love of God poured out on them. The newly burned stubble under their feet (cf. Micah 5:8) in parts of the pasture will give them no alarm, for all those who can harm them are ashes (4:3), and their paths lead on to God's green meadows and ever-flowing waters of life.

Behold! the Day comes! And whether it brings the fire of destruction or the sweet balm of healing depends on the character of those upon whom the light falls. As G. Campbell Morgan has written: "Can I say, 'Come' to Christ's announcement that He is coming? 'Behold, I come quickly'; can I say 'Come, Lord Jesus'? There is no test concerning holiness of life and character equal to that" (p. 130). The court case is ended here in Malachi and the recompense decreed.

Malachi 4:4–6

196

Yet the Book of Malachi does not end with 4:3 and its verdict for righteous and wicked. Instead, the prophet, who has acted the role of the priest-judge (see the Introduction) delivers a final priestly *torah* which in its mercy corresponds to the opening words of the Lord: "I have loved you and I love you still" (1:2).

The Day of the Lord lies in the future. Malachi therefore makes one last plea to his disbelieving and indifferent people. Appealing to the name of the nation's founder and mediator of their law, he urges his compatriots to turn in obedience to all God's teachings given to Moses at the mount of covenanting, here called Horeb after the manner of Deuteronomy. At the same time, Malachi announces the gracious words of God that even now, in the face of all their rebellion against him, God will not give up on his people. He is still working with them, and he will continue to do so in the hope that more of them will turn and be saved from the destruction of the Day. "I will send you Elijah before the great and terrible Day comes," promises God, "and as that prophet once turned the nation from its idolatry (cf. I Kings 18), so the new Elijah, working in the spirit and power of his predecessor (cf. Luke 1:17), will convert the hearts of fathers and sons (such is the meaning) to love and trust in me, your covenant King. And in such turning, my beloved people will avoid the death that comes from my curse upon them." (For the *ḥerem* or curse or ban, cf. Exod. 22:20; Lev. 27:28–29; Josh. 6:17; I Sam. 15:3; I Kings 20:42; Isa. 34:5). The words at the end of the book are, literally, ". . . lest I come and smite the land with a curse" (4:6).

Neither the Septuagint nor Hebrew liturgical tradition wished to end the Book of the Twelve Prophets with "curse," and so the Septuagint puts verse 4 after verse 6, while Hebrew liturgies often repeated verse 5 after verse 6—a practice followed in some versions of the Hebrew Bible. But

> The Old Testament does not end with a curse pronounced, but with a curse threatened, not with a declaring that hope is forever past, and that there can be no redemption and no deliverance, no further word, but with a statement intended to teach that God has not yet pronounced this curse, and that He does not desire to do so. . . . [It] is the last appeal of love, . . . aimed at averting calamity (Morgan, p. 113).

What about us Christians, the new Israel in Jesus Christ? Are Malachi's words concerning the coming of the Day of the Lord—the appearance of the Kingdom of God on earth, which was to be preceded by the work of Elijah—intended for us also? According to the Gospel of Matthew, they are indeed (11: 10–15): The messenger promised in Malachi 3:1 came (v. 10),

197

and he was in fact the new Elijah (v. 14). The warning has been given. The call to repentance and conversion has been issued. The Kingdom has broken into human history in the person of Jesus Christ (cf. Matt. 12:28). Now our decision about him determines our eternal life or death (cf. Matt. 12:32). And he will return to give his recompense and to bring the reign of God in its fullness (cf. Matt. 25; Rev. 22:12). Two decisions will be rendered, as Malachi said: one for the evildoer, one for the righteous (Rev. 22:10–11). And the final words of the New Testament show the yearning desire of this God of Malachi:

> The grace of the Lord Jesus be with you all. Amen. (Rev. 22:21 NEB).

BIBLIOGRAPHY

1. For further study

BALDWIN, JOYCE G. *Haggai, Zechariah, Malachi* (London: The Tyndale Press, 1972).

BRIGHT, JOHN. *A History of Israel,* Third edition (Philadelphia: The Westminster Press, 1982).

DAVIDSON, A. B. *The Books of Nahum, Habakkuk, and Zephaniah.* THE CAMBRIDGE BIBLE (Cambridge: at the University Press, 1920).

EATON, J. H. *Obadiah, Nahum, Habakkuk, and Zephaniah: Introduction and Commentary* (London: SCM Press, 1961).

GOWEN, DONALD E. *The Triumph of Faith in Habakkuk* (Atlanta: John Knox Press, 1976).

HANSON, PAUL. *The Dawn of Apocalyptic,* Revised edition (Philadelphia: Fortress Press, 1975, 1979).

MITCHELL, H. G., J. M. P. SMITH, J. A. BEWER. *A Critical and Exegetical Commentary on Haggai, Zechariah, Malachi, and Jonah.* INTERNATIONAL CRITICAL COMMENTARY (Edinbugh: T and T Clark, 1912).

PEROWNE, T. T. *Haggai and Zechariah* (Cambridge: at the University Press, 1886).

SMITH, J. M. P., W. H. WARD, J. A. BEWER. *A Critical and Exegetical Commentary on Micah, Zephaniah, Nahum, Habakkuk, Obadiah, and Joel.* INTERNATIONAL CRITICAL COMMENTARY (Edinburgh: T and T Clark, 1911).

2. Literature cited

ACHTEMEIER, ELIZABETH. "Righteousness in the Old Testament," *The Interpreter's Dictionary of the Bible* (New York, Nashville: Abingdon Press, 1962), IV, 80–85.

———*The Community and Message of Isaiah 56—66.* A THEOLOGICAL COMMENTARY (Minneapolis: Augsburg Publishing House, 1982).

———*Deuteronomy, Jeremiah.* PROCLAMATION COMMENTARIES. *The Old Testament Witnesses for Preaching.* Foster R. McCurley, editor (Philadelphia: Fortress Press, 1978).

ACHTEMEIER, PAUL J. *Romans.* INTERPRETATION: A BIBLE COMMENTARY FOR TEACHING AND PREACHING (Atlanta: John Knox Press, 1984).

CALVIN, JOHN. *Commentaries on the Twelve Minor Prophets.* Vols. III, IV, V, translated by J. Owen (Edinburgh: Printed for the Calvin Translation Society, 1948).

EATON, J. H. See listed in "For further study."

GADD, C. J., editor. *The Fall of Nineveh.* The newly discovered Babylonian Chronicles, No. 21,901 in the British Museum (London: Printed by order of the Trustees, 1923).

KLEINERT, PAUL. *The Book of Nahum,* translated and enlarged by Charles Elliott (New York: Scribner, Armstrong, and Co., 1874).

LUTHER, MARTIN. *Luther's Works*, Vols. 18, 19. "Lectures on the Minor Prophets," I and II, Hilton C. Oswald, editor (St. Louis: Concordia Publishing House, 1975).

MITCHELL, H. G., J. M. P. Smith, J. A. BEWER. See listed in "For further study."

PRITCHARD, JAMES B., editor. *Ancient Near Eastern Texts Relating to the Old Testament* (Princeton: Princeton University Press, 1950).

SADIE, STANLEY editor. *The New Grove Dictionary of Music and Musicians*. Vol. V. (London: The Macmillan Company, 1980).

SMITH, GEORGE ADAM. *The Book of the Twelve Prophets II*, Revised edition (New York: Harper and Brothers, 1928).

TAYLOR, CHARLES L., JR. "The Book of Habakkuk. Introduction and Exegesis," [pp. 973–1003]; "The Book of Zephaniah. Introduction and Exegesis" [pp. 1007–34]; TAYLOR and JAMES T. CLELAND. "The Book of Nahum. Introduction and Exegesis, and Exposition" [pp. 953–69]. *The Interpreter's Bible*, Vol. VI (New York, Nashville: Abingdon Press, 1956).

TREACH, RICHARD CHENEVIX editor. *Sacred Latin Poetry*, Second edition. (London; Cambridge: Macmillan and Co., 1864). Article on "Thomas of Celano."

3. Homiletical sources

ACHTEMEIER, ELIZABETH R., *Preaching as Theology and Art* (Nashville: Abingdon Press, 1984).

BERNANOS, GEORGES. *The Diary of a Country Priest*, translated from the French by Pamela Morris (New York: Macmillan Publishing Co., Inc., 1954, 1937).

BOWEN, W. E. *In the Beginning* (London: Hodder and Stoughton, 1939).

CHAPPEL, CLOVIS G. *Meet These Men* (New York, Nashville: Abingdon Press, 1956), pp. 72–82.

——*Chappell's Special Day Sermons* (Nashville: Cokesbury Press, 1936), pp. 134–46.

HOFFSIS, LARRY A. *Augsburg Sermons:* SERMONS ON THE OLD TESTAMENT, Series C (Minneapolis: Augsburg Publishing House, 1979), pp. 26–31.

JOWETT, J. H. *The Transfigured Church* (New York: Fleming H. Revell Co., 1910), pp. 128–37.

MACGREGOR, WILLIAM MALCOLM. "The Danger of Comparison," *Christ and the Church: Sermons and Interpretations* (London: Hodder and Stoughton, Ltd., 1937), pp. 210–22.

——"The Prince of Peace," *Jesus Christ the Son of God: Sermons and Interpretations* (Edinburgh: T and T Clark, 1907), pp. 77–89.

MORGAN, G. CAMPBELL. "The Children's Playground in the City of God" [pp. 256–67]; "The Divine Worker" [pp. 48–60]; "Jubilation in Desolation" [pp. 140–53]. *The Westminster Pulpit*, VI. *The Preaching of G. Campbell Morgan* (London: Pickering and Inglis, Ltd., n. d.).

——*Wherein Have We Robbed God? Malachi's Message to the Men of Today* (New York: Fleming H. Revell Company, 1898).

MORRIS, COLIN. *Mankind My Church* (Nashville: Abingdon Press, 1971), pp. 31–41.

SPURGEON, CHARLES HADDON. "A Luther Sermon at the Tabernacle" (Hab. 2:4); "Mercy, Omnipotence and Justice" (Nahum 1:3); "The Middle Passage" (Hab. 3:2); "A Sermon for the Time Present" (Zeph. 3:16–18); "The Sitting of the Refiner" (Mal. 3:3). *The Treasury of the Bible,* Vol. IV (Grand Rapids: Baker Book House, 1981).